**Crises can come in different forms —
and from different directions**

Crises can come from the outside—from the death of a loved one or a physical injury.

Crises can come from the inside—when an emotional vulnerability reaches the breaking point.

Crises can be part of the natural order of life—as one passes from childhood to adulthood to old age.

Or crises can seem to snap a life in two—as sometimes happens when one is divorced or fired or rejected.

But whatever the crisis, a person shouldn't have to handle it alone. This perceptive and resourceful guide will give you the skill, the sensitivity, and the methods with which to help.

CRISIS INTERVENTION

About the authors:

DONNA C. AGUILERA, Ph.D., is Associate Professor, Mental Health Nursing, at California State University at Los Angeles.

JANICE M. MESSICK, M.S., is Clinical Evaluation Specialist, Program Evaluation Service, at the Brentwood Veterans Administration Hospital in Los Angeles.

CRISIS

INTERVENTION

THERAPY FOR PSYCHOLOGICAL EMERGENCIES

DONNA C. AGUILERA, Ph.D.

Chairperson, Graduate Division Psychiatric Nursing,
University of Maryland,
Baltimore, Maryland

JANICE M. MESSICK, M.S., F.A.A.N.

Clinical Program Evaluation Specialist,
Veterans Administration Medical Center,
Los Angeles, California

A PLUME BOOK

NEW AMERICAN LIBRARY

MOSBY

TIMES MIRROR
NEW YORK AND SCARBOROUGH, ONTARIO

Publisher: Thomas A. Manning
Assistant editor: Nancy L. Mullins
Production: Barbara Merritt

MOSBY MEDICAL LIBRARY

This is a revised edition of a book previously published
by The C.V. Mosby Company, entitled *Crisis Intervention*.

NAL books are available at quantity discounts
when used to promote products or services. For information
please write to Premium Marketing Division,
The New American Library, Inc.,
1633 Broadway, New York, New York 10019.

SIGNET, SIGNET CLASSICS, MENTOR, PLUME, MERIDIAN, and
NAL BOOKS are published by The New American Library, Inc.,
1633 Broadway, New York, New York 10019, in Canada, by
The New American Library of Canada, Limited,
81 Mack Avenue, Scarborough, Ontario M1L 1M8.

Library of Congress Cataloging in Publication Data
Aguilera, Donna C.
Crisis intervention.
"A Plume book."
Bibliography: p.
1. Crisis intervention (Psychiatry) I. Messick,
Janice M. II. Title.
RC480.6.A38   1982b   616.89'14   82-3535
ISBN 0-8016-0086-3 (Mosby : pbk.)   AACR2

1 2 3 4 5 6 7 8 9   03/C/335

Printed in the United States of America

To
All from whom we have learned
and
All who will yet forever teach us

Foreword

Forty years ago, in the midst of celebration after a particularly exciting football game, the Coconut Grove night club in Boston suddenly burst into flames. Dozens of entrapped people lost their lives. The Boston community was stunned and shaken to its roots.

That event not only resulted in incredible suffering and loss of life, but also wrote an indelible page in the history of American psychiatry; it spurred Dr. Erich Lindemann of Massachusetts General Hospital to study in great detail the mourning reactions of bereaved people and to elaborate the theory and practice of *crisis intervention*.

Other events contributed to this concept. In World War II, we learned that many acute breakdowns of soldiers in action could be resolved by a short period of rest, abreaction (releasing tension through recalling a painful experience) and tranquilization, close to the front lines, with expectation of early return to active duty.

In civilian crises, too, as in the emotional casualties connected with bombing, we learned that proper attention to the acute phase could restore a person to equilibrium, forestall fixation of abnormal emotional states, and prevent long-term disability.

In the 1950s and 1960s, psychiatric practice began moving out of the hospital and private office, where mainly well-developed illnesses were being treated, into the community, where persons received help earlier, closer to home, with less disruption of ties to family, job, and natural support systems.

As a result, a host of problems of living came to psychiatric attention. Acute mourning reactions, as in the Coconut Grove disaster, were familiar; so were symptoms of mental distress associated with divorce or separation, loss of employment by firing or retirement, loss of security resulting from financial reverses, or loss of physical integrity from mutilative surgery. Suicidal attempts, acute situational depressions, homosexual panics, family crises, and acute reactions to alcohol or drug intoxication also were found to be common. In addition, community mental health practitioners saw persons suffering from stress involved with major turning points in life—such as marriage, leaving home to attend college, having a baby, joining the armed services, or facing a court battle. Often, however, problems did not come to the psychiatrist's office but were worked out for better or worse within the confines of the family, perhaps with help from friends, clergy, teachers, general practitioners, policemen, or lawyers.

This whole trend was greatly accelerated by the community mental health movement of the 1960s, to which none other than President John Fitzgerald Kennedy lent strong support. An exhaustive study of American systems of care for the mentally ill, pioneered by the American Psychiatric Association, had concluded that hospitalization for mental illness was excessive; hospitals were too big, remote, and custodial; treatment efforts were often inadequate, and social and community supports were too often neglected. A "bold new approach" to treating the mentally ill was outlined in a series of progressive laws that stressed construction and staffing of small mental-health centers in populated areas to provide early acute care of mental disability. Mobilization of a variety of volunteers and paraprofessional caregivers also was encouraged to bolster the work of the traditional team of psychiatrists, nurses, psychologists and social workers.

A variety of brief treatment techniques soon flourished: short-term psychotherapy, pastoral counselling, and use of a variety of neuroleptic drugs; and many suicide prevention centers, hot lines, drop-in centers, walk-in clinics, and family counseling services came into being. Widow-to-widow services and many other mutual self-help programs burgeoned in this period.

All these methods focussed primarily on the acute problem, with little or no attempt to effect major personality changes. The immediate objective was to bring the client back to his best level of functioning as soon as possible, with the least stigma, loss of status and position in family and society, and loss of productivity at work. Often help could be given by a nonpsychiatrist, even a nonprofessional.

In hundreds of the public mental health centers and programs created in recent years, increasing emphasis is being put on crisis intervention. Crisis intervention, brief therapy, family therapy, community support mobilization—all interventions directed at rapid resolution of emotional disequilibrium—will, in all probability, become even more popular in the future. This volume, by two highly sophisticated professionals, is an admirable and authoritative review of history, theory, and practice of crisis intervention, written in a most interesting and readable style. I recommend it to all those who are involved or will become involved with the mentally ill.

Milton Greenblatt, M.D.

Director, Neuropsychiatric Institute Hospital and Clinics.
and Professor and Executive Vice Chairman.
Department of Psychiatry and Biobehavioral Sciences.
University of California at Los Angeles: formerly Commissioner.
Massachusetts Department of Mental Health.

Preface

All of us are constantly being faced with the need to solve problems that arise in the course of our daily living experiences. Some you can solve almost routinely and with little stress or effort—the problem arises, you resolve it, and life goes on "as usual." In other instances, however, a problem arises but, despite your efforts, you cannot resolve it by yourself. Feelings of tension and anxiety increase as the problem persists, and you also become depressed by your failure to solve it. These symptoms interfere with your usual abilities to function—your life cannot go on "as usual." You are in *crisis*.

We have written this book because we saw the need for people to be able to recognize when they may be in a situation that could cause a crisis in their lives. We believe that an awareness of the basic theories of how crises may develop and how they may be resolved will be of value to anyone who is expected to deal effectively with the rapidly changing problems and demands of today's daily life experiences.

The beginning of this book provides information to help make you aware of the broad base of knowledge on which crisis theory is founded. We discuss various types of psychotherapy, how they are used in community psychiatry and by whom. The differences between various psychotherapeutic techniques are discussed in terms of their goals, activities of therapists, reasons for treatment, average time in treatment, and their general costs.

Various types of group therapy are reviewed in general and crisis groups in particular. A case study is included to demonstrate the use of crisis intervention in a group therapy session.

You are then introduced to the process of solving problems and how this could help you in coping with new or different experiences in your life.

Because crises arise from either situational or developmental events that commonly occur in life, the major part of this book deals with many such crises. Hypothetical case studies based on factual experience are included, along with brief theoretical material, to help you recognize when a crisis may happen to you, a family member, or someone else important in your life who may need your help. Among these cases are rape, divorce, suicide, alcoholism, cocaine abuse, burn-out, physical illness, child abuse, death and dying, and the hazards associated with the various stages in life.

We are indebted to many people who have been of assistance to us in writing this book. To our families, who were our kindest critics and strongest supporters, we owe a very special kind of debt.

Donna C. Aguilera
Janice M. Messick

Contents

Historical development of crisis intervention

The Chinese characters that represent the word *crisis* mean both danger and opportunity. Crisis is a *danger* because it threatens to overwhelm us or our families, and it may even result in suicide or a psychotic break. It is also an *opportunity* because during times of crisis we are most receptive to help from others in learning new or more adaptive methods for coping with stressful life problems. The outcome of a psychological crisis can be either emotional growth or emotional equilibrium. Prompt recognition of a crisis-causing situation may not only prevent the development of a serious long-term disability but also allow new coping patterns to emerge that can help us function at a higher level of emotional equilibrium than before the crisis.

All of us live in a state of emotional equilibrium, a state of balance. No matter what stresses we encounter in our lives, we always strive to maintain that balance in order to be comfortable and to function. When, for whatever reason, a stress becomes so great or a problem so difficult that our usual problem-solving skills do not work, the balance of equilibrium becomes upset. We are faced with a problem that we cannot solve, tension and anxiety increase, and we cannot function. This is considered to be a *crisis*. We must either find a means to solve the problem or adapt to nonsolution. In either case a new state of equilibrium will develop; it may be better or worse insofar as positive mental health is concerned. The outcome of crisis depends heavily on the kinds of support we receive from those on whom we usually depend to give us understanding and emotional support.

When we are in a crisis, we are at a turning point in our lives. We feel helpless and overwhelmed—caught in a state of great emotional turmoil—and feel unable to take action *on our own* to solve the problem.

It is important to have some awareness of the social and cultural factors that could precipitate crisis situations and their implications for daily life experiences.

Before the revolution in technology and industrialization most people lived on farms or in small rural communities. They were chiefly self-employed, either on their farms or in small, associated businesses. When sons and daughters married, they were likely to remain near their parents, working in the same occupations; in this way trades and occupations were a link between generations. Families therefore tended to be large, and because family members lived and worked together and relied chiefly on each other for social interaction, they developed strong loyalties and a sense of responsibility for one another.

Contemporary urban life, however, does not encourage or allow this kind of sheltered, close-knit family relationship. People who live in cities are likely to be employed by a company and paid a wage. They work with business associates and live with neighbors rather than with their immediate family. Because of housing conditions and the necessity of living on a wage, families in cities usually consist of parents and unmarried children.

These differences between rural and urban life have important repercussions with regard to individual security and stability. The large, extended rural family offered a large and relatively constant group of associates. Family size and the varying strength of blood ties meant that there was always someone to talk to, even about a problem involving two family members. But urban life is highly mobile. There is often a rapid turnover in business associates and neighbors, and there is no certainty that these relative strangers will share the same values, beliefs, and interests. All these factors make it difficult for people who live in urban situations to develop real trust and interdependence outside the small immediate family. In addition, urban life requires that people meet each other only superficially, in specific roles and in limited relationships rather than as total personalities.

These factors taken together mean that people in cities are more isolated than ever before from the emotional support provided by the family and close and familiar peers. As a result, there are no role models to follow—the demands of urban life are constantly changing, and coping behavior that was appropriate and successful several years ago may be hopelessly ineffective today.

This creates a favorable environment for the development of crises.

HISTORICAL DEVELOPMENT

Only in the past few decades has *crisis* been recognized as an identifiable emotional disturbance, the outcome of which will always have some effect on a person's state of mental health. The concept of crisis and the development of therapeutic approaches to its resolution are based on a broad range of theories of human behavior, including those of Freud, Hartmann, Rado, Erikson, Lindemann, and Caplan.

Although not all theories of human behavior depend on Freudian concepts— and we will be discussing only a selected few here—we have chosen to begin with the psychoanalytic theories of Sigmund Freud because they have formed the major basis for studies of normal and abnormal human behavior.

Freud was the first to identify and apply the principle of *causality,* or cause and effect, as it relates to an individual's mental makeup. This principle states that the ways we behave in various present situations have their causes, or basis, in our past experiences. Causality exists at all times, whether or not we are consciously aware of the reasons for our behavior.

Freud constructed a developmental, or *genetic,* psychology that theorized that all our present behavior can be understood in terms of our life history or past experiences, and that the crucial foundations for the various ways in which we will behave for the rest of our lives are laid down in infancy and early childhood.

Although the ego analysts have tended to go along with much of Freud's psychoanalytic theories, there are several areas in which they differ. As a group, however, they conclude that Freud neglected the direct study of normal, healthy behavior.

Heinz Hartmann, an early ego analyst, believed that Freud's psychoanalytic theories could provide a basis for understanding normal as well as abnormal behavior. He emphasized that methods of adaptation in early childhood, as well as the ability to maintain a functional level of adaptation to the environment in later life, cannot be ignored. He also believed that although behavior is strongly influenced by culture, a part of personality will always remain relatively free to develop independent of cultural influences and constraints.

Sandor Rado based human behavior on the principle of motivation and adaptation. According to this theory, the goal, or motivation, for all our efforts to adapt to our environment is *survival.* It follows, then, that our behaviors can be viewed in terms of how they will affect our welfare, not just in terms of cause and effect. We achieve adaptation through recurring interactions with the various cultural demands that we encounter in our daily lives.

We are constantly striving to increase our chances for survival. Rado's adaptational psychotherapy emphasizes the immediate present without neglecting the developmental past. His primary concern focuses on current failures in adaptational behaviors, what caused them, and what we must do to learn to overcome them.

Erik Erikson further developed the theories of ego psychology by focusing on the developmental stages of the ego and on the theory of reality relationships. He described the ego's development as being *epigenetic,* which means that there is an orderly sequence of development of the ego at particular stages, each dependent on the other for successful completion. Erikson perceived eight stages of psychosocial development spanning the entire human life cycle and with specific developmental tasks that must be solved in each stage. The solution that is achieved in each previous stage is then applied in subsequent stages. This theory is important because it offers an explanation of our social development as a result of our ongoing encounters with the realities of our social environment. Erikson's theories also have provided a basis for the work of others, who have further developed this concept of developmental crisis and who have begun serious consideration of situational crises and of how humans adapt to current environmental dilemmas.

Eric Lindemann's initial interest was in the development of approaches that might contribute to the maintenance of good mental health and help prevent emotional disorganization on a community-wide level. In his studies of bereavement among survivors of those killed in a large-scale disaster, he described both brief and abnormally prolonged grief reactions occurring in different individuals as a result of the loss of a significant person in their lives.

Based on his experiences in working with grief reactions, Lindemann concluded that it would be useful to further develop the concept of an emotional crisis. It was this work that led to the development of crisis intervention techniques. In 1946 he and Gerald Caplan established the first community-wide program for mental health to use these concepts. It was located in the Harvard area and named the Wellesley Project.

Caplan believes that the total emotional milieu of the person must be considered in an approach to preventive mental health. The material, physical, and social demands of reality, as well as the needs, instincts, and impulses of the individual, must *all* be considered as important behavioral determinants. Through his community work he evolved the concept of the importance of crisis periods in individual and group development.

EVOLUTION OF COMMUNITY PSYCHIATRY

Community psychiatry has rapidly emerged as a new field. New concepts and new problems continually arise in constantly changing cultures; thus community psychiatry is a broad, highly flexible field.

It is now generally agreed that there are decided differences between long-term, individual-oriented psychoanalytic therapy and short-term, reality-oriented psychotherapy as practiced in community psychiatry. Community psychiatry evolved from many disciplines in the field of mental health care. The social and behavioral sciences that developed during the first half of the century were almost all based on psychodynamic theories.

After World War II the general public's increasing awareness and acceptance of the high incidence of psychiatric problems created vast changes in attitudes and demands for community action. The discovery and successful use of psychotropic drugs provided opportunities for unlocking doors in psychiatric wards and for releasing patients for rehabilitation in their home setting.

Through a slow process of trial and error, widely different programs, each trying to deal with problems involving different cultures, interests, knowledge, and skills, began communicating and relating to other programs similarly begun. Disciplines became increasingly interdependent in working toward mutually recognized goals. New, allied disciplines developed; roles changed and expanded. There was a sharing of tasks, and traditionally established lines between disciplines became more flexible.

Day hospitals for the care of psychiatric patients were first established in the late 1930's. They began out of necessity rather than as an innovative treatment modality. A shortage of hospital beds at this time began to force the premature discharge of patients to their homes.

As the bed shortage continued, the concept of day hospitals spread rapidly. Soon other innovative programs were developed to help maintain the psychiatric patient in his home community. Among these were other part-time hospitalization programs such as night and weekend hospitals. They allowed patients to continue their work, school, family, and other usual roles and to return to the hospital for part-time therapy. Half-way houses and after-care rehabilitation homes also proliferated as other methods evolved to help rehabilitate psychiatric patients in the community. Almost all psychiatric hospitals now have some form of outpatient treatment clinics to provide a wide gamut of treatment services that formerly were available only in inpatient treatment programs in hospitals.

Changes in attitudes toward the mentally ill have paralleled innovations in treatment. The patient role has gradually changed from that of a passive recipient of care from treatment staff to that of an active partner and collaborator with treatment staff. As such, the patient is expected to assume an active role in treatment programs, in planning for the future, and in accepting a much greater degree of self-responsibility for behavior.

With this refocusing of psychiatric treatment programs toward community care, it was only natural that the general hospital should add to the various roles in which it serves the community that of becoming a focal point of preventive medicine and public health functions in psychiatry.

In 1958 a "trouble-shooting clinic" was opened by the City Hospital of Elmhurst, New York, a general hospital with 1,000 beds. This type of clinic is designed to offer first aid to emotional problems and is not limited to urgent crises. It provides walk-in, around-the-clock services for major psychiatric emergencies as well as for minor problems requiring short-term counseling and guidance.

In 1961 the California Department of Mental Health established the first state agency in the country to undertake the training of specialists in community psychiatry. It was recognized that clinics were needed to accommodate the great number of people in the community who conceivably could benefit from psychiatric treatment but had never been in contact with available services. Causes for their exclusion from treatment may have been differences in sociocultural attitudes toward mental illness, lack of communication, or a lack of recognition of their mental health needs by both the population and the existing agencies.

In January 1962 the Benjamin Rush Center for Problems in Living, a division of the Los Angeles Psychiatric Service, was opened as a no-waiting, unrestricted intake, walk-in crisis intervention center. The center currently operates under the aegis of the Didi Hirsch Community Mental Health Center. After more than 20 years of operation the Benjamin Rush Center has accumulated considerable evidence suggesting that persons who come to the center are generally different from those who typically seek treatment in a traditional clinic. The center's approach has been to bring forth persons who, although judged to be genuinely in need of psychiatric treatment, would not have sought traditional treatment because of a reluctance to consider themselves "sick," to assume the patient role, or to accept the stigma of psychiatric treatment.

The advent of community psychiatry in the early 1960's represented a major step away from institutionalized treatment of the mentally ill and toward preventive care for the emotionally vulnerable. On the basis of the unique needs of the populations they are trying to reach, community mental health programs have recognized the value of providing innovative, nontraditional services in preventive care.

Within a few years crisis-oriented services were being made increasingly available to populations at risk for a wide variety of stressful crisis-precipitating problems. Their primary goal is to reach people at early stages in the evolution of their crises; to facilitate resolution of the problem-causing increased tension and anxiety; and to help people return to emotional equilibrium at their former level or a higher level. Crisis-oriented treatment has become increasingly available to more people.

Physicians, nurses, and counselors functioning in psychiatric hospitals have done much to expedite their patients' return to independent functioning and to reduce their time spent as inpatients. Multilingual and multicultural clinics have proven effective in reaching non–English-speaking and foreign-born populations. The clergy have also become an immediate resource for many by providing pastoral counseling. They occupy a sensitive position in many communities and contribute much to the identification and resolution of potential crisis-causing problems.

Hot lines are another innovation in nontraditional treatment programs. It has been said, and perhaps not facetiously, that for every potential crisis-causing situation there is, or soon will be, a hot line. Hot lines are 24-hour crisis telephones that provide free counseling and a minimum of red tape, contacts with walk-in clinics if requested, and anonymity if the caller desires it. Almost all hot lines are staffed by volunteers who have received special training and who have ongoing professional supervision in their work. These services are becoming increasingly prevalent and attractive to people who feel the need for help with their problems in living but are either unable or unwilling to go to a traditional walk-in clinic.

Trends such as these are being repeated around the country as community mental health programs recognize the value of providing services in primary and secondary prevention unique to the needs of their particular clients. Increasing recognition is also being given to the need to provide more services for clients whose needs are for continuing support in rehabilitation after resolution of the immediate crisis.

PREVENTIVE MENTAL HEALTH

Preventive medicine is not a new concept in community care services, but the practice of prevention of mental illness on a community-wide basis has initiated a new era in psychiatric practice.

At the *primary* level prevention in mental health is accomplished by anticipatory planning, counseling, and guidance. Examples of such primary prevention are programs in marriage and family counseling, child guidance, expectant parent classes, and work with similar groups or individuals who may be faced with major changes in their lives. Through the practice of *primary* prevention vulnerable people in need of more intensive help may be identified and others may strengthen or even increase their levels of emotional equilibrium.

Secondary prevention in mental health care involves early case finding, diagnosis, and prompt treatment. Too often in the past less attention was given to this level of prevention in the community. Although case finding usually took place in the community, it was more often than not coincidental to general medical care. People were referred to psychiatric facilities either when the community could no longer tolerate or accept an individual's abnormal behavior or when an individual could no longer cope with the anxiety and stress of an emotional disturbance.

It is only within recent years that increasing recognition is also being given to the need to provide more community psychiatry services for those who require continuing support and rehabilitation. This is known as *tertiary* prevention. It includes halting further disability and providing rehabilitation toward the individual's maximum achievable level of mental health.

Until recently this level of prevention was relegated almost entirely to large institutional facilities, with little or no family and community participation. Increasing numbers of supportive services are now available in the community. These include half-way houses, vocational counseling and retraining programs, self-help groups, and many other innovative programs. Family and community members, as appropriate, are encouraged to participate in all phases of these rehabilitation programs.

Discerning the services most needed by potential clients and attracting clients are not major concerns confronting community mental health centers today. The major problem today for many centers is recruiting an adequate staff to meet the demands for services. Professionals and nonprofessionals alike are being recruited and specially trained to help fill the gaps between supply and demand for community mental health services.

PARAPROFESSIONALS

Almost all health care facilities employ persons who have had technical training to prepare them to assist professional staff in patient treatment programs. They are called *paraprofessionals*. Each profession has developed its own training programs and is responsible for supervising its own paraprofessionals. Their work titles usually include the name of the profession (physician, nursing, social work, psychology, etc.) and such added designations as "assistant," "technician," or "aide."

Increasing numbers of paraprofessionals are receiving additional training and education to function as mental health assistants and counselors in specialty programs. In general, the functions of the paraprofessional staff should not be determined by the scope of their education and training alone. They must also be determined by the amount of professional supervision and consultation time that a program is willing and able to provide. Inappropriate use of paraprofessionals in new community programs could easily perpetuate the past patterns of providing second-class services to those who cannot afford treatment elsewhere. The public has become quite sophisticated in its understanding of human rights to equal care and treatment. It will not accept less much longer.

NON-MENTAL HEALTH PROFESSIONALS

Non-mental health professionals such as medical professionals, teachers, lawyers, clergy, policemen, firemen, and social and welfare workers are also being recruited into liaison activities with community programs. All of them serve as the official caretakers within our communities and have in common their traditional role of helping people in trouble. In the course of their daily work these highly skilled individuals function on the front lines of preventive mental health care. They are frequently in contact with individuals or groups who are in potential crisis situations because of a loss or the threat of a loss in their lives. Often these official community caretakers become the initial contact for a person in crisis.

NONPROFESSIONAL VOLUNTEERS

Many nonprofessional volunteers are being used in other than traditional volunteer roles in community health centers and are being provided specialized training to become meaningful members of treatment teams. For example, crisis hot lines, initially established by professionals, rely heavily on trained nonprofessional volunteers to maintain their 24-hour-a-day, 7-day-a-week operations. The potential danger of hot lines for both clients and volunteers is lack of close professional supervision. For the client there is always the danger that an unskilled volunteer may be responding solely with personal intuition and bias. For the volunteer without professional supervision there is always the danger of becoming overwhelmed by increased tension and anxiety when confronting situations for which he has no special problem-solving training or past coping experiences on which to draw.

WHERE TO FIND HELP

Where do you begin to look for help when you suddenly find yourself feeling overwhelmed and unable to cope with a problem in your life? To begin with, where you live may be a major determining factor. In general, mental health professionals tend to cluster in large urban areas where both private and community psychiatry services are more accepted and used. However, increasing numbers of mental health teams have incorporated traveling clinics to rural areas on a regularly scheduled basis. Both state- and county-sponsored mental health agencies can be easily located in your local telephone directory or by getting in contact with a local medical agency for a referral.

Mental health programs operate under a wide variety of names. Their names may or may not indicate the kinds of help they provide. For example, it is not difficult to determine the kinds of problems with which *suicide prevention centers, child guidance clinics,* and *marriage and family counseling programs* deal. Most hot lines likewise have easily identifiable names.

Larger, multiservice community centers tend to operate under generalized names such as the "Big Town Mental Health Center" or the "City Hospital Mental Hygiene Clinic." These names indicate that they provide help for emotional, not medical, problems. Further information as to exactly what services these centers provide can be easily obtained by telephone or personal contact with the staff.

It may be helpful to seek advice for referrals from professional community caretakers such as physicians, attorneys, clergy, school teachers and counselors, policemen, and firemen. All these people have clearly identified helping roles in the community. They have both the experience and the knowledge to help solve problems related to their areas of expertise, and they can provide referrals to others as needed.

Finally, there are many other people that you may have never consciously identified as having a significant helping role in your daily life. These may be family members, particularly the ones you know you can depend on when there is a troublesome problem to solve. They may also include close friends, the bartender down the street, the hairdresser, or the friendly neighbor. What they all may have in common is the ability to be good, objective listeners whom you can trust to come up with logical, reality-based advice for helping to solve a problem.

Different types of therapy

Each of us encounters problems of some sort as we go through life—some minor and others that seem to be major. Frequently just discussing the problem with someone else and gaining a different perspective will help solve the problem. At other times this does not work and there is a need to seek professional help before the problem can be resolved.

The purpose of this chapter is to familiarize you with the different types of psychotherapy so that intelligent selection, according to individual needs, can be made. It not only describes *types* of therapy, but *who* does them, *what* educational background different therapists should have, *how much* therapy may cost, and *where* one may find the different types of therapists. Also discussed are some of the problems that may require professional help and which kinds of problems usually respond to which types of psychotherapy.

Psychotherapy as a form of treatment has many definitions. Areas of difference are usually methods, goals, length of therapy, and indications for treatment. Psychotherapy of all types is a set of procedures for changing behaviors; it is based primarily on the relationship between two or more people.

PSYCHOANALYSIS AND PSYCHOANALYTIC THERAPY

Psychoanalysis is concerned with theory (primarily Sigmund Freud's) as well as with techniques. The traditional approach in psychoanalytic therapy is nondirective. The therapist is a passive observer who follows the lead of the patient's verbal expressions as they unfold before him. For example, a patient may say, "I remember the first time my father spanked me." The therapist may respond with, "Go on," or "Do you remember how you felt?"

The situation and techniques in psychoanalysis can best be described by the following eight factors:

1. Exclusive reliance during the hour on the patient's free associations for communication

2. Regularity of time, frequency, and duration of appointments; clearly defined financial agreement
3. Three to five appointments a week (this was originally six, with daily appointments strongly recommended)
4. Recumbent position, "the couch," with the analyst sitting behind the client, out of sight
5. Confinement of the analyst's activity to interpretation of what the patient says or an occasional question
6. Analyst's emotional passivity and neutrality
7. Analyst's abstention from advice or any other direct intervention or participation in the patient's daily life
8. Use of a procedure that is guided largely by the patient's free association from day to day and in which there is no immediate emphasis on curing symptoms

In psychoanalytic psychotherapy the therapist is more active than in psychoanalysis. The therapist interacts more with the patient and does not interpret as completely. The most helpful attitude is one of calm. This differs from the neutral attitude of the analyst in psychoanalysis. It is believed that a calm, helpful, and interested attitude of the therapist provides support for the patient in dealing with tensions, sustains contact with reality, and provides gratifications and rewards in the therapeutic relationship. These, in turn, provide incentives for the patient to continue to deal with emerging unconscious material.

Psychoanalytic psychotherapy procedures are usually divided into two categories based on the methods they use; they are usually referred to as supportive (suppressive) and uncovering (exploratory, expressive) procedures. The aim of the uncovering procedure is to intensify the ego's ability to handle repressed, unconscious, emotional conflict situations. Through transference the patient relives early interpersonal conflicts in relation to the therapist. Supportive and uncovering procedures overlap, but it is not difficult to distinguish between them. Primarily, supportive methods of treatment are used when impairment of the ego is temporary and is caused by acute emotional distress. There are five tasks in the supportive procedure:

1. Gratifying dependency needs of the patient during stress situations, thereby reducing anxiety
2. Reducing stress by giving the patient an opportunity to relive (in feeling, action, or imagination) the situation that originally caused the conflict (this process is called abreaction)
3. Giving intellectual guidance by objectively reviewing with the patient his acute stress situation, thus helping the individual gain a proper perspective of the total situation
4. Supporting the patient's neurotic defenses until his ego can handle the emotional discharges

5. Actively participating in changing or manipulating the life situation (for example, encouraging the patient to change his job or residence) when this may be the *only* approach in the circumstances

Psychoanalysis and psychoanalytic psychotherapy require many years of intensive training on the part of the therapist. The aspiring therapist must graduate from medical school, complete a residency in psychiatry, undergo years of analysis himself, and pass state board examinations to become board certified. This is one of the main reasons that there is a limited number of these therapists and that psychoanalysis is so expensive. Depending on geographical location, psychoanalysis may cost from 50 to 150 dollars an hour—with three or four sessions a week. In large metropolitan cities on the East and West coasts the fee is higher than in smaller cities in the South and Midwest. This is why most analysts work in large cities in private practice.

In summary, the goal of psychoanalysis is that of restructuring the personality; the focus of treatment is the genetic past (origin, development) and the freeing of the unconscious. Psychoanalytic psychotherapeutic procedures are usually divided into two categories—supportive (supressive) and uncovering (exploratory or expressive) procedures. The therapist's role is nondirective and that of a passive observer. This type of therapy is indicated for individuals with neurotic personality patterns. The length of the therapy is indefinite and depends on the individual and therapist. Psychoanalysis can last for years and is very expensive.

BRIEF PSYCHOTHERAPY

Brief psychotherapy as a treatment form developed as the result of the increased demand for mental health services and the lack of personnel trained to meet this demand. Initially much of it was conducted by psychiatric residents as part of their training. Later psychiatric social workers and psychologists became involved in this form of treatment.

Brief psychotherapy has its roots in psychoanalytic theory but differs from psychoanalysis in terms of goals and other factors. It is limited to removing or alleviating specific symptoms when possible. Intervention may lead to some reconstruction of personality, although it is not considered as the primary goal. As in more traditional forms of psychotherapy, the therapy must be guided by an orderly series of concepts directed toward beneficial change in the patient. It is concerned with the degree of abatement of the symptoms presented and the return to or maintenance of the individual's ability to function adequately. To attain this goal, the individual may choose to involve himself in a longer form of therapy. Another goal is assistance in preventing the development of deeper neurotic or psychotic symptoms after catastrophies or emergencies in life situations.

Free association, interpretation, and the analysis of transference are also used successfully in a modified manner. Free association is not a basic tool in short-term therapy. It may arise in response to a stimulus from the therapist. Interpretation is modified by the time limit and the immediacy of the problem. Although it may occur in brief psychotherapy, it is commonly used with medical or environmental types of intervention.

It is believed that positive transference should be encouraged. It is crucial in brief therapy that the individual see the therapist as likable, reliable, and understanding. The individual *must* believe that the therapist will be able to help if treatment goals are to be accomplished in a short period. This does not mean that negative transference feelings are to be ignored, but it does mean that these feelings are not analyzed in terms of defenses.

In brief psychotherapy the therapist assumes a more active role than in the traditional methods. Trends not directly related to the presenting problem are avoided. The positive is accentuated, and the therapist acts as an interested, helpful person. The difficulties faced by the patient are circumscribed. The environmental position of the patient is used by the therapist to help the patient evaluate the reality of the situation in an attempt to modify and change it. Productive behavior is encouraged.

Diagnostic evaluation is extremely important in short-term therapy. Its aim is to understand the symptoms and the patient dynamically and to formulate hypotheses that can be validated by the historical data. The result of the diagnosis will enable the therapist to decide which factors are most susceptible to change and to select the appropriate method of intervention. Part of the evaluation should be the degree of discrepancy or accord between the patient's fantasies and reality. His probable ability to tolerate past and future frustrations should also be considered; the adequacy of his past and present relationships is also pertinent. The question "Why do you come now?" must be asked and means not only "What is it that is going on in your life that distresses you?" but also "What is it that you expect in the way of help?" It is reasonable to assume that a request for help is motivated by emotional necessities, both external and internal, which are meaningful to the patient. Short-term goals can be beneficial for *all* patients.

After determining the causes of the symptoms, the therapist elects the appropriate intervention. Interpretation to achieve insight is used with care. Direct confrontation is used sparingly. An attempt is made to strengthen the ego by increasing the patient's self-esteem. One facet of this approach is to help the patient feel that he is on a level with the therapist and that he is no less worthwhile nor are his problems more unusual than those of others. This technique not only relieves the patient's anxiety but also facilitates communication between the patient and the therapist. Other basic procedures include the following: catharsis, drive repression and restraint, reality testing, intellectualization, reassurance and support, counseling and guidance to move the patient along a line of behavior, and conjoint counseling.

The ending of treatment is an important phase in brief therapy. The patient should be left with a positive transference and the feeling that he may return if the need arises. The learning that has taken place during therapy must be reinforced to encourage the patient to realize that he has begun to understand and solve his own problems. This has a preventive effect that will help the patient to recognize possible future problems.

As an adjunct, drug therapy may be used in selected cases. This is in contrast to pure psychoanalysis, where such is seldom used. Environmental manipulation is considered when it is necessary to remove or modify an element causing disruption in the patient's life pattern. Included might be close scrutiny of family and friends, job and job training, education, and plans for travel.

Brief psychotherapy is indicated in cases of acutely disruptive emotional pain, in cases of severely destructive circumstances, and in situations endangering the life of the patient or others. Another indication involves the life circumstances of the individual; if he cannot involve himself in the long-term therapeutic situation, which implies a stable residence, job, and so forth, brief therapy is advocated to alleviate disruptive symptoms.

It is imperative that the patient feel relief as rapidly as possible, even during the first therapeutic session. The span of treatment can be any reasonable, limited number of sessions but usually is more than six. Most clinics expect the number of visits to be under twenty. Treatment goals can be attained in this short period if the patient is seen quickly and intensively after requesting help. Circumstances associated with disrupted functioning are more easily accessible if they are recent. Only active conflicts are amenable to therapeutic intervention. Disequilibrated states are more easily resolved *before* they have crystallized, acquired secondary gain features, or developed into highly maladaptive behavior patterns.

CRISIS INTERVENTION

Crisis intervention extends logically from brief psychotherapy. The minimum therapeutic goal of crisis intervention is psychological resolution of the individual's immediate crisis and restoration at least to the level of functioning that existed before the crisis period. A maximum goal is functioning above the precrisis level.

A crisis is characteristically self-limiting and lasts from 4 to 6 weeks. This constitutes a transitional period, representing both the danger of increased psychological vulnerability and an opportunity for personality growth. In any particular situation the outcome may depend to a significant degree on the ready availability of appropriate help. On this basis the length of time for intervention is from 4 to 6 weeks, with the median being 4 weeks.

Since time is at a premium, a therapeutic climate is generated that commands the concentrated attention of both therapist and patient. A goal-oriented sense of commitment develops in sharp contrast to the more modest pace of traditional treatment modes.

Generic approach

The generic approach focuses on the characteristic course of the *particular kind of crisis* rather than on the psychodynamics of each individual in crisis. A treatment plan is directed toward an adaptive resolution of the crisis. Specific intervention measures are designed to be effective for all members of a given group rather than for the unique situation of one individual. Recognition of behavioral patterns is an important aspect of preventive mental health.

It has been suggested that knowledge of patterned behaviors in transitional states during intense or sudden change from one life situation to another might provide a basis for the management of these states and the prevention of subsequent mental illness. Examples are studies of individual responses to community disaster, migration, and retirement of pensioners.

Generic approaches to crisis intervention include direct encouragement of adaptive behavior, general support, environmental manipulation, and anticipatory guidance. In brief, the generic approach emphasizes (1) specific situational and maturational-developmental events occurring to significant population groups, (2) intervention oriented to crises that are related to these specific events, and (3) intervention carried out by non–mental health professionals.

This approach has been found to be a feasible mode of intervention that can be learned and implemented by nonpsychiatric physicians, nurses, social workers, and so forth. It does not require a mastery of knowledge of the intrapsychic and interpersonal processes of an individual in crisis.

Individual approach

The individual approach differs from the generic in its emphasis on assessment, by a professional, of the interpersonal and intrapsychic processes of the person in crisis. It is used in selected cases, usually those not responding to the generic approach. Intervention is planned to meet the unique needs of the individual in crisis and to reach a solution for the particular situation and circumstances that precipitated the crisis. This differs from the generic approach, which focuses on the characteristic course of a particular kind of crisis.

Unlike the case in extended psychotherapy, there is relatively little concern with the developmental past of the individual. Information from this source is seen as relevant only for clues that may result in a better understanding of the present crisis situation. Emphasis is placed on the immediate causes of disturbed equilibrium and on the processes necessary for regaining a precrisis or higher level of functioning. The inclusion of family members or other important persons in the process of the patient's crisis resolution is another area of differentiation from most psychotherapy.

In comparison with the generic approach, the individual approach emphasizes the need for greater depth of understanding of biological, psychological, and sociological processes. The intervention is oriented to the individual's unique situation and carried out only by mental health professionals.

Several attitudes are important adjuncts to the specific techniques. In essence, they comprise the general philosophical orientation of therapist and patient necessary for the full effectiveness of the intervention.

1. It is essential that the therapist and the individual view the work being done as the treatment of choice for crisis intervention.
2. Accurate assessment of the presenting problem, *not* a thorough diagnostic evaluation, is essential to an effective intervention.
3. Both the therapist and the individual should keep in mind throughout the contacts that the treatment is sharply time limited and should persistently direct their energies toward resolution of the presenting problem.
4. Dealing with material not directly related to the crisis has no place in an intervention of this kind.
5. The therapist takes an active and sometimes directive role in the intervention. The relatively slow paced approach of more traditional treatment is inappropriate in this type of therapy.
6. Maximum flexibility of approach is encouraged. Such diverse techniques as serving as a resource person or information giver and taking an active role in established liaison with other helping resources are often appropriate in particular situations.
7. The goal toward which the therapist is striving is explicit. His energy is directed entirely toward returning the individual to at least his precrisis level of functioning.

Steps in crisis intervention

1. The initial session may be spent finding out what the problem is; in other words, what in the patient's life is different or changed. What are the symptoms of stress? Is the patient extremely anxious or depressed (the two cardinal symptoms of a crisis)? How disruptive are the symptoms? For example, can the patient still function at work or at home? Is he unable to sleep? Has he lost his appetite? If so, how much weight has he lost? (A loss of 7 pounds a month indicates severe depression.) Does the patient talk about suicide? If so, does he have a *plan* or is he just thinking about it (suicidal ideation)? If he has a plan, does he have a *method,* and how lethal is the method? Does he have a loaded gun or a tall building or bridge picked out? Can he tell *when* he plans to do it? For example, after his wife goes to work? The therapist must also find out whether the patient is homicidal. Questions that are asked are those to find out *who, when, how,* and *why.* If the plan, method, and time are specific, the patient must be referred to a psychiatrist for evaluation and hospitaliza-

tion. In some states, by law, the intended victim must also be notified.

2. Usually at the end of the first session the therapist has assessed the patient and the problem. The therapeutic interventions are then discussed. The patient is told what crisis intervention can and cannot do. It *can* restore the patient to his precrisis level of functioning; it *cannot* bring about major changes in personality structure.

3. Intervention techniques depend on the skills, creativity, and flexibility of the therapist. The therapist will have a very direct approach. There is no time and no need to go into the patient's past history in depth. The focus is on the "here and now"—reality orientation. Sometimes the patient can see no relationship between the problem (the crisis) and the symptoms being experienced. In this case the therapist can provide the "link" between the crisis and the symptoms by describing the connection.

An immediate goal of intervention is the reduction of tension the patient is feeling. This can be done by providing means for him to recognize suppressed feelings and bring them out in the open—in a safe environment—with the therapist. If the crisis has been caused by the loss of someone significant (through termination of a relationship, separation, or death), the therapist may suggest the possibility of bringing new people in the life-space to fill the void. This is known as "repeopling the social world." It is very effective if supports and gratifications provided by the "lost" person in the past can be achieved—to a similar degree—from new relationships.

4. The last phase is the resolution of the crisis and planning for the future. The therapist will reinforce those appropriate coping mechanisms which the patient has used with success to reduce tension and anxiety. Assistance is given, as needed, in making realistic plans for the future. There is usually a discussion of ways in which the present experience may help the patient cope with future crises.

Summary

Crisis intervention is usually conducted by psychologists, psychiatric social workers, and psychiatric nurses in community mental health centers who have been taught how to deal with patients in a crisis situation. All have either a doctoral (Ph.D.) or master's degree and have completed an internship at a crisis center. The centers are usually a part of a state's mental health or outpatient centers. The majority of large hospitals in metropolitan cities have a walk-in crisis outpatient center.

The goal of crisis intervention is the resolution of an immediate crisis. Its focus is on the genetic present, with the restoration of the individual to his precrisis level of functioning or possibly to a higher level of functioning. The therapist's role is direct, suppressive, and that of an active participant. Techniques are varied, limited only by the flexibility and creativity of the therapist. Some of these techniques include helping the individual gain an intellectual understanding of his crisis, assisting the individual in bringing his feelings into the open, exploring past and present coping mechanisms, finding and using situational supports, and anticipatory planning with the individual to reduce the possibility of future crises. The indications for this type of therapy are an individual's (or family's) sudden loss of ability to cope with a life situation. The average length of treatment is from one to six sessions, and, depending on the center, the cost of treatment may range from 0 to 50 dollars.

Group therapy concepts in crisis intervention

GROUP CONCEPTS

From birth the individual is a member of a group composed of himself and his parents. Life becomes a succession of group memberships, expanding from the basic family unit to peer groups, play groups, and groups in school, business, and church. An individual may remain in a group permanently or temporarily, voluntarily or involuntarily, directly or indirectly, but will usually participate in some form of group activity until death.

A helpless infant depending on the actions of others for survival progresses through intellectual, emotional, and social development. Forms of behavior that communicate feelings, needs, and ideas develop through interactions with others. At the same time, perceptions and reactions toward the feelings, needs, and ideas of others develop.

It has been suggested that an individual's behavior can be controlled and influenced by the forces of groups of which he is a member and that he becomes what he is because of the roles, status, and functions that are taken or given in them. Interpersonal skills are neither inherited nor instinctive but are acquired through a continual learning process involving use of all the senses. Facial expressions, vocal tones, body movements, odors, and touch are all part of the language of interpersonal communications. Since human beings communicate through nonverbal as well as verbal clues, deprivation of any of the senses could lead to distorted perceptions of the actions and responses of others.

Experiences that bring feelings of comfort and satisfaction are usually tried again, whereas those which result in frustration and discomfort are avoided whenever possible. Thus progressive learning is based on past experiences. If a child's first important group, the immediate family, fails to provide gratifying, positive interpersonal learning experiences, his future psychosocial development could be impaired. For example, the child who has never learned how to obtain gratifying feelings of approval from his family may be less than secure in establishing relationships with authority figures in other groups later (such as with teachers in school). He may also experience difficulties in his early peer groups, where beginning competition and leadership skills are first learned.

In recent years practical and scientific knowledge has been synthesized to form new concepts about the manipulation of group structures and group processes to effect change, both on the group and on its individual members. In psychiatry there has been a shift of emphasis from considering man as a biological entity to considering him as a biological, psychological, and sociological entity. Movement has been increasingly away from an organism-centered to a social-centered conceptualization of personality dynamics. Other professions and social institutions have also been increasingly aware of the effects of group influences on the individual.

During and immediately after World War II there was an increased recognition of the necessity to meet the special needs of groups of people for whom individual care was impossible. This contributed to a rapid rise in the development and acceptance of group therapy and other therapeutic groups in the military, veterans' hospitals, and state and private institutions and clinics. Since then an increasing variety of therapy groups has been developed in community and institutional settings, not only for patients with psychiatric problems, but also for people unable to cope with many situational and maturational-developmental problems and stresses in daily life.

THERAPY GROUPS

Simple definition of the term *group therapy* is difficult because of the wide variety of concepts, methods, and interpretations of its meaning. A group involves, primarily, more than one person. Group therapy could mean, simply, a treatment given simultaneously to more than one person. When the group goal of effecting a change is included, the definition of group therapy becomes more complicated because consideration must then be given to the methods and processes of group and individual action and to the wide differences in group accomplishments.

Some writers propose a classification of group therapies in terms of involvement of intellectual, emotional, or action factors. Others suggest classifications based on concrete activities. One approach to understanding the differences between the many types of therapy groups has been to focus on their purposes and results. Two main categories are suggested: *social group work* and *group therapy.*

Another approach to classifying therapy groups is to focus on the concept of depth in therapy for differentiating between types of psychotherapies. The concept of depth in therapy is a controversial one, and there is apparently no absolute criterion for determining the absolute values of any one method in relation to another. The absence of accurate measuring devices makes it difficult to measure quantitatively changes in the psyche, functions, and attitudes resulting from therapy, and comparisons among methods could be misleading.

If the choice of method and course of psychotherapy is determined by the nature and intensity of individual needs, it is suggested that psychotherapies be differentiated by means of the level of a person's psyche that requires change. On the basis of this concept psychotherapy has been differentiated into the main categories of *counseling, guidance,* and *psychotherapy.*

Social group work

In social group work the purpose is to achieve a common group goal with the aid of a leader. A project or an activity is used to unite the members, and the chief result is socialization. Examples are recreational groups, calling for teamwork and sportsmanship; rhythm and game groups; and sociodrama, in which symptomatic behavior is indirectly touched on by participants through play acting. In this way discussions of feelings and behavior can be directed toward the *part* that is acted out, not toward the participant himself. Scouting and camping groups for children and adolescents are other means of fostering socialization and group-unifying activities.

In all social groups the leader serves as a director, discusser, or counselor. He must have skills in special areas, and his understanding of the dynamics of personality is secondary in importance to his understanding of group action and cultural patterns and mores. He is usually directive in his method of leading group activities along a prescribed course.

Counseling

Counseling is reality oriented and focuses on solving specific problems arising from situational or interpersonal difficulties. The counselor is not required to be a trained psychotherapist but should have a greater knowledge than the patient of the factors affecting the situation. The role is to direct actively toward the finding and acceptance of a solution to an immediate difficulty while not intentionally exposing the patient's feelings or attitudes for the purpose of changing them. It is assumed that once the solutions are made clear, the ego will be able to function adequately toward solving the problem. The interviews are comparatively brief, and the sessions terminate as soon as the immediate specific difficulty is resolved. This method is least effective in group use.

Guidance

Guidance is a reality-oriented approach that may be used when a person is incapable of coping with increased stresses because the emotional significance of a specific problem begins to affect simple ego functioning. The aims and techniques are toward holding or reducing anxiety to a tolerable level and preventing disorganization. The focus is on correcting feelings and requires a professionally trained person with a sound understanding of psychodynamics and experience in psychotherapy that will enable the professional to work at this deeper level. The therapist's role is to supply clarification and support through empathy, acceptance, and permissiveness, thus enabling a patient to bring conflicting feelings about the specific problem into conscious awareness and to ventilate them without increasing anxiety, guilt, or fear.

This approach may require a much longer time and more sessions than required in the counseling approach because there is a need to prevent additional stress and discomfort. The patient is confronted with personal feelings and may be expected to change some perceptions, attitudes, and behaviors.

The use of groups appears to accelerate the guidance process, particularly when people with problems of a similar nature are brought together. There is mutual identification with the problem area, and interactions occur rapidly. Members can possibly provide each other with greater support of self-esteem through empathy, acceptance, and permissiveness than the therapist alone could provide. Negative feelings of being alone in needing help with a problem are alleviated.

Guidance has been found particularly effective in dealing with adolescents, persons with marital problems, families, and parents of handicapped children. The therapist's role in the group requires the ability to use skills necessary for psychotherapy and the ability to recognize and avoid threatening areas for each member while working with the group as a whole. Feelings and behaviors are explored only as they are significant to the reality of each member's life situation. Unrestricted exploration of feelings is avoided.

Group psychotherapy

Group psychotherapy is intended to make fundamental personality changes and to investigate reasons for personal emotional problems. Unlike counseling or guidance, it does not aim to solve a single specific situational problem. Rather group psychotherapy aims toward correction of intrapsychic processes that will make the patient more capable of dealing with many problems.

The group approach is based on concepts of individual psychotherapy. Free association and unrestricted exploration of emotions are encouraged. Unlike the case with social or guidance groups, there is no one specific group goal; each member has his own specific aims and expectations as to what the group experience can offer. Cohesiveness of members develops from the stresses and pain they experience as they focus on emotional problems, traumatic memories, and uncovered feelings as well as from mutual identification with specific reality problem areas. Efforts to minimize these feelings by resorting to gamelike activities are not permitted. Rather than avoiding threatening areas, the therapist takes relatively few precautions and encourages ventilation or catharsis of feelings. General therapeutic goals for patients with functional illness are to relieve tensions and anxiety, help them to gain some insights into their problems, assist them in resolving some of their conflicts, and support them in replacing inappropriate behaviors with appropriate ones.

Group therapy uses a variety of techniques to obtain its general aims, and therapists often differ in their leadership roles. Some actively direct, whereas others deem it more therapeutic to take a passive, indirect role to a degree that the group appears to be self-directed.

Although there is a relationship between technique and theory, few present-day techniques have been derived *solely* from theory. The therapist will undoubtedly be testing out certain theories, hypotheses, psychodynamics, and group dynamics; this is an intrinsic part of a professional scientific role. At the same time the therapist also has the role of "healer" by assuming responsibilities to help individuals solve concrete problems encountered in their daily living.

Some therapists focus on the psychodynamics of individual behavior; others focus on group dynamics. Sometimes the focus will remain on the theoretical, intellectual level rather than on the specific individual behavioral responses taking place in the immediate interactions of the group. More often than not there is a combination of both, and no one method can be proven to be better or worse than another.

The therapist will communicate to patients the purpose of the group and the principles or rules under which members will operate. The patient's acceptance of this mode of therapy is determined in large part by whether he sees it as meeting his needs and whether he will be able to function under the principles of the group's operation. For example, a person's basic difficulties may stem from early negative experiences in his primary family, and as a result, avoidance reactions to group contacts could further increase his anxieties. Not only might this lead to increasing areas of conflict, but the necessary positive transference experience would be unlikely. Selection criteria for members vary widely according to their needs, the availability and special areas of expertise of qualified therapists, and the purpose of the groups. These factors may also influence the size of membership. There is no general agreement as to the number of sessions needed to accomplish specific goals.

The group process provides more than one person with whom the individual may identify and test out reactions to past experiences. The therapist is most likely to be seen as the parental role figure. Other group members with whom interactions take place are sibling role figures. In this way group psychotherapy provides, on a small scale, a situation in which a problem in interpersonal relationships can be exposed; a setting for action, reaction, and interaction in a therapeutic environment; and a setting in which distorted perceptions of interpersonal experiences in the past can be revealed and examined. Varied interpersonal stimuli will be received from more than one source, and increasing opportunities for a transference experience to take place and to be worked through will occur. A transference experience occurs when a person reacts to someone in the present as he did to someone in the past. This occurs because everyone has a tendency to carry into the present attitudes and impressions gained from past interpersonal experiences. Although the present person may possess only one or two of the characteristics of the past person, a generalized distortion of the relationship can be triggered. He becomes the recipient of the emotional responses and reactive behaviors that, in reality, were learned in the past relationship.

One therapeutic goal is to modify and clarify feelings, and feelings must be labeled and then verbalized in order for this to take place. The group provides an incentive in this area by open discussion during which patients are stimulated by the fact of emotions expressed by others and by the opportunity to relate their own problems to others in the group. Changed or new behavioral responses can be tried out, observed in action, reflected, and the dynamics explored for cause-and-effect reactions. Opportunities to increase coping capacities are important because they improve the person's ability to resolve emotional issues and interpersonal problems that create conflicts.

For the individual, group experience is primarily an emotional one, and through interactions with other members the patient is confronted by relationships that may be supportive, critical, or a combination of the two. Members are encouraged both to criticize and support each other, support occurring most often through mutual acceptance and empathic responses. The presence of others is perceived as a protection against being the only object of the therapist's attention. Acceptance by a peer group rather than by just one person, the therapist, is reassuring, and feelings of being different and isolated are counteracted by the discovery that one's feelings and problems may be shared by others. It is generally agreed that intragroup support is essential to the growth of a therapy group. Group interaction should help the members to achieve insight into past behavior and to gain self-awareness in learning to adapt to more positive and satisfying interpersonal experiences in the future.

CRISIS GROUPS

The term *group therapy* may refer to any two individuals who are in therapy together with a therapist. Certain terms that may be unfamiliar to those who have not been involved in conducting therapy will be clarified. *Individual crisis intervention therapy* refers to therapy in a one-to-one relationship with the therapist (see Case study: Edward, p. 47). *Conjoint therapy* refers to therapy that is conducted with a husband and wife who are seen by the therapist together (see Case study: Laura, p. 40). *Family therapy* is therapy for the members of a family who are involved or affected by the crisis situation (see Case study: Mary, p. 118). *Collateral therapy* refers to therapy for almost any two individuals who are involved in a crisis: mother and son, father and son, mother and daughter, father and daughter, boyfriend and girlfriend, friends, roommates, and so forth (see Case study: Bob, p. 121). *Crisis group* refers to unknown and unrelated individuals who meet as a group with a therapist to work together toward resolution of their individual crises through group interaction (see Case study: Opal, p. 27).

Treatment goals

The goal of a crisis group is to return the individual members of the group to at least their precrisis level of functioning and possibly to a higher level with an increased ability to solve problems. The focus of treatment (like that of crisis intervention individual therapy) is the present and the problem that is of concern at the time the individual requests help. Treatment deals with the stresses and factors that are either absent or ineffective in the present crisis situation and is directed toward helping the members to achieve a resolution of their crises. With the therapist, the members explore the crisis, past coping skills (what they usually do when they cannot handle anxiety, tension, or stress), situational supports (whom they usually turn to for help), and what is going on at the present time that is preventing them from solving their problems. The group members usually quickly become a cohesive group, actively involved in helping other members develop new coping skills and find situational supports. The therapist keeps them aware that the number of sessions for each individual is limited to six, using such methods as reminding them that a certain member has only two more sessions left.

Selection of members

The determination of whether individuals requesting help in a crisis situation would benefit more from group therapy than from individual therapy is initially left to the discretion of the intake worker who sees the patient first. It might be that a group is being formed or that an ongoing group is oriented toward problems similar to the one in which the patient is involved. For example, there may be groups of couples having marital problems, parents having problems that involve their children, persons trying to break the drug habit, and adolescents having problems such as with family, drugs, or juvenile authority. Another consideration is whether another member can be added to the group. The crisis group is open ended. Because its members enter and leave at different times, some will be beginning in the group, some will be half through, and some will be terminating. Five to eight members is usually considered the best size for a crisis group, although the size can fluctuate weekly as some members are absent or are terminated and new members are added. The therapist who conducts the group will control its size by limiting the number of intake interviews scheduled each week.

Some crisis groups have differing rather than common problems as their focus. Individuals may be included in one of these groups if the intake worker believes that they would benefit more by interaction in a group than in a one-to-one relationship. It may be decided that part of a person's problem is the result of inadequate interpersonal relations. The individual may be a social isolate by choice or by necessity, and his problem may be that he has never been able to establish satisfactory relationships with others because of low self-esteem, poor self-concept, or a real or imagined handicap. The individual may be new to the area or functioning in a new job or school and having difficulty meeting and making friends. Such individuals would benefit from a group experience. Groups dealing with different problems may also be the choice for individuals who might resist accepting the "advice of experts" but would be more agreeable to changing faulty coping skills through group pressure.

If it is thought that a person would benefit from group therapy, he is told the time and day the group meets and is asked whether he would be willing to participate. If he agrees, he is given an appointment for a pregroup interview with the therapist who will be conducting the group. In this interview the therapist assesses the individual and makes the final decision of recommending group or individual therapy. Determinations are made of the stressful event or events that caused the crisis, the symptoms that are present, and the degree of disruption that the crisis is creating in the patient's life. If group therapy is the treatment of choice, the therapist discusses the format of the sessions. The time element (six weekly sessions that last for 1½ to 2 hours), the necessity for focusing on immediate problems, and the fact that some members will be new to the group and others will be terminating are explained. If the group has members with a common problem area, a brief explanation may be made of who is in the group. This technique helps those seeking help to relax and assures them that their problem is not unique, that they are not alone, and that they can expect other members of the group to understand and help them reach a solution to their problem.

Format of sessions

The format of sessions is highly individual, not only with the therapist but also with the physical environment or setting where the groups meet. Members may be asked to wait in a reception room until the scheduled hour, when they enter the office or room that has been assigned, or the members may go directly to the assigned room and, in some cases, "start" the session informally before the therapist arrives.

In the first part of the group session the therapist briefly introduces new members and asks them to tell why they came for help. The other members then tell the reason they are there and usually add at what stage they are in therapy and what they believe is being accomplished in the group.

Therapist's role

The role of the therapist is active and direct. He functions as a participant leader in the group sessions, helping the members to focus on the problem areas under discussion by restricting and diverting general social conversation and lengthy discussions of past occurrences that have no relevance to the present crises of the patients in the group. He also acts as group facilitator and must be alert to the quiet, passive members and encourage their participation. Conversely, he must control and direct highly verbal and dominant members without completely silencing them as participants. The therapist must be skillful in understanding and acting on nonverbal clues from the members of the group. An example of this is the silent wife who appeared to the group to be calm and unruffled while her verbal, aggressive husband, in an angry tirade, told the rest of the group about the problems he was having with their son, who never talked to him, refused to mind, was never home, and so on. The therapist, observing the wife's nonverbal behavior (tense posture, hands folding her handkerchief over and over, lips tightly compressed—as if she did not dare to speak), interrupted the husband politely but firmly and asked the wife directly if this was the way their son acted toward his father. The wife looked at the rest of the group, and they encouraged her, saying that she should know her son better than his father because she was with him more. Thus encouraged by the therapist and the group, she replied that their son did act this way toward his father and she believed that he had every reason to do so because he had no respect for him. Turning to her husband, she said, "Why should he? Every time he sees you, you are either drunk or mad at something, and you are always fighting with him."

As a brief overview of how group therapy functions by using crisis intervention techniques, a case study is presented showing how the therapist and the group members interrelated in resolving their crisis.

It was initially believed by the intake worker that Opal would benefit more from group therapy than from individual therapy. She was by choice a social isolate and in all probability would resist efforts to modify her behavior with her daughter because she strongly believed that she was "right" and a "good mother." Cindy, in turn, would benefit from group therapy with those of her own age group to gain their support or to have her actions invalidated by them. They were scheduled for their pregroup interview with the therapist.

CASE STUDY: OPAL

Opal, 48 years of age and a grandmotherly appearing woman, came to a crisis intervention center for her pregroup interview with the therapist, accompanied by her 14-year-old daughter, Cindy. Cindy and her mother had been referred to the center for therapy by juvenile authorities. Cindy had run away from home and had been picked up by the police while trying to hitchhike to a well-known commune in northern California. When Opal was notified that Cindy had been found and was at the police station, she refused to go there, saying to the officer, "You had better keep her; I can't do anything with her!" She was told to come to court the next morning.

Cindy was held overnight in a juvenile hall. This was apparently a terrifying experience for her. She said that she had shared a room with two other girls but had been too frightened to sleep because they threatened to kill her if she "reported on their lesbian activities." She stated she would do anything to avoid going to juvenile hall or a similar corrective institution.

Cindy was very attractive, and she was mature socially as well as physically. Soft spoken and poised, she was of above average intelligence with A and B grades in school, and she enjoyed tennis and playing the piano. She was well liked by her teachers but had few friends in her peer group.

Cindy told the therapist that she thought her mother's standards were too rigid and that she tried to keep her isolated from her own age group. Opal refused to let Cindy participate in social activities or dating and would even wait for Cindy to get out of school and "walk" her home.

Opal said that Cindy had been a "good" girl—very obedient and so forth—until recently, and she could not understand her present behavior. When questioned about Cindy's father, Opal became angry and defensive and said they had been divorced for 6 years. She implied that she had "married beneath her" and that Cindy's father drank too much and had difficulty keeping jobs. It was the small amount of alimony and support for Cindy that had forced them to move from their original "middle-class" neighborhood to their present, low socioeconomic area. She was apparently attempting to isolate Cindy from the "undesirable elements and people" in the environment. She saw herself as a "good" mother who was trying to maintain middle-class morality while living in a lower class neighborhood.

The therapist introduced Opal to the other members of the group and asked her to state the problem she was having with Cindy. She repeated her previous remarks about Cindy's running away and what she had done and said to the officer. When asked what had preceded Cindy's running away, she became quite verbal. She said Cindy had asked to go to a neighborhood teen social center where a dance was being held. Opal refused, feeling that "Cindy was too young . . . she would meet the 'wrong' kind of people . . . the events were not properly chaperoned. . . . " While Opal was watching television in the living room, Cindy sneaked out of the house, went to the dance, and got back without being found out. The next day a neighbor informed Opal that her daughter had seen Cindy at the dance.

Opal immediately went to school, had Cindy called out of class, and confronted Cindy with the information. Cindy admitted she had attended the dance and that she would sneak out again if she got the chance. Opal slapped her, and Cindy ran from the school crying. When Cindy failed to come home that evening, Opal reported her missing to the police. Cindy was picked up the next afternoon. (Opal's previous method of coping, by denying the reality of the situation and by trying to isolate herself and Cindy from their environment, was no longer effective. Cindy was growing up and demanding more freedom and independence.)

Some of the members of the group responded to Opal's comments by making superficial supportive statements such as, "It sure is difficult to raise kids these days!" and, "The kids must be acting this way because of the kind of world we live in." Others suggested that she was too rigid, "You have to give the girl some freedom . . . she's not a baby anymore . . . you can't keep her a prisoner." Another offered alternate ways of coping, suggesting, "You don't have to give in all the way, but give her a chance; if it doesn't work, then try something else." One member reminded her that her present behavior had *caused* Cindy to run away. Others challenged her with, "If you don't like the neighborhood, move. No one is keeping you there!" and, "If you don't have the money, go to work instead of staying home and playing the good mother."

At first Opal reacted with hostility toward the group's suggestions and confrontations. She still maintained her rigidity and saw her actions and behavior as justified. She rationalized them by stating firmly that she couldn't care less what other people think, she knew she was right. Later, when the group members began making suggestions for different ways of maintaining discipline and still allowing Cindy some freedom, she responded with, "I'll consider it." She reacted warmly to those members who made supportive statements or suggestions and directed most of her remarks toward them. To the members who made negative statements, she responded in a coldly aloof manner and avoided conversation with them if she could.

In subsequent sessions Opal became more comfortable with the group members and felt less threatened. She began to adopt some of their suggestions in coping with Cindy. When the suggestions "worked," she always expressed her thanks to the member who had made the suggestion. She soon dropped her superior attitude toward group members and was able to express her feelings of guilt over slapping Cindy. She stated that she rarely had to punish Cindy because she was usually able to reason with her. She still maintained her "good mother" role in the group, and the group accepted her as an authority figure because she was very verbal and intelligent. They still challenged her rigidity and inconsistency about not wanting to work while Cindy was in school. She believed that she and her daughter were beginning to understand each other a little better.

The group members worked cohesively and focused sharply on specific problem areas. By the end of the third session they were interacting freely, testing new coping methods and reality testing within the group.

Before Opal's fourth group session the therapist had a pregroup interview with Ralph. His problems with his son appeared to be so similar to Opal's that the therapist thought he would be a valuable addition to the group and would benefit from the group experience. In the pregroup interview with the therapist Ralph expressed great concern over his son's changed behavior and appeared genuinely at a loss as to why he should now be presenting problems. He had run away from home and been picked up by authorities. Ralph said he had tried hard to be a "good father" since his wife had left him 5 years ago, and he stated repeatedly how much he loved his son and what a good boy the son had always been before running away. Ralph appeared to be a very mild mannered man and was quiet almost to the point of shyness.

He entered the group at Opal's fourth session. After being introduced, he began talking about his son and his problems with him. Very matter-of-factly, with little emotional expression, he calmly stated, "I'm a good father, I love my son, I can't understand why he has changed. I've beaten the hell out of him since he was 5 years old, and with the buckle end of the belt half the time, and he still won't mind." The group members were shocked into silence. The therapist, recognizing this, remained silent to observe the responses of the individual members to this attitude about disciplining a child.

The group recovered from the state of shock over Ralph's announcement and immediately began to attack him verbally. Opal emerged as their "leader" in the attack. The comments were personal and cutting. Ralph countered their attack by becoming hostile and just as verbally aggressive. It was obvious that the focus of the group was, at this time, shattered because the group had deviated from the problem areas to attacking an individual's attitude and character. The therapist stopped the "debate" and confronted the group with this behavior. After a discussion period the group, at the insistence of the therapist, began to redirect the focus to areas of concern. Opal, as the group leader, began to explain to Ralph how the group functioned and brought him up to date on the problems they had been working on together. Ralph remained silent for most of the rest of the session, giving his opinion only if asked directly by a group member or the therapist.

(THERAPIST'S NOTE: Ralph's attitude and statements in the pregroup interview were totally different from those displayed in the group. The therapist was caught completely unaware by Ralph's change in behavior. It was a very valuable learning experience for the group *and* the therapist!)

By Opal's sixth session she had apparently resolved her crisis with the help of group support. She and Cindy were getting along well together. (This information was verified by Cindy and her therapist.) She admitted that minor problems occasionally occurred but that she and Cindy were usually able to reach an agreeable compromise. She became friendly with several members of the group; they even visited each other's homes. Thus Opal was able to overcome her illogical isolation of herself and Cindy from their low-income community. The most dramatic and encouraging change in Opal's behavior was apparent when she announced in the last session that through the encouragement and help of another member, she had gotten a part-time job as a secretary at a local community college. She had worked 3 days and, as she stated it, "I love it! I've never been happier, and Cindy is so proud of me!"

It was at this session that the therapist and the group reviewed the progress and work they had done in the previous sessions to help Opal resolve her problem. Opal expressed some reluctance over terminating with the group. She was reassured by the members that they would "keep in touch." In an attempt to overcome her feeling of loss, she invited the entire group to her house for cake and coffee after the session. Everyone accepted the invitation.

SUMMARY

In group therapy patients get to see things from different perspectives. They learn that their problems are not unique, nor too different from those of others. They receive support from the other members and give support in turn. They learn that they are not alone in trying to solve a problem. Instead of one "therapist," they have five or eight peers who can give them suggestions and help. The presence of others also serves as a protection against being the sole object of the therapist's attention.

How to solve problems
using crisis intervention

You are constantly faced with a need to solve problems in order to maintain equilibrium. When you are faced with an imbalance between the difficulty (as you perceive it) of a problem and your available repertoire of coping skills, a crisis may occur. If alternatives cannot be found or if solving the problem requires more time and energy than is usual, disequilibrium, or emotional imbalance, occurs. Tension rises and discomfort is felt, with associated feelings of anxiety, fear, guilt, shame, and helplessness.

One reason for understanding crises is to increase your skills in solving problems. This does not mean that you are expected to find an answer for every problem. However, you should be able to have a ready and knowledgeable competency in problem solving. It is not enough to be able to recognize a hazardous, crisis-causing situation. You must also be able to use problem-solving skills to return to a level of emotional equilibrium that is equal to or better than it was before your crisis.

Solving a problem requires you to learn to use a logical sequence of reasoning for any situation that requires you to answer a question for which you have no immediate source of reliable information. This process may be either conscious or unconscious. Usually the need to find an answer or solution is felt more strongly when such a solution is most difficult.

The process of solving problems follows a structured, logical order of steps, each step depending on the preceding one. In the routine decision making required in daily living, this process is rarely visible. Most people are unaware that they usually follow a defined, logical sequence of reasoning in making decisions, although they may note that some solutions seem to be reached more easily than others. Finding out what time it is or deciding which shoe to put on first rarely calls for long, involved reasoning, and more often than not a question arises and the answer is found without any conscious effort.

FACTORS AFFECTING PROBLEM SOLVING

Depending on past experiences related to the immediate problem, you may be more adept at finding some solutions than others. Both internal and external factors affect the problem-solving process, although initially there may be only a temporary lack of concrete information. For example, when you find yourself lost because of a missing road sign, how much finding the right directions means to you in terms of your physical, psychological, and social well-being could affect the ease with which you find them. Anxiety will increase in proportion to the value you place on finding a solution. If you are driving only for pleasure, for example, you may feel casually concerned; but if you are under stress to be somewhere on time, your anxiety may increase according to how important your arrival is to your immediate goals.

When anxiety is kept within tolerable limits, it can be an effective stimulant to action. It is a normal response to an unknown danger; experienced as discomfort, it helps you to mobilize your resources in meeting the problem. But as anxiety increases, there is a narrowing of perceptual awareness, and all perceptions are focused on the difficulty. When problem-solving skills are available, you are able to use this narrowing of perceptions to concentrate on the problem at hand.

If a solution is not found, anxiety may become more severe. Feelings of discomfort become intensified, and perceptions are narrowed to a crippling degree. The ability to understand what is happening and to make use of past experiences gives way to concentration on the discomfort itself. You become unable to recognize your own feelings, the problem, the facts, the evidence, and the situation in which you find yourself.

Although problem solving involves a logical sequence of reasoning, it is not *always* a series of well-defined steps. It usually begins with a feeling that something has to be done. The problem area is generalized rather than specific and well defined. Next you search your memory in an attempt to come up with ideas or solutions from similar problems that have been encountered in the past. This is "reproductive problem solving," and its value greatly depends on past successes in finding solutions.

When no similar past experiences are available, you may next turn to "productive problem solving." Here you are faced with the need to construct new ideas from more or less raw data. You will have to go to sources other than yourself to get facts. For example, when looking for the road sign, you may find someone nearby who can give you the needed new data—directions to the right road. If there is no one nearby, you will have to find some other source of information. You may resort to trial and error and, with luck and patience, find the way yourself. Finding a solution in this way may meet a present need, but the information gained may not always be applicable to solving a similar problem in the future.

YOU AND YOUR PROBLEM

When you are in a crisis situation, you must use logic and background to define your problem and seek appropriate help as needed. The crisis approach to problem solving involves assessing yourself and your problem, planning how to solve the problem, putting the plan into action, resolving the crisis, and finally, anticipatory planning to avert crises in similar situations in the future.

The first thing you must do is find out just what the crisis-causing event was and what factors are interfering with your ability to solve problems at this time.

It is important that you define the problem clearly before taking any action. It is equally important to find someone to use as a "sounding board," someone you can depend on and trust to listen, to feed back what you say, and to help you sort out the real from the unreal facts of the situation as you perceive it.

Some of the questions to ask yourself are, "What else do I need to know about the situation?" and "What must be done?" The more specifically the problem can be defined, the more likely you will be on the trail to the "correct" answer.

Clues should be investigated to highlight and explore the problem or what is happening in your life. Think carefully over recent past events that may have affected your life as it is now or as you want it to be in the future. Use your observational skills to obtain factual, reality-based data. It is important to know what has happened in the immediate situation. How you have coped in similar past situations may affect your present behavior. Determine your level of anxiety, expressive movements, emotional tone, verbal responses, and attitudinal changes.

It is important to remember that your task is that of focusing on the immediate problem. There is neither the time *nor the need* to try to go into your past history in depth.

The questions to be dealt with focus around, "What has recently happened in my life that is *different? When* did it happen?" In crisis the precipitating event usually has occurred no more than 10 to 14 days before an individual's tension and anxiety reach the point where he feels overwhelmed, helpless, and hopeless about ever resolving the crisis. Frequently the precipitating event occurs the day or the night before the crisis. It could be almost anything—for example, threat of divorce, discovery of extramarital relations or that a son or daughter is taking drugs, loss of boyfriend or girlfriend, loss of job or status, or unwanted pregnancy.

The next area on which to focus is *your* perception of the event. What does it mean to you? How do you see its effect on your future? Do you see the event realistically, or do you distort its meaning?

The next questions you should focus on concern your available situational supports. What person(s) in your family or social circles can you depend on to provide you with emotional support during this stressful time? Is there someone with whom you feel particularly close that you could rely on at this time? Crisis resolution is sharply time-limited, and the more people who can appropriately help you, the better. Also, if others are involved and familiar with the problem, they can continue to give you support after the problem situation is resolved.

The next step is to decide what you usually do when you have a problem you cannot solve. What are your coping skills? Ask yourself the following: Has anything like this ever happened to me before? How do I usually deal with tension, anxiety, and depression? Have I tried the same method this time? If not, why not? If the usual method was tried and it did not work, *why?* What might reduce my symptoms of stress?

Something to reduce stress is usually thought of; coping skills are very individual. Methods of coping with anxiety that have not been used in years may be remembered. One man recalled that he used to work off tensions by playing the piano for a few hours, and it was suggested that he try this method again. Since he did not have a piano, he rented one; by the next week his anxiety had reduced enough to enable him to begin problem solving.

One of the most important questions that you must answer is, "Do I feel like killing myself or someone else?" Severe feelings of depression are common in crisis-causing situations. You feel helpless, hopeless, and trapped in a situation with no way out that is acceptable to you and your life values and goals. You may blame yourself to the point of considering suicide as the *only* way of resolving the situation, or you may blame someone else to the point that you may consider homicide as the *only* way of resolving the situation. Thinking along these lines, even fleetingly, is an *abnormal* response to stress. You must make contact with someone for *professional* help.

PLANNING FOR PROBLEM SOLVING

After identifying the crisis-causing event and the factors that are influencing your state of disequilibrium, you will begin to plan your strategies for resolving the problem. First, you must determine how much the problem has disrupted your life. Are you still able to go to work? Go to school? Keep house? Care for your family? Are these activities being affected? This is the first area to examine for the degree of disruption. How is your state of disequilibrium affecting others in your life? How does your wife (or husband, boyfriend, girlfriend, roommate, or family) feel about this problem? What do these others think you should do? Are they upset?

This is basically a search process in which information is collected. It requires the use of cognitive abilities and recollection of past events for information relative to the present situation. The last phase of this step is essentially a thinking process in which alternatives are considered and evaluated in the context of past experience and knowledge as well as in that of the present situation.

You begin to develop tentative solutions as to *why* the problem exists, and you should anticipate coming up with more than one answer. In the study of behavior it is important to look for causal relationships, for experiences in your past that could be influencing how you are responding in the present situation. These could provide clues to your disturbed equilibrium.

DEFINE THE PROBLEM, NOW SOLVE IT

After the necessary information is collected, the problem-solving process continues. Define the problem based on all the *facts* that have been collected. Talk it out with someone, or write it out in detail. Reflect on it. Look for missing or unfounded bits of information. This helps to clarify the problem and encourages focusing on the immediate situation. Explore possible alternative solutions to the problem that might help reduce your symptoms caused by stress. Select and try out what appear to be your best tentative solutions. Evaluate the results; if none of them appears to have been effective, begin again to work toward finding others.

Your appraisal of how effective you are becoming with your problem solving must be objective and impartial to be valid. Just feeling less anxious or less depressed does not mean that you are doing a good job. Have someone else who knows you well answer some of these questions: How are you functioning in your various life roles now? Better than before? The same? Or worse than before? Answers to these questions will provide you with clues as to how effective your planning is toward resolution of the crisis-precipitating problem.

FACTORS AFFECTING YOUR USUAL LEVEL OF FUNCTIONING

Whenever a stressful event occurs in your life, certain recognized factors can affect how well you maintain, or return to, your usual level of emotional equilibrium. These factors are perception of the event, available situational supports, and coping mechanisms.

No stressful event can be so clearly defined in your life that you can immediately determine what caused it. Internalized emotional changes occur at the same time as the externally caused stress. Some stressful events may cause a strong emotional response in one person yet leave another unaffected. How you respond to stressful events is greatly determined by these factors. Strengths or weaknesses in perception, situational supports, or coping mechanisms can be directly related to the onset of a crisis and to how well you resolve it.

Why do some people go into crisis when others do not? Let us take the example of Sue and Mary, two students. Both fail a final examination. Sue is upset but does not go into crisis. Mary, however, *does* go into crisis. Why do

Sue and Mary react differently to the same stressful event? What "things" in their present lives make the difference?

WHAT IS YOUR OPINION OF WHAT JUST HAPPENED?

Subjective meaning—what a stressful event means to you personally—plays a major role in determining both the nature and degree of coping behaviors. Differences in subjective meaning, in terms of how you see the event as a threat to an important life goal or value, account for large differences in coping behaviors.

If you perceive the event realistically, you will be able to recognize a relationship between the event and feelings of stress. Problem solving can be appropriately oriented toward reduction of tension, and your successful solution of the stressful situation will be more probable.

If your perception of the event is distorted, you may have no recognition of any relationship between the event and the feelings of stress. Thus your attempts to solve the problem will be ineffective, and your tension will not be reduced.

What does the event mean to you? How is it going to affect your future? Can you look at it realistically, or do you distort its meaning? For example, Sue saw failing the examination as the result of not studying enough or of concentrating on the wrong material, and she decided not to make the same mistake again. Mary, on the other hand, thought that failing the examination made *her* a failure; she felt threatened and believed she would never graduate from college.

USE THOSE CRUTCHES

By nature, human beings are social and dependent on others in their environment to supply them with reflected appraisals of their own worth. As you establish life patterns, certain appraisals are more significant to you than others because they tend to reinforce the perception that you have of yourself.

Loss, threatened loss, or feelings of inadequacy in a supportive relationship may leave you in a vulnerable position, so that when confronted with a stressful situation, the lack of situational support may lead to a state of disequilibrium and possible crisis. Any perceived failure to obtain adequate support to meet psychosocial needs may provoke, or compound, a stressful situation. The receipt of negative support could be equally detrimental to your self-esteem.

Situational supports are those persons who are available in the environment and on whom you can depend to help solve the problem. Sue talked to her roommate about her feelings over failing the exam; she even cried on her shoulder. She also called home for reassurance from her family. In effect, *someone* had been found for support during this stressful event. Mary did not feel close enough to her roommate to talk about the problem. She had no close friends whom she trusted. Fearing their reaction, she did not call home to tell her family about failing. Mary did not have *anyone* to turn to for help; she felt overwhelmed and alone.

COPING MECHANISMS

Through the process of daily living you learn to use many methods to cope with anxiety and reduce tension. Your life-style is developed around patterns of response that you have learned and established to cope with a wide variety of stressful situations. Your life-style is highly individual, and it helps you protect and maintain your equilibrium.

Tension-reducing mechanisms can be obvious or subtle and can be consciously or unconsciously activated. They have been generally classified into such behavioral responses as aggression, regression, withdrawal, and repression. Your selection of a response is based on which of these actions successfully relieved your anxiety and reduced tension in similar situations in the past. Through repetition it may pass from conscious awareness during its learning phase to a habitual unconscious level of reaction as a learned behavior. In many instances you may not be aware of *how,* let alone *why,* you react to stress in given situations. Except for vague feelings of discomfort, the rise and consequent reduction in tension may pass almost unnoticed. When an unfamiliar stress-producing event arises and learned coping mechanisms are ineffectual, discomfort is felt on a conscious level. The need to "do something" becomes the major focus of activity, narrowing your perception of all other life activities.

Available coping mechanisms are what people *usually* use when they have a problem. Some sit down and try to think it out or talk it out with a friend. Some cry it out, get drunk, or try to get rid of their feelings of anger and hostility by swearing, kicking a chair, or slamming doors. Others get into verbal battles with friends. Some react by temporarily withdrawing from the situation to reassess the problem. These are just a few of the many coping methods people use to relieve tension and anxiety when faced with a problem. Each has been used at some time in the developmental past of the individual, found effective to maintain emotional stability, and become part of his life-style in meeting and dealing with the stresses of daily living.

Sue talked to her roommate about her problem; this reduced her tension and anxiety. She was able to solve the problem and decided that for the next exam she would study more over a longer time. Her tension and anxiety were reduced, equilibrium was restored, and she did not have a crisis.

Mary withdrew. She had no coping skills, and her tension and anxiety increased. Unable to solve the problem and unable to function, she went into crisis.

Situational crises

Whenever stressful events occur that threaten a person's sense of biological, psychological, or social integrity, some degree of disequilibrium and the possibility of a crisis result. Several factors affect the balance of equilibrium, and the absence of one or more could make a state of crisis more imminent.

When an instinctual need or a sense of integrity is threatened, the ego characteristically responds with anxiety; when loss or deprivation occurs, the response is usually depression. On the other hand, if the threat or loss is viewed as a challenge, energy is more likely to be mobilized toward purposeful problem-solving activities.

That which may create only a feeling of mild concern in one person may create a high level of anxiety and tension in another. Recognized factors influencing a return to equilibrium are the perception of the event (what it means to the person), available coping mechanisms, and available situational supports. Crises may be avoided if these factors are operating at the time of the stressful event(s).

Behavior patterns that might be anticipated in response to common stressful situations have been studied. The results provide valuable clues to anticipatory planning for prevention as well as intervention in crisis situations. The crisis situations that have been studied include combat neurosis, relocation through urban renewal, rehabilitation of families after tornado disasters, hospitalization of children and adolescents, crises of unwed mothers, separation anxiety of hospitalized children, and death and dying. These studies suggested that there are certain patterned phases of reactions to unique stressful situations through which select groups of people can be expected to pass before equilibrium is restored. Preventive techniques of community psychiatry focus on anticipatory intervention to prevent crises that could result from inappropriate responses as individuals attempt to return to equilibrium.

In this chapter, stressful events that could cause a crisis have been selected on the premise that each could affect some member of a family, regardless of its socioeconomic or sociocultural status. The case studies are not all-inclusive of the many situational crises with which an individual may come in contact. It is also important to recognize that the theoretical material preceding each case study is presented as an overview, relevant to the crisis situation.

In order to clarify the steps in crisis intervention, much extraneous case study material has been eliminated. In crisis a person may be confronted with *many* stressful events occurring simultaneously. He may have no conscious awareness of *what* occurred, let alone which event requires priority in problem solving.

PREMATURITY

The birth of a premature baby is a stressful situation. Even when anticipated, there is a sense of emergency both at home and in the hospital when labor begins. In the hospital both staff and parents feel anxiety for the welfare of the newborn infant.

Researchers have identified the following four phases, or tasks, the mother must work through if she is to come out of the experience in a healthy way.

1. She must realize that she may lose the baby. This anticipatory grief involves gradual withdrawal from the relationship established with the child during the pregnancy.
2. She must acknowledge failure in her maternal function to deliver a full-term baby.
3. After separation from the infant as a result of the newborn's prolonged hospital stay, she must resume her relationship with the baby in preparation for his homecoming.
4. She must prepare herself for the job of caring for the baby through an understanding of his special needs and growth patterns.

After delivery the infant is hurriedly taken to the premature nursery. The parents have barely had a glimpse of their new son or daughter and have had no opportunity to reassure themselves about the infant's condition. The infant is isolated from everyone except the medical personnel during his hospital stay, and the parents, denied physical contact with the child, cannot allay their anxieties. There is a realistic danger that the baby will not live or will not be normal. Often physicians and nurses talk about the baby in guarded terms, not wanting to give false reassurance, so the parents' anxiety may last for days or weeks.

The way in which the family reacts to this period of stress is crucial in determining whether a crisis will develop. Studies of families who have experienced the stress of a premature birth show that some have managed very well and that some mothers were not apprehensive about caring for the baby despite the special attention required. In these families the relationship between husband and wife was found to be good; they seemingly had adjusted to the new member of the family, and their relationship was not threatened by the increased responsibility.

Other families studied appeared to be in a state of crisis although the premature infant was out of danger. In those cases the relationship between the husband and wife was determined to be unstable. The baby was cared for by an overly apprehensive mother who often seemed unconcerned about important things such as his weight gain, whether he was eating adequately, and his immediate prognosis.

It has been hypothesized that women who are most disturbed when there is real danger to the baby deal with this stress most effectively. Women who showed symptoms of a crisis were those who seemingly denied the existence of any danger. They did not question the information given them or the reassurances of the treating personnel. In fact, they seemed to encourage a conspiracy of silence, avoiding any confrontation with feelings of fear, guilt, and anxiety.

Parents experience many emotions when a new baby arrives, even when the child is full term. The mother is called on to meet additional demands on her time and may feel hostility toward the new baby. Usually, however, the strong feeling of a mother's love ensures repression of any resentment she may feel and the guilt it inspires. The usual activities of the father are not as directly interrupted, so his resentment is usually less than that of the mother and is more often aroused by jealousy of the attention that his wife gives to the baby.

The following case study concerns a young mother of a premature baby. Clues from the initial interview indicated that she was acknowledging herself to be a failure for not delivering a full-term baby. Intervention focused on relieving the immediate causes of her anxiety and depression and helping her to adapt to subsequent phases in the characteristic responses to a premature birth.

CASE STUDY: LAURA

Laura and Peter were a young couple who had been married for 3 years. Peter, 5 years older than Laura, was the oldest of four children. Laura, a petite young woman, was an only child. They had a 2-year-old daughter and a 2-month-old son who was born prematurely.

Peter's company had transferred him to another city when Laura was 7½ months pregnant; she went into labor the day after moving into their new home 100 miles from their home town, where both their families lived. She delivered their son in a private hospital with excellent facilities, but under the care of an obstetrician previously unknown to her as a result of their recent move. She was upset by the strangeness of the hospital, by the new physicians, and by the precarious physical condition of the son she and Peter had been hoping for. Laura did not want to discuss her fears with her physician because she did not know him or with the nurses because they "always seemed so busy." She also thought that since she had had a baby before, she should know the answers to all the questions she had in mind.

After she and Peter brought their son home from the hospital, Laura had episodes of crying and was experiencing symptoms of anxiety, including insomnia. She felt physically exhausted and increasingly fearful concerning her ability to care for her son. No matter what she did, the baby slept only for short periods and was more fretful when awake than their daughter had been. Because of the baby's small size, Peter was afraid to help with his care, so Laura was responsible for all his physical care.

Peter's mother arrived for a visit "to see how the new baby was doing." She had been critical of Laura's intention to move at the time of Peter's transfer, advising that Laura should wait until after the baby's birth. Laura had now begun to think that she should have followed that advice. Her mother-in-law and she often had talks about the rearing of children. Laura had begun to have confidence in her own mothering abilities as a result of her daughter's good health and average development, but now she was doubtful because of her apparent inability to care for her new son.

The event that caused the crisis was the visit of a mother-in-law who was critical of Laura's ability to care for her new baby. "I can't understand why the baby cries so much. You must be doing something wrong. My children always slept through the night by 2 months of age and took long naps during the day," was typical of the mother-in-law's constant comments. Peter seemed reluctant to take sides against his mother, so Laura received little support from him in dealing with these criticisms. She was finally unable to cope with her feelings of inadequacy, which were intensified by her mother-in-law's visit, and as a result became extremely upset, cried uncontrollably, and was unable to care for the baby at all. Peter's employer commented to him that he seemed upset and asked whether there was anything wrong at work. Peter told him that the problem was not his job, but Laura's behavior since the birth of the baby. His employer recommended that they seek help at a nearby crisis center.

The goal of intervention determined by the therapist at the crisis center was to assist both Laura and Peter in exploring their feelings about the premature birth of their son, their changed communication pattern, and the lack of support Peter was giving Laura.

During the first few weeks of therapy Laura was able to discuss her feelings of inadequacy in the mothering role and to tell Peter of her anxieties about their son, of her fears that he would be abnormal, and of her belief that the premature birth was her fault because she had insisted on moving with Peter at the time of his transfer. Peter, in turn, could tell Laura of his feelings of guilt at not being able to help more during the move and also of the blame he placed on himself because the labor was premature. The therapist assisted them in seeing the reality of the situation—although the move may have been a factor in the premature onset of labor, there could have been other causes.

Peter discussed his insecurities about the handling of such a small baby; Laura was then able to tell him that she felt the same way, and she feared she might be doing something wrong with this baby. The therapist gave them information about the differences in the behavior of and the care required for a full-term infant and a premature infant. She reassured Laura that she was doing well and that in time the baby would adjust to more regular hours. She encouraged Peter to help his wife so she could get more rest; in turn Laura helped Peter to gain confidence in holding and caring for their new son.

As Peter became comfortable in caring for the baby, he was encouraged to share the responsibility of caring for him in the evenings. This enabled Laura to get more physical rest. Peter's emotional support helped her to relax, and she began to sleep better.

The therapist discussed their need to continue to improve communications between them. It was stressed that they must reestablish a pattern of social activities with each other. They were assured that their new son could survive for a few hours with a competent baby-sitter while they went out to dinner or to play cards with other couples.

Most of their energies and concern during the past 2 months had been concentrated on their son. It was recommended that they also devote some additional time to their 2-year-old daughter. This was a stressful time for her too! Since her mother and father could not give her their sole attention, she would be competing for time with her new brother, and the feelings of sibling rivalry would emerge. She would need to feel that her position in the family—that is, a daughter and their firstborn—was also unique and important. Time should be planned for her to have some activities with her parents.

This would emphasize that she was "old" enough to be included in their activities.

They were warned to expect some acting-out behavior and possibly some regressive behavior in her bids for "equal" attention.

During their last visit Laura and Peter were assured they could return to the center if they felt the need for help with a problem.

Summary

This case study concerned a young mother unable to cope with problems of an unexpectedly premature baby. Assessment of the stressful events causing the crisis indicated that Laura regarded herself as a failure for not delivering a full-term baby. This was reinforced by the criticisms of her mother-in-law and the lack of situational support from her husband.

In the assessment phase focus was maintained on the immediate area of stress that could have caused the crisis. After determining a possible cause-effect relationship, a goal for intervention was established. Laura was encouraged to ventilate her feelings of guilt and inadequacy in the present situation. A realistic awareness of the event developed as the therapist provided information leading to an intellectual understanding of the relationship between the event and the resulting symptoms of stress. The husband was brought in as a situational support, and new as well as previously successful coping skills were used in resolving the crisis.

CHILD ABUSE

Only in the past century have the rights of children been considered cause for legal interventions, and only in the past few decades have state laws in this country mandated the reporting of physically abused or neglected children.

Professionals, generally, do not agree on one definition of child abuse or neglect. Some see it in terms of a problem of individual children, whereas others suggest that it is a broad problem of society as a whole. The development of a consensus for one definition is further complicated by the wide diversity of culturally accepted child-rearing methods, some of which result in physical or psychological harm to the child. Each culture has its own values and practices associated with child abuse. Some acts of abuse are based on superstition and folklore and are done "for the good" of the child, such as deliberately inflicting pain and injury as a method of removing evil influences or promoting healing. Others are based on societal practices that support the rights of the parents to inflict corporal punishment on their children.

The clinical signs of the *battered child syndrome* include bruises, abrasions, lacerations, broken bones, burns, abdominal and chest injuries, and eye damage. Frequently, examination of new injuries yields clinical evidence of past injuries. Some children receive a single violent injury; others receive a long series of violent injuries.

Child neglect involves the parents' *intentional* failure to meet the child's basic needs for physical or psychological survival. These needs include food, shelter, clothing, hygiene, medical care, and appropriate supervision to protect the child from dangers in the environment. *Intent* is an important factor in determining a case of child neglect. The parents' economic situation and the availability of resources needed by the child must be considered.

Sexual abuse of children has received increasingly serious attention during the past decade. It has been suggested that this is not a new problem, but rather one that is only now being publically exposed and legally addressed.

There are probably as many causes for child abuse as there are symptoms. Abusive parents have been characterized as immature and unable or unwilling to assume their adult roles in the parent-child relationship. Some studies have suggested that parents of abused children have themselves been abused as children. One's methods of child rearing are usually quite similar to those learned from one's parents. Some people may not know of any way to deal with their children other than with anger and violence.

Recent, severe stress is a fairly common factor in families in which child abuse has been identified. Stresses include such things as the death of a loved one, economic crisis, relocation to a new community, and any important loss or threatened loss that could require changes in one's life-style.

Aggressiveness toward children seems to vary cross-culturally. For example, corporal punishment in the schools is a historically sanctioned form of discipline in most states in this country. Many countries now consider the practice as a form of child abuse and have established social and legal sanctions against it.

Another set of symptoms has also been associated with child abuse. These include signs of physical and psychological growth deficiencies with little or no evidence of an organic cause. Occasionally, parents may even allow their child to die of starvation. It has been suggested that some mothers are unable to meet their children's nutritional and emotional needs. The cause may be failure to develop an adequate mother-infant relationship, which promotes nurturing behavior in the mother; a mother's severe emotional problems; or some real or imagined abnormal, negative qualities in the child that interfere with the mother's development of a nurturing relationship with the child.

CASE STUDY: FRANK AND MARTHA

Frank and Martha, a young married couple with four small children, originally went to their parish priest for family counseling because they felt that their marriage was becoming a "disaster." After meeting with them, he advised them to seek professional help at a nearby community center.

Frank was an unskilled laborer who worked for an airline as a maintenance man. He had finished the eighth grade in school; Martha had finished 9 years of school and had worked in a garment factory until right before the birth of their first child. Frank was 16 years old and Martha 15 when they married. Their first child, a son, was born within a year. Three more children, one boy and two girls, were born by the time Martha was 20 years old. Ever since their marriage they had lived in a house owned by Frank's mother. Their only recreation was watching television. Frank usually worked 6 to 7 days a week. The airline had cut back on services 3 weeks ago, and Frank's job had been cut to 3 days of work a week.

Frank was very angry and suspicious at the beginning of the session, and Martha appeared frightened and was reluctant to talk. When asked why they had come to the center, Frank replied that he thought his wife was crazy; he then began to explain her "crazy" behavior. The afternoon before, Martha had caught their oldest child (Joe, 9 years old) playing with matches behind the house. She flew into a rage, pulled him into the house, and burned his arm by holding it over the flame of the kitchen stove. Frank's mother walked in while Joe was screaming. The grandmother learned what had happened, and she grabbed Martha and forced her arm over the flame so she "could see how it felt." When the therapist asked Martha whether this were true, she nodded her head and began to cry. She said, "I just don't know what came over me. The kids had been under my feet all day. I'd counted on Joe to help keep an eye on them for me—and I suddenly find him with matches. He could have burned the house down! I don't think I've ever been so angry in my life. It frightens me to remember how I felt and what I did."

Frank took Joe to a nearby hospital emergency room. He said that the doctor asked Joe a lot of questions about the injury, but Joe told him only that he had been playing with matches when it happened.

Martha had a fairly large blistered area on her arm. She said that it was painful and asked whether a doctor at the center could take care of it while she was there. A medical consultation was arranged, and while Martha was being seen by the doctor, the therapist met with Frank.

When Frank was alone with the therapist, he dropped his defensive attitude and showed his true concern for Martha's irrational behavior. When questioned about Martha's usual manner of coping with problems, he stated that he really did not know—usually she just "blew up" at him, and since it did not bother him, he ignored it. However, during the past few months she had begun to "blow up" at the children, too.

At first he thought it was just because it was summer vacation and the children were around the house and "under her feet" most of the time. Because of cuts in the city budget, the neighborhood free day camp was not available this year for Joe. They were not able to afford the cost of sending him to another one, where several of his friends were going.

Recently Frank had learned that Martha had begun to do more than just yell at the children and threaten them with punishment. Last week he came home unexpectedly early and discovered that she had locked herself in the bedroom and was "crying hysterically." She blamed it on the children's behavior; they did not seem to do anything she asked them to do anymore, "and when I hit them with one of your leather belts, they just ran out of the house." She said that she had never done anything like this to their children before, and she was frightened at her own behavior. That evening Martha and Frank went to see their parish priest and arranged to begin meeting with him regularly for family counseling. When the priest was told what Martha had done to Joe, he told them they should have professional help, and, when they agreed, he arranged for the appointment at the community center today.

Frank stated that he loved his wife and children and believed that Martha loved him and the children. When asked what he and Martha usually did together and with the children for pleasure, he said, "Are you kidding? I work 6 or 7 days a week—hard! I come home and I'm tired; I have a few beers, eat, and usually fall asleep in front of TV." When asked what Martha usually did, he stated that she took care of the house and kids.

When Martha returned from the medical consultation, the therapist repeated what Frank had told her. Martha said, "That's true . . . that's *all* I do: take care of his mother's crummy house and the kids!" Frank jumped on this immediately: "You have never gotten along with my mother . . . you hate her!" Martha said that she did not hate her, she just did not *like* her "always butting into our business and you always taking her side against me and the kids! I've told you I don't like living in her house, where she can walk in and out any time she wants to; I want a place I can call my own. We pay her rent; we can pay rent someplace else and get a better house too!"

Frank said, "You never told me you didn't want to live in Mother's house." Martha said, "I have, but you never listen!"

When asked about the possibility of moving, since Martha was unhappy with the living arrangements, Frank said that his mother would not understand, but that Martha and the kids meant more to him than anything.

The therapist refocused on the problem that had brought them to the center. She again asked Martha about burning Joe's arm. Martha said, "I was tired and upset; all I ever hear are the kids yelling and Frank's mother butting in and telling me everything I'm doing wrong with the kids and the house, and Frank never tries to help or even listen to me. I just felt like I was cracking up!"

Frank was asked whether there were any way he could help Martha. It was explained that it can be very exhausting taking care of four small children every day without a few hours off. The therapist pointed out to Frank that his work kept him in contact with people all day, whereas Martha had no contact with anyone except his mother (who was an added irritant) and the children. Martha said that if she could look forward to talking with him when she was upset, or even if she could go over to a friend's house for a few hours once or twice a week, "anything to get away for a few hours!" she knew she would be all right.

Frank very reluctantly said that he could put the kids to bed one night for her so she could go to a friend's house. The therapist said that it sounded like a fine idea and that it might be good for them both if they could get out for a few hours together once in a while to talk things over. Their reaction was a cautious silence.

When they came for their next session, it was obvious that they had had a good week. They were talking together quite animatedly when the therapist came into the waiting room to get them for their appointment. She remarked how good and happy they looked. Martha started talking about their week: Frank had put the kids to bed one night, as he had said he would, and she had gone to a friend's house to visit. She said it was really great to be out for a few hours. When Frank was asked how he had managed with the children, he looked embarrassed and said, "It was a mess! I don't know how she ever manages them all; no wonder she gets so tired!" Frank could not get the children to go to sleep—or even stay in bed—without Martha there to control them. He finally brought them all into the living room to watch television, and when they fell asleep, he carried them one by one to bed. The highlight of the week came when Frank told his mother not to come to the house and bother Martha. He had said that if she did, he and Martha would find another house and move. Martha felt so much better that she backed down a bit and told her mother-in-law that she could visit them, but to call before coming. The therapist cautioned them that there would be good weeks and bad weeks and told them that if they began to talk *with* each other rather than *at* each other when problems arose, they could work out solutions more easily.

At the next session Martha had apparently stabilized, and she and Frank were relaxed and comfortable with each other and the therapist. Frank began by saying that they both believed that they were capable of handling their problems now and did not want to return for more visits. He said that he could now understand Martha's feelings of being "hemmed in" and "trapped" when she was with the children constantly, all day and every day. He said a friend at work had invited them for dinner the Saturday before, and instead of refusing, as he usually did, he had accepted. He asked his mother to stay with the children, and he and Martha went to dinner. He said that as he watched Martha laughing and talking, he realized how much he had missed their being together alone "like before we were married. I watched her and realized how pretty and young she really is and how much I love her. I'm going to do everything I can to help her with the kids. I know we can make it now!"

They had already made plans with their parish priest to begin participating in a special group that he met with every week to discuss their family daily living problems and share ideas for solving them.

Summary

Frank and Martha's early marriage and rapidly increased responsibilities of parenthood had forced them into adult roles before they were emotionally ready to handle them. As their family increased in size, they were less able to spend time alone together. Frank had to work long hours to make enough money to keep up with their expenses. He expected Martha to be responsible for all problems at home. That was the way his parents had shared their family responsibilities, and he saw no reason to change things. Martha had never really objected to the way they lived, so he had always thought things were fine at home.

During the past month, with the children home all day long, Martha had begun to feel increasingly isolated, trapped in her house, and overwhelmed by her responsibilities as a parent. The loss of income caused by the cutback in Frank's work compounded her feelings. Fearful of their future security and unable to discuss it with anyone, she became increasingly tense and anxious and easily frustrated and angered by any problem. As she later described it, "I would fly off the handle at the simplest things—I couldn't stop myself." Still emotionally immature, she was unable fully to accept the adult responsibility of parenthood. When her son Joe had failed to accept the responsibility of keeping an eye on the other children for her, she lost control of her feelings and reacted impulsively and violently toward him.

Frank and Martha's response to crisis intervention and their plans to continue in family counseling provide positive signs that this single incident of child abuse may not be repeated.

STATUS AND ROLE CHANGE

Throughout life the individual is constantly in the process of joining and leaving social groups related to family, occupation, recreation, education, church, and so forth. *Status* in each of these groups is determined by the relative rights and duties that society assigns to the position held in the group. *Role* is determined by the expectations of society that the individual will carry out the duties of his position. If the member's position in the group is changed, his status and role also change.

There are four interrelated meanings of the term *role.* The first, *role expectation,* is what society expects of the individual. *Role conception* means *how* the individual perceives the effect of the role on his self-concept. He defines the role according to his perception and his needs, which are influenced by life goals, basic values, and congruency with other roles he is expected to perform. *Role acceptance,* like role conception, is highly subjective. Not all roles are willingly accepted, nor are they willingly altered. The political process is one example of the kind of pressure that society can exert to force a role change. Reciprocal role changes occur for all who are dependent on the winner's (and loser's) new status. *Role performance* depends on role expectation, conception, and acceptance. The performance of the role will meet the expectations of society only to the degree that there has been mutual communication and understanding throughout the process. The greater the disagreement in any area of understanding, the greater the possibility of failure in the performance.

A person tends to understand his role from his view of how it relates to his self-concept. The "self" may be defined as the individual's image of himself built through what he thinks others are judging him to be. It is also derived from the reflected values that others place on him and the values that he places on himself in his societal roles. As new evaluations are understood, he is obliged to reconcile these new concepts with preexisting ones. Increasing conflictual appraisals of the self result in increased tension and anxiety, leading to a state of disequilibrium.

A person tries to avoid accepting a role that might threaten the security of his self-concept. Various defense mechanisms are used to escape conflict and to ensure the integrity of self. Danger occurs when an unacceptable change in role is forced by society and cannot be avoided. For example, in the sudden death of a husband, the existing role of wife ceases to exist; the position is gone and its status with it. Without a husband there is no wife role. Similar unavoidable losses may occur in occupations and other groups; for example, when a business closes or a position is abolished, certain roles no longer exist.

The individual's feelings of loss are in accordance with the value that he places on the role. Effects of the loss are viewed in relation to the self-image, and this involves consideration of the negative factors that might cause conflicting appraisals from others. The greater the conflict between self-concept and expectations as a result of role change, the more painful is the decision-making experience.

Role changes related to loss of status are particularly critical because they represent a direct threat to self-esteem and may encourage the development of a negative self-concept. If defensive coping mechanisms such as projection or rationalization prove ineffective in protecting the integrity of the self, anxiety and tension will arise and the person's life will be disturbed.

CASE STUDY: EDWARD

Edward requested help at a crisis center on the advice of his attorney. He was in a state of severe depression and anxiety. He described his symptoms as insomnia, inability to concentrate, and feelings of hopelessness and failure. He was a well-dressed man, 47 years old, who looked older than his stated age because of tense posture, a dull, depressed facial expression, and a rather flat, low tone of voice. Married for 22 years, he had three children, a daughter 13 years old, and two sons, 8 and 10 years old.

His symptoms had begun about 3 weeks previously, when his company closed its West Coast branch and he lost his job. His symptoms had increased in intensity during the past 2 days to the point that he remained in his room, lying in bed and not eating. He became frightened of his depressed thoughts and feared completely losing control of his actions.

During the initial session he told the therapist that he had never been without a job before. Immediately after graduation from college 22 years before he had started his own advertising agency in New York City. It had expanded over the years, and he had incorporated it, retaining controlling interest and the position of company president. On several occasions he had been approached by larger companies with merger proposals. About a year ago one of the "top three" advertising companies offered him the presidency of a new West Coast branch, which he could run with full autonomy, gaining a great increase in prestige and salary. All expenses were to be paid for his family's move to the West Coast.

Edward saw this as a chance to "make it big"—an opportunity that might never come his way again. His wife and children, however, did not share his enthusiasm. Sophie had always lived in New York City and objected to his giving up his business, where he was "really the boss." She liked the structured security of their life and did not want to leave it for a new life that she thought would be alien to her. The children sided with her, adding personal objections of their own. They had known only city life, had always gone to the same schools, and did not want to move "way out West." Despite this resistance, he accepted the job offer. His business friends admired his decision to take the chance and expressed full confidence in his ability to succeed. Selling out his shares in his own company to his partner, he moved West with his family within a month.

In keeping with his new economic status and the prestige of his job, he leased a large home in an exclusive residential area. He left most of the responsibility for settling his family to his wife and became immediately involved in his new job. He described Sophie's reaction to the change as being "everything negative that she told me it would be." The children disliked their schools, made few friends, and did not seem to adjust to the pace of their peer group activities. His wife could not find housekeeping help to her liking and consequently felt tied down with work in the home. She missed her friends and clubs, was unable to find shops to satisfy her, and was constantly making negative comparisons between their present life-style and their previous one. Edward felt that there had been a loss of communication between them. His present work was foreign to her, and he could not understand why she was having so many problems just because they had moved. Her attitude was one of constantly blaming everything that went wrong on his decision to move West and to a new job.

About a month ago the company suddenly lost four big accounts. Although none of these losses had been a result of his management, immediate retrenchment in nationwide operations was necessary to save the company as a whole. The decision was made to close the newest branch office—Edward's branch. No similar position was available in the remaining offices, and he was offered a lesser position and salary in the Midwest. He was given 2 months in which to close out his office and make a decision.

Sophie's attitude toward these sudden events was a quick, "I told you so." She blamed him for their being "stranded out here without friends and a job." He said that he was not a bit surprised by her reaction and had expected it. He had been able to "tune out" her constant complaints in the past months because he had been so occupied by his job, but now he was forced to join her in making plans for the family's future and in considering their tenuous economic status. He thought he had been able to hold up pretty well under the dual pressures of closing out the business and planning for his family's future security.

A week ago his wife found a smaller home that would easily fit into their projected budget until he decided on a new job. He had felt a sense of relief that she had calmed down and was "working *with* me for a change."

Two days ago, however, their landlord had threatened a lawsuit if they broke the lease on their present home. Sophie became hysterical, blaming Edward for signing such a lease and calling him a self-centered failure who had ruined his family's lives. "Suddenly I felt as though the bottom had fallen out of my world. I felt frozen and couldn't think what to do next, where to go, and who to ask for help. My family, my employees, everyone was blaming me for this mess! Maybe it *was* all my fault."

Until now Edward had always experienced successes in his business and home life. He usually anticipated and overcame minor setbacks with little need for guidance from others. Now, for the first time, he felt helpless to cope with a stressful situation alone. The threat of having to fulfill the lease on a house he could no longer afford not only destroyed his plans for his family, but also broke off what little support he had been receiving from his wife. His feelings of guilt and hopelessness were reinforced by the reality of the threatened lawsuit and the loss of situational support.

Because of his total involvement in his new work, Edward had withdrawn from his previous business and family supports. The sudden loss of his job threatened him with role change and loss of status for which he had no previous coping experiences. Perceiving himself as a self-made success in the past, he now perceived himself as a self-made failure, both in business and in his parent-husband roles.

When asked about his coping methods in the past, he said that he had always had recourse to discussions with his business friends. He now felt ashamed to contact them, "to let them know I've failed." He had always felt free to discuss home problems with his wife, and they usually had resolved them together. Now he seemed no longer able to communicate with his wife. When questioned whether he was planning to kill himself, he said, "No, I could never take *that* way out. That has never entered my mind." After determining that there was no threat of immediate suicide, the therapist initiated intervention.

One goal of intervention was to assist Edward in exploring unrecognized feelings about his change in role and status. His loss of situational supports and lack of available coping mechanisms for dealing with the present stressful situation were recognized as areas in need of attention.

In the next 4 weeks, through direct questioning, he began to see the present crisis as a reflection of his past business and family roles. Edward had perceived himself as a strong, independent, self-made man, feeling secure in his roles as boss, husband, and father. He now felt shame at having to depend on others for help in these roles. Coping experiences and skills learned in the past were proving to be inadequate in dealing with the sudden, unexpected, novel changes in his social orbit. The loss of support from his wife added to his already high level of tension and anxiety. This resulted in failure of the coping methods he had been using with marginal success and it caused the crisis.

After the fourth therapy session Edward's depression and feelings of hopelessness had diminished. His understanding of the situation had become more realistic, and he realized that the closing of the branch office was not the result of any failure on his part. In fact, he thought that he would have decided to close the office had he been in charge of the overall operation. He further recognized the great importance he had placed on the possibility that this job was his "last chance to make it big." His available coping skills had not lessened but had, in fact, been increased by the experience of the situation.

By the fifth week Edward had made significant changes in both his business and family life. He had been able to explore his attitudes about the need to be "the boss" and his sense of shame in being dependent on others for support in decision making. He was now able to understand the stressful events realistically and to cope with his anxieties.

He met with his landlord and resolved the impending lawsuit, breaking the lease with amicable agreement on both sides. His family had already decided to move into a smaller home, and his wife and children were actively involved with the planning. He contacted business friends in the East and accepted one of several offers for a lesser position. He would return East alone, and his family would follow when he had reestablished himself. His wife and children decided to do this rather than repeat the sudden move into an unsettled situation that they experienced a year before.

He felt pride that his friends had competed for his services rather than giving him the "I told you so" that he had been dreading.

Before termination of the therapy Edward and the therapist reviewed the adjustments and the tremendous progress he had made in such a short time. The therapist emphasized that it had taken a great deal of strength for Edward to resolve such an extremely ego-shattering experience. He was also complimented on his ability to recognize the factors he could change, those he would be unable to change, and his new status in life.

He viewed the experience as having been very disturbing at the time, but believed he had gained a great deal of insight from it. He believed that he would be able to cope more realistically if a similar situation occurred in the future. He was pleased with his ability to extricate himself from a seemingly impossible situation.

In discussing plans for the future, Edward stated he no longer believed he had lost his chance for future advancement. He was realistic about past happenings and the possibility that such a crisis could occur again. He was relieved about his family's rapid adjustment to the lower status of his new position. They were happy to be returning to family and friends on the East Coast.

He expressed optimism about again rising to a high position in business, concluding with, "I wonder if I could ever really settle for less."

Summary

Edward's crisis was caused by a sudden change in role status (loss of his job) and threatened economic, social, and personal losses. Assessment of the crisis situation determined that he was depressed but not suicidal. Because he was overwhelmed by a sense of failure in both business and family roles, his understanding of the events were distorted. Having no previous experience with personal failure of this scope, he was unable to cope with his guilt and depression. His wife's actions reinforced his low self-esteem, and she withdrew as situational support.

Realistic understanding of the event developed as the therapist assisted Edward in exploring and ventilating unrecognized feelings; he was able to gain insight into relationships between his symptoms of depression and the stressful events. His wife resumed her role of situational support as his new coping skills were successfully implemented in resolving the crisis.

RAPE

The word *rape* arouses almost as much fear as the word *murder.* In a sense it kills both the rapist and his victim. The rapist dies emotionally because he can no longer express or feel tenderness or love, and his victim suffers severe emotional trauma.

Women have nightmares about being sexually assaulted; they anguish over what to do. They can either resist, hoping to fend off the rapist, or they can obey his commands, hoping he will leave without seriously injuring or killing them.

Definitions of rape usually include terms such as *forcible or unlawful carnal knowledge* and *against the will* or *without the consent* of the victim. For our purposes rape is defined as forcible carnal knowledge of a woman without her consent and against her will.

Rape, although an overtly sexual act, is actually an act of physical dominance and violence in which sex is used as the weapon. Viewing the victim of rape as a victim of violence promotes a more objective and nonjudgmental approach to the victim. The victim of any other type of physical violence is never treated with the type of emotional, superstitious approach that the victim of rape must endure.

The victim of rape is the victim of medical and cultural myths. The medical myth insists that a healthy adult woman cannot be forcibly raped with full penetration of the vagina unless she actively cooperates.

The medical myth does not seem to consider emotional reactions, such as fear and panic, or logical reactions, such as submissiveness to ensure life. Neither does the use of weapons, fists, or threats by the offender seem to have a role in the medical myth. The medical myth springs from the cultural myth that "whatever a man does to a woman, she provokes." The low esteem that society in general holds for women is reflected in both the medical and cultural myths.

Sociological studies reflect that the most typical rape victim is between 15 and 24 years of age, of the same race as the offender, and of low socioeconomic status. The initial contact for the rape or the rape itself occurs in the approximate neighborhood of the offender and the victim.

Some researchers classify the victim's emotional reactions to rape into the following phases: phase I, acute reaction; phase II, outward adjustment; and phase III, integration and resolution. Others classify the rape trauma syndrome into an acute phase (disorganization) and a long-term process (reorganization).

Crisis intervention seems to be an ideal model for use with rape victims. Rape is a sudden, overwhelming experience for which the usual coping mechanisms probably are inadequate. The victim needs an opportunity for emotional catharsis, reality testing for self-blame, active support on a short-term basis, and someone who will assist in identifying the situational supports available. Crisis intervention seems to be well defined to reach this group of people.

Crisis intervention is also increasingly available in the area where rape victims are initially brought to the attention of the health care system—the emergency room. Prompt referral and active intervention in the emergency room may prevent deterioration of the victim's emotional status.

The crisis caused by rape seems to be approachable by the generic type of crisis intervention. A characteristic course of behavior results, and specific interventions seem to be effective with the majority of the victims. The generic approach is not best for victims with compounded reactions because of a history of physical, psychological, or social problems. For such people a physician, therapist, or agency probably should handle the case.

To be a genuine victim in our society, one must have people available who accept and acknowledge that something extremely disruptive has occurred in one's life. In other words, the victim's claim to having been victimized needs to receive confirmation from others.

There are three basic types of rape. The first type is rape involving persons who know one another, for example, neighbors, separated husbands and wives, fathers and daughters, and prostitutes and dissatisfied clients. The second type is gang rape, in which two or more men, usually young men, rape one woman. These encounters follow various patterns. It is the third type, the stranger-to-stranger rape, that women fear most, and it is this type of rape that follows an identifiable pattern, which we will now discuss.

First, a potential rapist looks for a woman who is vulnerable to attack. Rapists differ in defining who is vulnerable. Some look for victims who are handicapped or who cannot react appropriately or swiftly to the threat of rape. Such men might prey on retarded girls, old women, sleeping women, or women who are intoxicated.

Other rapists look for environments that are easily entered and relatively safe. They make certain that the victim is alone and that they will not be interrupted. Rapists of this type often commit the crime in run-down sections of town, where many women live alone.

Rapists often select their victims long before they approach them, and they usually are very consistent in how they do it; they repeat the same pattern over and over again. Rapists seem to have a sixth sense for identifying women who live alone, and they are especially good at finding isolated streets, laundromats, or theater restrooms that draw unsuspecting victims.

Housing that is easy to enter and the isolation of the victim are two obvious factors that make women particularly vulnerable to rape, but women who are usually friendly and who like to help others are also courting danger. Teachers, nurses, volunteers, and other women who have learned to serve others, to be charitable, and to give of themselves are especially vulnerable to rape.

A woman's first act of resistance should be to refuse to help or be helped by strange men. It is not wise to stop on a street to give a man a light or to explain street directions. It may be rude but it is much safer to state firmly, while continuing to walk, "I don't have a match," or "I don't know." Do *not* smile and say, "I'm sorry but . . . " and so forth.

Women should refuse to let a stranger into their apartment or home to make an emergency phone call or for any other reason. These may be ploys, and there are hundreds of clinical case histories and police reports to validate this method of entry for the purpose of rape.

After finding a vulnerable target, the rapist proceeds, in essence, to ask his victim, "Can you be intimidated?" If she can, he then threatens her life. For example, a rapist may approach a victim on the street and ask her for a light. If she provides it, he may ask her an intimate question. If she reacts submissively or fearfully, he knows he has intimidated her and that she likely will submit to his demands.

This testing phase is crucial for the rapist. If he guesses incorrectly about whether a woman can be intimidated, he will lose the opportunity to rape her, and if he is incorrect about the victim's situation, he may be caught, convicted, and sentenced to a penitentiary. The rapist tests his victim's responses to threats with intimidations such as "Don't scream!" "Don't shout!" or "Take your clothes off!"

The safest stance for a woman alone—either on the street or in her home—is to be aloof and unfriendly. This is her first line of resistance to rape.

When a rapist attacks a woman without warning, for example, climbs into her bedroom while she is asleep or pulls her into a dark alley, the woman must decide whether to use direct methods of resistance or to submit.

In the third, or "threat," stage of rape the rapist tells his victim what he wants from her and what he will do to her if she refuses to cooperate. Most important, he tells her what reward she will receive if she submits. Typically he says he will kill her if she does not cooperate and that he will not hurt her if she does. If the victim is terrified, immobilized, or hysterical, the rapist may reassure her. He will repeatedly promise her that nothing will happen to her if she does as he tells her. He may express concern for her health or future relationships with her husband or boyfriend.

The final stage of rape is the sexual transaction itself. Vaginal intercourse occurs in less than 50% of rapes; anal or oral intercourse is common. In this stage the rapist's fantasy life is in full bloom. Here he imprints his unique personality on the crime. Some rapists create a false identity and describe a nonexistent person to the victim; others reveal a split personality by telling the victim, "It isn't really me doing this," or "I can't help it."

Most rapists fall into one of two categories. One type includes those who are usually victims of what analysts call ego splits. They are married, young, employed, and living a life that you could not describe as typical of a person who is mentally ill. However, their family life is disturbed; they cannot relate successfully to their wives or parents, and as youngsters they had problems with an older sister, cousin, or aunt.

After the crime these men deny their behavior. Typically they say, "I don't remember," "It wasn't me," or "I felt like I was watching a movie." If they do not harm their victims, these rapists often get a suspended sentence or are sent to reformatories where they can get work releases and return to the community in a matter of months. The courts generally give them a second chance on the condition that they receive psychotherapy. Most rapists fall into this category.

The other type of rapist is a predator. Often he goes into a place to rob it. In the course of the crime he enters a bedroom where he finds a lone woman sleeping. On the spur of the moment he decides to rape her. These men are out to exploit or manipulate others, and sometimes they do it through rape.

The rapist who requires his victim to pretend to respond sexually has often failed to please his wife or lover. On a deeper level he may be trying to maintain his shaky defenses about his own sexual inadequacy.

Most rapists have narcissistic and self-centered relationships with women. They have only a minute awareness of their partner's social needs or of the social situation itself.

A rapist also writes his diagnostic signature in the sign-off, or termination, stage of rape. A rapist who assumes the victim will report the crime terminates the rape by trying to confuse the woman. He will say, "Don't move until you count to 100." Then he will go into another room and wait to see if she moves. A minute later he will reenter the room, and if the victim has moved, he will berate her for failing to follow his directions. He may do this several times. Other offenders act guilty or apologetic when they leave. They plead for the victim not to call the police. Still others threaten future harm if the victim calls for help.

Unfortunately, most rapists can neither admit nor express the fact that they are a menace to society. Even convicted rapists who are serving long prison terms deny their culpability; they tenaciously insist that women encourage and enjoy sexual assault. These men will say they are the greatest lovers in the world.

CASE STUDY: ANN

Ann, an attractive, 26-year-old legal secretary, was brought to the crisis center by her employer. That morning on her way to work she had been raped. After being raped, she returned to her apartment, showered, changed her clothes, and calmly went to work.

At approximately 11:30 AM she matter-of-factly announced to her employer that she had been raped and told him the details. He was shocked and horrified. He asked her to go to the hospital for treatment and to notify the police. She stated very unemotionally that she was "fine" and had only numerous superficial cuts on her breasts and abdomen and would continue working. By midafternoon she appeared to her employer to be in a state of shock and was acting disoriented and confused. He drove her to the crisis center, where she was seen immediately by a female therapist who had expertise in working with rape victims.

The therapist offered Ann a cup of coffee, and Ann accepted. While they were drinking their coffee, the therapist quietly asked Ann to tell her what had happened. Ann began to sob. The therapist handed her some tissues, put her arms around her shoulders, held her close, and told her that she understood how she was feeling. Gradually Ann calmed down and stopped crying. She then said, "I feel so filthy. I feel I should have resisted more. I am so confused." She was reassured that these feelings were normal and was asked to tell what happened.

Ann stated that she always got up early and took the bus to work, since it was very convenient, and she arrived before anyone else was in the office. She liked to get her desk "in order" for the day and make the coffee so that she could serve coffee to the attorney she worked for when he arrived. She smiled slightly and said, "He isn't fit to talk to until he has finished his second cup of coffee in the morning—he commutes in from a suburb, and he has to battle the traffic for at least an hour or an hour and a half." The therapist smiled and asked her to continue. She took a deep breath and stated that this morning she got up as usual and rode the bus to work. As she was walking from the bus stop to her office building, approximately three blocks, a man walked toward her. He was tall, attractive, and well dressed. When he approached her, he smiled and said, "Can you tell me where Fifth Street is?" She returned his smile and said, "You are going the wrong way. It's the next street up" (pointing in the direction she was walking). He thanked her and, turning around, fell into step with her and started talking about the weather—"what a beautiful morning" and other "small talk." They had walked approximately 100 yards when he suddenly pulled out a knife, shoved her against a car, put the knife to her throat, and said, "Don't scream or I'll kill you. Get in the car." At this point in her story Ann began to tremble and tears rolled down her cheeks. The therapist said, "How frightening! What did you do?" Ann said, "I was so shocked and terrified, I thought he *would* kill me. So when he opened the car door, I got in."

Ann continued to tell what had happened. Keeping the knife firmly at her waist, the man made her slide over to the driver's seat, ordered her to start the car, and told her where to drive (an isolated area near the river). He then made her get into the back seat and undress. He started caressing her and talking obscenities to her, telling her how he was going to make love to her "like no other man could." Ann said she began to cry and plead with him, but it only seemed to make him angry. He began making small cuts on her breasts and abdomen and kept saying he would kill her if she did not cooperate. Ann said that he acted "spaced out" and had a glazed look in his eyes, as if he were not really raping her *personally*—just somebody.

Ann stated that after he raped her, he seemed to "come to" and started to cry, saying, "I'm so sorry; I didn't mean to hurt you. Please forgive me. I just can't help it. Please don't tell anyone." Ann got dressed, and he helped her into the front seat and kept asking her whether she was all right and generally expressing concern for her well-being. He asked whether he could drive her someplace, and Ann asked him to drop her off approximately four blocks from her apartment, telling him she was going to a girlfriend's to "clean up." He dropped her off and again begged her not to tell anyone and to please forgive him. Ann said that when she was certain he had driven away, she walked to her apartment in a daze. All she could think about was taking a shower to "get clean again" and to change her clothes completely to try to erase her feelings of degradation. She stated that she thought she should go to work "to keep her mind off it." It was only later in the afternoon as she "relived" the events in her mind that she began to feel terribly guilty over not "resisting" or "fighting back" when he first pulled the knife. She said (with a tone of great remorse), "I didn't even scream!"

The therapist thought that Ann should go to the hospital immediately for treatment of her numerous cuts and for determination of the presence of spermatozoa in the vagina and that then she should report the incident to the police. After this had been done, she should return to the center to meet with the therapist and continue her mental catharsis. The therapist explained to Ann that someone from the rape hot line would stay with her while she went to the hospital and gave her report to the police. Ann was assured that the therapist would arrange for Ann to be examined by a female physician and interrogated by a female police officer. Ann agreed to go, and a member of the rape team was called to accompany her and then return her to the center.

When Ann returned, she was pale and trembling but apparently in control of her emotions. Again she was offered coffee, which she accepted, and she and the therapist discussed how things "had gone" at the hospital and with the police interrogation. Ann stated that the experience was definitely *not* pleasant but that it was not as bad as she had expected, and added, "Thank God I didn't take a douche!"

The therapist asked Ann whether she would like to contact a friend or family member and possibly have this person spend the night with her, since she was still very frightened by her experience. Ann turned even paler and exclaimed, "Oh my God . . . Charles!" She was asked, "Who is Charles?" She replied, hesitantly, "My fiancé." The therapist asked Ann whether she could call Charles and tell him what happened. Ann began to cry and said, "I am so ashamed. He will probably hate me; he probably will never want to touch me again. What have I done?" She was comforted by the therapist and told that *she* had done nothing wrong. She continued to cry and berate herself. The therapist gave her a mild sedative and asked her to lie down and rest. Twenty minutes later Ann asked the therapist to call Charles and tell him what had happened *but* said that she did not want to see him until she knew how he felt about her being raped. The therapist agreed and asked for Charles's telephone number.

The call was placed to Charles, and a brief explanation was given by the therapist about Ann being raped; the therapist told Charles that Ann was physically unharmed but psychologically very traumatized. Charles responded with concern and anger and asked whether he could see Ann. He was told to come to the center and ask for the therapist.

Charles arrived extremely upset and angry. The therapist took him to her office and explained fully what had happened to Ann and what had been done for her. He started to cry and to curse, stating, "My God—poor Ann!" and "I'll find that dirty bastard and kill him!" The therapist allowed him to ventilate his feelings of pity and anger, and he began to calm down. When he seemed calmer, he was asked, "Does this change your feelings for Ann?" He appeared startled and said, "No, I love her. We are getting married!" He was told that Ann was afraid he would not love her anymore. He replied, "It wasn't *her* fault. Of course I still love her!"

It was explained that after being raped a woman usually feels "guilty," "unclean," and very fearful of intimacy with another man, even though she may love him very much. The therapist added that Ann needed his strength, love, and constant reassurance that nothing had changed between them. He listened and said, "I'll do *anything* I can to help her forget this."

The therapist asked whether he sometimes stayed overnight at Ann's apartment, and he answered, "Yes, often." If Ann agreed, would he spend the night with her and hold her (if she would let him), touch her, reaffirm his love for her, and speak about their coming marriage but not attempt sexual intercourse unless she asked him to? He agreed and asked to see Ann. The therapist asked for a few minutes alone with Ann first.

Ann was lying on the couch staring at the ceiling when the therapist entered. She turned her head and looked fearfully at the door. The therapist smiled, sat down by Ann, held her hand, and said, "I like *your* Charles. He is a fine young man. He will probably break down that door if I don't let him in to see you!" Ann said, "What did he say?" The therapist replied that he had stated he loved her very much and that he would do *anything* to help her forget, that it was not her fault, and that he would like to "kill the bastard who hurt you." Ann said, hesitantly, "Are you *sure*?" The therapist replied firmly, "*Positive*! Now comb your hair and put some makeup on so I can let him in!" Ann smiled weakly and complied.

Charles entered the office, took Ann in his arms, and held her gently, stroking her hair and face, saying, "I'm so sorry, my love. Let me take care of you. Everything is going to be all right. I love you—you are the most precious thing in my life." Ann cried softly on his shoulder. The therapist said, "Why don't you two go home and get some rest, and I'll see you both next week." Ann and Charles agreed and left with their arms around each other and Ann's head on his shoulder.

(*Note*: The therapist had listened to Ann's account of the rape and the modus operandi with increasing feelings of helplessness and anger because in the past 3 months she had worked with two other rape victims who had described the same details but with one major difference: the first victim had only one minute cut on her throat, which she received when he pushed her against the car; the second victim had several small superficial cuts on her breasts; and now the third victim [Ann] had numerous cuts on her breast and abdomen. The rapist was obviously becoming increasingly violent with each rape.)

The next sessions were spent in collateral therapy with Ann and Charles. The focus was on ventilation of their feelings and helping Ann begin to express anger toward her rapist. By the end of six sessions they had resumed their normal sexual activities and had advanced their wedding date 3 months. Charles thought he was living at Ann's apartment because he wanted to be with her as much as possible; therefore they agreed to get married sooner than they had planned.

Summary

Since rape is so emotionally traumatic, Ann's situation was treated as an emergency by the therapist. The sooner intervention begins with a rape victim, the less psychological damage will occur.

Most women are totally unprepared for rape; therefore it is a new traumatic experience to cope with, and previous defense mechanisms are usually ineffective to resolve the crisis.

Ann greatly feared total rejection by her fiancé (a very real and common occurrence). This is why the therapist saw both Ann and Charles in collateral sessions, in which they both would have a chance to explore and ventilate their feelings together. Had Charles been unable to accept Ann after the rape, the therapist would have seen him alone to help him through *his* crisis.

The event, rape, was perceived by Ann as being her fault because she did not resist immediately and did not scream. These feelings are common in women who have been raped. Usually everything occurs so rapidly, and the ever-present fear of being killed or seriously injured tends to immobilize the victim.

Addendum

Four months later a patient was referred to the center because he was on probation for rape, and he became the same therapist's patient. When questioned about how and why, as he described his modus operandi, the therapist *knew* he was the one who had raped Ann and the two other victims. After the rapist discussed his feelings—guilt, shame, and helplessness in controlling his actions—the therapist asked about his background and family. This new patient, Phillip, described his childhood as one deprived of affection. His mother had left his father, and he was reared by an "old-maid aunt" who was very cold, undemonstrative and—to him—uncaring and rigid.

When questioned about his present living circumstances, he stated that he was happily married and had three small children. When asked why he felt the need to rape, he stated, "I don't know." He began to cry and said, "Please help me. I can't help myself."

When the therapist asked whether his wife knew that he was on probation for rape, he said, very hesitantly, "No, but I *know* she thinks something is wrong with me." The therapist told Phillip that she had worked with three of his victims, and she thought that he was becoming increasingly violent, as evidenced by the increasing use of the knife and the sight of blood to stimulate him.

Phillip stared intently at the therapist and said with amazement in his voice, "My God, don't you hate me? I hate myself." The therapist was able to admit that her bias was toward his victims, but that she felt he needed help because she was afraid he might kill his next victim. He admitted that he did not know whether he *would* or *would not* kill someone.

The therapist then asked him how his wife and children would feel if they found out he was a potential murderer. He shuddered and said, "Help me! I don't know what to do!" The therapist stated that he should tell his wife about being on probation and about the rapes, and then the therapist would do all she could to get him help. He agreed and called his wife and asked her to come to the center.

His wife arrived, and Phillip, with the therapist present, told her what he had done and the possibility of what he could do in the future. She began to cry and said, "I've *known* something was wrong, but I didn't know what." She turned to the therapist and asked, "What can we do?" The therapist was very candid and stated that Phillip should be at a well-known maximum security prison where he could receive consistent, intensive psychiatric therapy in order to protect the reputation of their family and to protect the community.

They agreed with this decision. The therapist then called the judge and told him the facts. He agreed that maximum security was needed and said he would send a car to transport Phillip to the facility.

It must be noted that *rarely* does a therapist work with rape victims and then with the offender. It was extremely difficult to remain "cool, calm, and collected" while Phillip related his modus operandi; however, he too was a "victim" and needed help, and help he did receive.

SUBSTANCE ABUSE
Cocaine

Cocaine is a vegetable alkaloid derived from leaves of the coca plant. It is often referred to as Coke, C, snow, happy dust, white girl, etc. Cocaine is fast becoming the all-American drug. No longer is it a sinful secret of the moneyed elite or an elusive glitter of decadence in raffish society circles. Today, in part because it is such an emblem of wealth and status, cocaine is the drug of choice for millions of solid, conventional, and upwardly mobile citizens—lawyers, businessmen, students, bureaucrats, politicians, secretaries, bankers, real estate brokers, and waitresses.

Superficially, cocaine is a beguiling and relatively risk-free drug—so its devotees innocently claim. But cocaine is no joke. Although in very small and occasional doses it is no more harmful than equally moderate doses of alcohol or marijuana, the euphoric lift, the feeling of being confident and on top of things that comes from a few brief "snorts," is often followed by a letdown, and regular use can induce depression, edginess, and weight loss. As usage increases, so does the danger of paranoia, hallucinations, and a total physical collapse. And usage does tend to increase.

Cocaine is classified as a narcotic, as are opium, heroin, and morphine. The last three are "downers," which quiet the body and dull the senses, whereas cocaine is an "upper," a stimulant, similar to amphetamines. It increases the heartbeat, raises the blood pressure and body temperature, and curbs the appetite. Unlike such downers as heroin and Quaaludes, cocaine is physically nonaddictive. It can, however, damage the liver, cause malnutrition, and increase the risk of heart attacks. Coming down from a high may cause such deep gloom that the only remedy is more cocaine. Bigger doses often follow, and soon the urge may become a total obsession. This pattern can lead to a psychological dependence whose effects are not all that different from addiction. There is growing clinical evidence that when cocaine is taken in the most potent and dangerous forms—injected in solution or chemically converted and smoked in a process called freebasing—it may become addictive.

A cocaine high is an intensely vivid, sensation-enhancing experience; there is *no* evidence, as claimed, that it is an aphrodisiac. There *is* evidence that the sustained use of cocaine can cause sexual dysfunction and impotence. Even casual sniffing can lead to more potent and potentially damaging ways of using cocaine and other drugs. Many cocaine users take sedative pills such as Quaaludes to calm them down after the high and to take the edge off their yearning for more cocaine. A few smoke marijuana for the same purpose or mix their cocaine with heroin in a process called speedballing or boy-girl. The latter produces a tug-of-war in which the exhilaration of cocaine is undercut by the heroin.

A few middle-class users who dabble with heroin in conjunction with cocaine smoke it rather than inject it—this they believe prevents addiction. This is *false;* heroin, however used, is a fiercely addictive drug. Treatment centers are receiving an influx of well-dressed, well-to-do men and women who have gravely underestimated heroin's effects. One of cocaine's biggest dangers is that it diverts people from normal pursuits; it can entrap and redirect people's activities into an almost exclusive preoccupation with the drug.

There is little likelihood that the cocaine blizzard will soon abate. A drug habit born of a desire to escape the bad news in life is not likely to be discouraged by the bad news about the drug itself. Middle-class Americans will continue to succumb to the powder's crystalline dazzle. Few are yet aware or willing to concede that, at the very least, taking cocaine is dangerous to their psychological health.

CASE STUDY: RONALD

Ronald came to the crisis center and told the intake worker, "I don't think I have a problem, but my wife insisted that I come. *She* thinks I need help." He was assigned to a therapist.

The therapist came to the reception room, introduced herself, and asked Ronald to come to her office. He was of average height but very thin, well dressed in a three-piece suit, and quite good looking. He was asked by the therapist to tell her about himself and his family, since he had stated that he did not have a problem. He smiled pleasantly and said, "Please call me Ron—Ronald is much too stuffy; only my mother calls me Ronald." The therapist replied, "Of course, Ron, tell me more about yourself and why you came to the center."

Ron sat back in his chair in a very relaxed manner and began to talk. He stated that he was 38 years old, an attorney in international law who worked with a large bank, that he was married, his wife's name was Margaret ("I call her Maggie") and she was 32 years old, they had two children, Theodore (Ted), age 10, and Priscilla, age 7. He continued by saying, "Maggie insisted that I get some psychiatric help—I don't think I need any." Asked why his wife thought he might need some help, he commented, casually, "I travel a great deal, I work hard, and I use coke to relieve some of the stress, but I can control it. It gives me a great boost physically, and if I get too high, I can always take a downer." He was asked how long he had been using coke. Again, very casually he responded, "About 2 years—Maggie is just too old-fashioned, everyone uses it. When we go to parties, it's always available; everyone uses it—*except* Maggie."

The therapist asked, "Does your wife think you have changed since you have been using coke?" He answered defensively, "*She* says I have, but I don't think so. Last night I got too high and was getting ready to take a downer when she saw me and called me a drug addict. I know coke isn't addicting, but she doesn't believe me." The therapist asked, "How does she think you have changed?" He hesitated and then replied, "She says that our sex life is lousy—but it *isn't* the coke, it's just that I'm working too hard and traveling too much."

He was asked if he had increased his use of cocaine in the past 2 years. He replied, "Yes, but that's normal. Everyone says so. It just takes more for me to get high." The therapist responded, "It *is* an expensive habit. Do you have any difficulty getting cocaine or affording it?" He smiled and said, "Don't forget, I travel all over the world, and I have very *good* connections."

Ron was then asked, "Since you have increased your use of cocaine, have you changed the way in which you use it?" He responded, "Well, yes, I used to just sniff it, now I smoke it, it's more effective that way." He was asked how he was feeling in general. Angrily he said, "I feel *fine!*" The therapist replied, "Oh? Sleeping well? Appetite good?" He responded sarcastically, "What are you, a psychic?" The therapist replied, "No, Ron, not psychic, but I have worked with other patients who have used cocaine. I know what they were feeling, and I suspect you are feeling the same way."

Ron got up and started pacing around the office and said, "Damn it, you are just as nosey as Maggie. Have you talked to her [*paranoid*]? Listen, I can handle this. *So what* if I've lost weight, *so what* if we have a lousy sex life, *so what* if I am not sleeping much—what the hell is it to you?" The therapist responded calmly, "Ron, you came here for help. Don't you want help?" He replied, "I guess Maggie is right. I do have a problem, and I guess I do need some help." The therapist said, "Ron, won't you sit down so we can talk about it?"

Ron stopped pacing, sat down, looked at the therapist, and said, "God, I am such a fool! No wonder Maggie said she would divorce me if I didn't get help. I have been lying to myself and trying to make *you* believe I don't have a problem. I know my habit is out of control. It started so slowly, and then it just snowballed." He stopped abruptly, laughed bitterly, and said, "How is *that* for an analogy—snow—snowballed? What do I do now, check into some funny farm?" The therapist replied, "No, not a funny farm, Ron. You do have some vacation time available, don't you?" He replied, "Vacation time, we haven't had a vacation in 5 years. I can take all the time I want—or need! What did you have in mind?"

The therapist explained that there was an excellent substance abuse hospital, more like an exclusive country club, that he and his wife could go to. He would be evaluated and helped with his problem, Maggie would rest and attend group therapy so she could understand what he was going through. He listened and said, "When can I go?" The therapist responded, "Why don't you call Maggie and ask her? Also, what about the children, who would take care of them?" Ron said, "No problem, we have a live-in housekeeper and my mother, a widow, lives with us. She would love nothing better than having Ted and Priscilla all to herself for awhile."

The therapist smiled, dialed an outside line, and said, "Talk to Maggie now! Do you want me to leave the room?" Ron replied, "God, no! I need you to help me explain, in case I panic." The therapist agreed to stay, and Ron talked to Maggie. He told her where he was and what had been discussed and asked whether she would go with him to his "special resort." She apparently responded favorably; Ron looked at the therapist, grinned, and said, "When can you get us a reservation?" She responded, "How about tomorrow morning—check in before 11:00?" Ron repeated this to Maggie and she apparently agreed because he said, "Tell Mother that we are going to the French Riviera for a rest!" He laughed and said, "I am on my way home to pack. See you soon."

Ron looked at the therapist and exclaimed, "Thank God for Maggie—and you! How can I ever repay you?" The therapist responded, "Get well and stay that way." She added, "Of course, you can always make a donation to our center, we could use the money." Ron stood up, shook hands, and said, "To whom do I give my check?" The therapist smiled and said, "To the receptionist. Good luck, come back if you need us again!"

Summary

Ron was an intelligent attorney, who because of some need—stress or peer pressure—became psychologically addicted and possibly physiologically addicted to cocaine. He denied that his habit had changed his life, but his wife knew that he needed help and insisted that he come to the center. Through direct questioning the therapist was able to convince Ron that he did indeed have a problem. He was referred to a substance abuse hospital for treatment and intensive psychotherapy.

Three months later the therapist received a telephone call from Ron's wife, Maggie. Maggie asked the therapist to have dinner at their home to meet the children and to see Ron and how he had changed. She added, "Also, we have never met, although I feel that I really know you. Ron has spoken of you so often." The therapist agreed, and a date was set for the following Friday.

The therapist arrived at their home and was warmly greeted by Ron, who looked even more handsome. He was tanned, had gained approximately 10 pounds, and had a sparkle in his clear blue eyes. She was introduced to Maggie and to Ted and Priscilla. Maggie greeted the therapist with a hug, saying, "At last I get to meet you—welcome to our home." Maggie was a very attractive, suntanned, petite blonde. The children solemnly shook hands and were very well behaved. The therapist was escorted to the living room where she, Ron, and Maggie had a glass of wine and some hors d'oeuvres, which the children passed with a great deal of care and pride.

Dinner, served by the housekeeper, was delicious. The conversation was light and interesting. Nothing was said about Ron and Maggie's trip to the "Riviera." Ron's mother regaled everyone with stories of the children's many accomplishments and how very much Ted was like his father. After dinner the children went upstairs with their grand-mother to read some stories. The therapist and Ron and Maggie returned to the living room to have coffee.

After Maggie poured the coffee, Ron asked the therapist, "How do you think I look?" The therapist replied, smiling, "Fantastic! And I thought you were handsome when we *first* met!" Everyone laughed. Ron continued, "It was *not* easy, but with Maggie with me, giving me support, I made it. We both just wanted to let you see how happy we are *and* how healthy." The therapist stated, "It is very obvious that you are happy *and* healthy. I wish you both the very best."

ALCOHOLISM

Each year alcoholism accounts for an estimated 7% of all adults over the age of 18. A more shocking statistic is the steadily increasing number of children, sometimes 10 years old or even younger, who are being identified and treated for alcoholism. In recent years there has also been a marked increase in the number of women identified as alcoholics. It has been suggested that this may not represent an actual increase in the number of women who are becoming alcoholics but may be due to changing social attitudes, which now permit women to be more public with their drinking problems.

Alcoholism has been described as a condition in which a person is consistently unable to stop drinking alcoholic beverages and, once started, cannot stop until intoxicated. Generally, this is a repetitive condition and usually creates physical, psychological, and social problems for both the drinker or for others.

Dependence on the consumption of alcohol has been considered a symptom, a disease, and a combination of the two. The specific cause is still unknown. Some researchers have investigated whether alcoholism is inherited, or biologically transmitted, from parents to children or whether alcoholism is actually an expression of the role identification and imitative behaviors occurring in a child's family environment in which one or more family members is an alcoholic.

Alcohol is addictive, and it is similar to many other addicting substances. The stages towards addiction involve concomitant physical, psychological, and social changes in the individual. Prealcoholism usually begins with socially motivated drinking. Gradually this changes to drinking to reduce personal tensions, and, as tolerance for alcohol builds, consumption increases in order to achieve the same comfortable effects. The person gradually moves from social to surreptitious, avid drinking. There is a preoccupation with alcohol, yet an avoidance of discussing it in social groups. Blackouts begin to occur. This phase may last from several months to several years. In the next phase the person progresses to conspicuous drinking, loss of behavioral controls, and weakening or destruction of social and family relationships. Alcohol becomes the sole mechanism for dealing with daily living problems. If untreated, the person will slowly progress to a stage of chronic alcoholism, which is evidenced by marked symptoms of physical, psychological, and social deterioration.

Many psychosocial theories have been developed to help explain why a person becomes an alcoholic and why some continue to drink despite treatment whereas others stop drinking. It is generally agreed that many individuals resort to drinking as a method of adjusting to psychosocial demands or inner emotional needs when other methods of coping prove to be inadequate or unavailable.

For such individuals, alcohol may become a primary aid for managing personal tensions. Some drink excessively in reaction to stress in order to relieve anxiety and depression but stop as soon as the stressful situation is resolved. Reactive drinking has also been noted as a coping method used to reduce the tensions of maturational crises. Some start drinking heavily and persistently at an early age and handle alcohol well until the generalized effects of prolonged alcohol abuse catch up with them later in life. Often such persons seek treatment *only* when their drinking has created a crisis in their lives—and resume drinking as soon as the crisis has been resolved.

Many others, however, persist in their drinking and stop only when their physical, psychological, and/or social deterioration results in enforced abstinence from alcohol (such as external controls imposed by hospitalization for physical and psychological disorders, imprisonment, parole). For persons such as these, facing the *future possibility* of permanent disability, imprisonment, or even death is less stressful than facing the *present reality* of coping without alcohol.

CASE STUDY: MARK

Mark, aged 20, came to the Student Health Center at a West Coast university early one morning. He appeared to be very tense and anxious and had a strong odor of alcohol on his breath. While waiting to be seen by the physician, he paced restlessly about the reception room, avoiding conversation with anyone. He had been seen as a patient there several times in the past year for various minor physical complaints. He said that he had come this time because for the past few days he had had trouble sleeping, an upset stomach, and a headache that he could not get rid of.

Almost as soon as he entered the physician's office and sat down, he began to cry and said, "I think I must be going crazy. Here I am, an honor student, and I can't even remember what I read anymore. I can't concentrate on anything, and I'm going to fail my finals next week. My wife kicked me out. I might as well be dead! What's wrong with me?"

After a few minutes he stopped crying and was able to provide more information about himself. Mark was in his junior year at the university. He had come there from the Midwest and entered the university on a scholarship 3 years ago. A year ago he had married Barbara, who was also 20 years old and a fellow student. Until the past 2 months he had maintained a high scholastic average. He said that he and Barbara had had a good marriage until a few months ago, when they both began to feel the pressures of heavy class schedules. He had thought things would get better, though, once the semester was over and they could go away on vacation.

Mark was asked to briefly describe his family life before he came to the university. He replied that his father had been an alcoholic and had died in a traffic accident when Mark was 12 years old. He went on to describe his father as a person who was known by all his friends and business acquaintances as a "great guy," an upstanding civic leader, always very social and well liked, heading up committees, and so on. Mark and his mother, however, *also* knew him as a man who, at home, would drink excessively, easily lose control of his temper, and be very verbally abusive.

His mother had never remarried, and, because his father had invested his money well while he was alive, she had never needed to seek employment after his death. As Mark described her, she had always been a dependent, passive type who never complained about her husband's behavior when he drank and became abusive. Whenever Mark complained about his father's drinking, she was quick to make excuses for him and to defend his behavior.

She covered up for her husband whenever he was drinking heavily, and Mark grew up with the understanding that his father's alcoholism was a "family secret" not to be known to anyone outside their home.

Mark recalled that it was at times difficult for him to listen quietly when people would tell him what a great father he had and how much he should try to be like his father when he grew up. "There were times when he really was the greatest person in my life—and there were other times when I used to wish I had someone *else* for a father. Those were the times when he began his heavy drinking and we had to 'cover up' for him, so no one else would find out."

Mark's father had not been drinking when he was killed in the traffic accident, and the accident was not his fault. His car had been crushed by a truck whose driver had run a red light. He had died instantly. Mark stated that his mother really surprised everyone with how well she handled the personal and business details related to the funeral and settlement of his father's estate. He said that she did all her crying alone, at home, but always pulled herself together in public and didn't seem to want a lot of sympathy from anyone. She told Mark that she did not plan to move or make any great changes in the way they lived. She continued to attend her various club and church groups, go out to dinner with family friends, and entertain friends at home as usual.

About 6 months after his father's death Mark first noticed that his mother seemed to be drinking a little more than usual. "At first," he said, "she started having a little nightcap before going to bed to help her sleep. This was right after my father died, and she was having a rough time getting used to not having him there anymore." By the time Mark first noticed that she was drinking more heavily, she was already consuming up to a quart of alcoholic beverages a day. As he eventually learned, she would begin with an eye-opener as soon as she got up in the morning and then arrange her daily social schedule to space her personal and social drinking evenly throughout the day. In this way she attempted to fool both herself and her friends into thinking that she drank less than she actually did.

By the time he was 15 years old Mark observed that his mother was acting almost exactly like his father had. She had become actively involved, as a volunteer, in many cultural and civic groups and, like his father, was well respected and admired by everyone. She had also become a "secret alcoholic" like his father. It became his responsibility to "cover" for her whenever she was too drunk to answer the telephone or keep an appointment.

His mother died suddenly 3 years ago, during the summer after he graduated from high school. The cause of her death was listed as cirrhosis of the liver. His mother's attorney, an old family friend, had been designated as Mark's guardian in the event of her death while he was still a minor. Mark's mother had already approved Mark's plans to attend this university, so he moved to the West Coast that fall. He found an off-campus apartment to share with three other freshmen and lived with these three men until his marriage to Barbara a year ago.

On further questioning, Mark revealed that he had drunk some amount of alcoholic beverages daily for most of his life. Beer or wine was always available in his home, and his parents usually let him have a small glass with his meals whenever he wanted one. By the time he graduated from high school he was drinking up to a quart of beer and/or wine daily, and on occasion he drank stronger liquors. He said that this never interfered with his studies, that he got top grades, and that he never really got drunk—just felt good."

When Mark came to the university, he continued to drink about the same amount. This did not change very much after his marriage, until 6 months ago when he had started to drink more, adding a few nightcaps of whiskey before bedtime. Recently, however, he was finding it increasingly difficult to get started in the morning without an eye-opener. He began to miss some of his early morning classes frequently, and in the past few weeks his wife had become quite critical of his behavior and said that she was finding it difficult to live with him. Recently she informed him that in her opinion he was drinking too much and upsetting their guests with his rude behavior. She warned him that unless he cut down on his drinking, she did not want to live with him any more; either he or she would have to move out if his present drinking behavior continued.

Two nights ago they had had several friends in for dinner. Mark stated that, except for drinking a couple of beers, he had no memory about the rest of the evening. The next morning (yesterday) Barbara told him that he had been unusually rude to everyone and had started a fight with his former roommates. She informed him that he would have to find some place else to live as soon as final examinations were over next week. She reminded him that he had been warned several times before and that *this* time she really meant it.

Mark told the physician that he had spent all yesterday trying to figure out what to do. He still had one more final exam to take this week, one for which he had not yet prepared properly. Last night he had gone for a walk along the beach, had walked out to the end of a fishing pier, and suddenly had a very strong urge to jump into the ocean. "I suddenly realized what a mess I'd been making of my life—that I was behaving exactly like my parents had. I was expecting my wife to cover up for me just as I had been expected to do for them. The only difference is that Barbara won't play that game for me—and she's right. Why *should* she lie for me? This is *my* problem, not hers!"

He then covered his face with his hands and began to sob deeply. "I wanted to die then and there. I knew that I may have lost Barbara forever. I have never felt so helpless and alone in my life. I couldn't figure out what to do next. I nearly *did* go over the side, and it scared the hell out of me! That's why I'm here today. I'm afraid of what I might do if I start drinking again. I need help to get my act together again."

Mark said that he had already had "two or three shots of whiskey" to give him the courage to come to the center. He admitted to being severely depressed and, when asked whether he thought he might try suicide again, said, "I honestly don't think so. I really scared myself last night and did a lot of thinking about myself afterwards. I've never felt so mixed up and so helpless in my life, but I'm not ready to give up and die yet."

When asked what he usually did to handle tension and anxiety in the past, he answered, "When I was a kid back home I could always get into sport activities or talk it out with friends who'd known me all my life. Since my mother died, I've never gone back there. I haven't much time for sports now because of all my studies, so I usually grab a couple of beers or a shot of whiskey to calm my nerves and get some sleep. Lately, though, that hasn't been helping as much as it did before."

The physician's assessment was that Mark's major problem was alcoholism which, in turn, had caused a highly stressful situation in his life. During the past 6 months Mark's drinking habits had moved from the stage of social drinking into that of conspicuous drinking, destruction of his social relationships, and memory blackouts. No longer able to control his drinking, he was now threatened with the loss of his remaining close situational supports and the possibility of failure in his school classes. His perception of the situation was distorted both by the physical effects of alcohol on the senses and by his increased tension and anxiety. In addition, he was in emotional crisis. The physician believed that this crisis might serve as the impetus for Mark to obtain treatment for his alcoholism, which he had never openly sought before. The outside pressures of his wife and peer group combined with his internal pressures to succeed in school were providing strong motivators for him to control his drinking habits. These influencing factors would be strongly supported and reinforced as part of his therapy.

During their meeting the physician explored with Mark his past drinking habits and how he had handled stressful situations in the past. A pattern of increased drinking whenever he became tense, anxious, or depressed emerged clearly as Mark discussed his past. It was pointed out that his increasing physical complaints, although minor right now, could be symptoms of organic damage caused by alcohol addiction. As he described his relationships with his parents and his feelings about their problems with alcohol, it became apparent that he was functioning under the attitude (learned from his parents' behavior) that alcoholism per se was not the major problem. The major problem as perceived by them was how to keep one's drinking habit a family secret. As a child he had joined in the conspiracy with his parents. As an adult he found himself alone with no one to play this deception game with him. His wife and friends were threatening to reject him completely unless he changed his behavior. Faced with the realities of their demands, he was also suddenly faced with the realization that he had never learned any other ways to keep from feeling uncomfortably tense or anxious when things got stressful in his life.

By the end of their meeting the physician had determined that Mark, although very remorseful, was not suicidal. However, because of his recent prolonged and heavy drinking and his temporary loss of situational supports, Mark's admission as an inpatient to an alcoholic treatment program was arranged. The purpose was to provide Mark with medically supervised withdrawal from his alcohol addiction and professional support services to help him and his wife through the acute phases of his rehabilitation. When this was achieved, the next step would be to help them make connections with community resources that have been established specifically to help alcoholics and their families maintain their rehabilitation.

Summary

In this instance the physician used crisis intervention methods to help Mark focus on and identify the problem that caused his emotional disequilibrium. He provided situational support to help reduce Mark's anxiety and to help him begin to gain an intellectual understanding of the stressful situation and to recognize his need for help. The physician made no effort to resolve the situation or to schedule further meetings with Mark for this purpose. His primary goal during the meeting was to use the opportunity created by Mark's crisis and subsequent appeal for help to motivate him to enter an alcoholic treatment program and obtain the long-term psychotherapy that he needed.

PHYSICAL ILLNESS
Heart attack

Diseases are known to have their places as well as their times. Primitive societies have been characterized by health problems related to recurrent famines, and urban societies, until recently, by epidemics of infectious disease. Modern industrial societies are characterized by a new set of diseases: obesity, arteriosclerosis, hypertension, diabetes, and anxiety. Arising from these are two of the three greatest disablers and killers of our own place and time: coronary heart disease and stroke. In recent years increasing concern has focused investigation not only on the etiology and epidemiology of cardiac disease, but also on factors affecting recovery.

The unexpected recognition that one has heart disease is usually a crisis event for an individual. The disease may also be chronic, persisting throughout life and precipitating a series of crises both for the patient and for his family.

The conceptualization of the recovery process in heart disease as a response to crisis provides strategic advantages in approaching the problem. It leads to focusing on the kinds of adaptive and maladaptive mechanisms that patients employ in coping with this illness, on the stages of recovery, and on the resources that patients use and require at each stage. Viewing response to coronary heart disease as a problem that can be approached through crisis intervention permits the use of concepts and formulations inherent in crisis theory.

In a discussion of the rehabilitation of patients with cardiac disease, a report by the World Health Organization distinguishes between phases of the recovery process in terms of time and coping tasks. In the first phase the patient spends approximately 3 weeks in bed with minimal physical activity. In the next phase the patient spends approximately 6 weeks at home with a variety of sedentary activities. In the third phase, which lasts from 3 to 6 months, the patient gradually reenters the occupational world.

The recovery process has also been viewed in terms of the emotional adaptation of the patient. In this view the first phase is marked by initial shock and the second by appreciation of the full extent of the disability. In the third phase there is "recovery from the lure of hospital care," and in the fourth and final phase there is "a facing of independent, unsupported, competitive life."

Among the most obvious and critical determinants of the outcome of the recovery process are the severity of heart damage, the degree of impairment, and the physiological resources of the patient. Although cardiac damage has much to do with setting limits on performance and affecting levels of adjustment, studies of physiological factors alone contribute only partially to understanding the recovery process. Research on the importance of the premorbid personality of the patient as a determinant of adjustment to illness suggests that this is also an important factor in the recovery process.

Other important factors bearing on the recovery process include the various psychological mechanisms that the patient uses in handling the illness. If the recovery process is viewed as a response to a crisis situation, then the individual mechanisms used by patients appear particularly important in the resolution of the crisis. The significance of emotional response to disease has often been underlined in discussing the elements that determine recovery. The way in which a crisis is handled emotionally may significantly influence the eventual outcome of a case in terms of the extent of recovery and the degree of rehabilitation achieved. It is essential to deal with the anxieties associated with the diagnosis and symptoms of heart disease if the therapy of cardiac disease is to attain its optimum effect.

A common view is that during the acute phase of any serious illness the patient's emotional state is characterized by fear, since the illness threatens his total integrity as well as his sense of personal adequacy and worth to others.

Heart disease has several unique features. Associated as it is with sudden death, it is viewed by the patient and his family as an immediate and severe threat to life. Even in the most stable patients the onset of heart disease is associated with an onslaught of anxiety. During the first days of illness the patient with heart disease must assume a passive role, and some believe that this tends to compound his anxiety. Physical restriction usually increases feelings of helplessness, vulnerability, and depression. The patient is thus handicapped in using defense mechanisms that should ultimately help him to adjust to his altered status.

Although coping responses vary widely, there appears to be a core of relatively uniform responses of adjustment. For example, depression and regression have often been reported as the initial reaction to the illness. Some patients display aggression and hostility, placing the blame for the illness on external factors. Some deal with the threat to life by denying the illness.

It has been suggested that certain coping responses are appropriate at one stage of recovery but inappropriate at another. The same response may function constructively for some patients but hinder recovery for others. There is disagreement at present as to the role denial plays in recovery. Some regard denial, which may lead to noncooperation with the physician, as a response of self-destruction. Others consider that denial arises from a belief in the integrity of the self and the invulnerability of the body; they regard it as constructive and believe that it is associated with the maintenance of health.

Since each patient reacts individually in this life-threatening situation, the therapist will in all probability see a variety of coping responses. It is not the therapist's role to change a patient's pattern of coping but to understand that this reaction to illness is part of the individual patient's defense.

One's basis for action in health and disease is a composite of many things. One crucial variable is the way that one sees or understands the situation and all the social ramifications that accompany it. These perceptions are conditioned by socialization in a sociocultural context. How a patient responds to disease is influenced by what he has learned, and the content of that learning has been determined by the norms and values of the society in which he lives. The significance that a patient attaches to the disease, his attitude toward medical practitioners, his willingness to comply with medical advice, and his management of his life after the heart attack are all influenced by the attitudes and beliefs that he has learned.

Pertinent to the recovery process is the conceptualization of the "sick role," or social role, with its own culturally defined rights and obligations. Although a person may be physiologically ill, he is not recognized as legitimately ill unless his illness fulfills the criteria or standards set by society. Once defined as legitimately able to be in the "sick role," he is confronted with certain expectations. He is expected, for example, to seek help and to make an effort toward becoming well. In turn, he has the right to expect certain kinds of behavior in others toward him, including a willingness to permit him to relinquish his normal social role responsibilities.

Willingness to accept the sick role may mean that a patient with heart disease is likely to follow the regimen of his physician and to care for himself in ways that will maximize his recovery. Reluctance to accept the sick role may also influence the recovery process favorably. A patient may be anxious to avoid being defined as sick. Like the willing patient, he may follow the therapeutic regimen in order to shorten the period of incapacity. On the other hand, reluctance to view himself as sick may lead a patient to comply minimally with medical advice and to attempt full activity before he is physically able to do so.

In essence, social and cultural standards and expectations may have a strong influence on the action a patient with cardiac disease may take concerning his health status.

CASE STUDY: SAM

Sam, aged 43, was chairing a board meeting of his large, successful manufacturing corporation when he developed shortness of breath, dizziness, and a crushing, vicelike pain in his chest. The paramedics were called, and he was taken to the medical center. Subsequently he was admitted to the coronary care unit with a diagnosis of impending myocardial infarction.

Sam was married and had three children: Steve, aged 14; Sean, aged 12; and Liza, aged 8. He was president and majority stockholder of a large manufacturing corporation. He had no previous history of cardiovascular problems. His father, however, died at the age of 38 of a massive coronary occlusion; his oldest brother died at the age of 42 of the same condition; and his other brother, still living, was a semi-invalid after suffering two heart attacks—one at the age of 44 and the other at the age of 47.

Sam was tall, slim, suntanned, and very athletic. He swam daily, jogged every morning for 30 minutes, played golf regularly, and was an avid sailor who participated in every yacht regatta, usually winning. He was very health conscious and had annual physical checkups, watched his diet, and quit smoking to avoid possible damage to his heart, determined to avoid dying young or becoming an invalid like his brother.

When he was admitted to the coronary care unit, he was conscious. Although in a great deal of pain, he seemed determined to control his own fate. While in the coronary care unit he was an exceedingly difficult patient, a trial to the nursing staff and his physician. He constantly watched and listened to everything going on around him and demanded complete explanations about every procedure and medication he received. His sleep consisted of brief naps, and only when he was totally exhausted. Despite his obvious tension and anxiety, his condition stabilized. The damage to his heart was considered minimal, and his prognosis was good. As the pain diminished, he began asking when he could go home and when he could go back to work. He was impatient to be moved to a private room so that he could conduct some of his business by telephone.

Sam denied having any anxiety or concerns about his condition, although his behavior contradicted this denial. Recognizing that Sam was coping inappropriately with the stress of illness, his physician requested that a therapist whose expertise was crisis intervention work with Sam to help him through the crisis period.

The therapist agreed to work with Sam for 1 hour a week for 6 weeks. Their first session was scheduled the second day of his stay in the coronary care unit.

The therapist reviewed Sam's chart and talked with his physician before the first session in order to gain an accurate assessment of Sam's physical condition and to find out some factors (socioeconomic status, marital status, family history, and so on) that would help her assess Sam's needs.

In the first session the therapist observed Sam's overt and covert signs of anxiety and depression and determined, through discussion with him, what hospitalization meant to him, his usual patterns of coping with stress, and his available situational supports. Through direct questions and verbal feedback she was able to elicit the reasons for his behavior and his reactions to the illness and to the confinement in the coronary care unit.

Observing his suntanned, youthful appearance and the general physical condition of a very active and persistent athlete, the therapist questioned him about his life-style and patterns before hospitalization. Sam was adamant about his "minor" condition and the possibility of curtailed activity. He stated that he was very aware of his family's tendency toward cardiac conditions but said, "I have always taken excellent care of myself to avoid the possibility of becoming a cardiac cripple like my brother." Apparently he was not too concerned about the prospect of dying; in fact, he might prefer it to the overwhelming prospect of being a useless, dependent invalid.

He expressed concern about the time he might have to spend in the hospital. When questioned about this concern, he stated, "I *have* to be in good shape by the second of December [in approximately 3½ months]—I've entered the big yacht race, and I plan to win again!"

When he was asked how his wife and children were reacting to his illness and hospitalization, Sam's facial expression and general body tension relaxed noticeably. He smiled and said, "My wife, Ann, is simply unbelievable; she takes everything in stride. She is always cool, calm, and collected. She even met with the board of directors and told them to delay any major decisions until I return—but that any minor decisions she could handle!"

The therapist asked whether she could meet his wife. Sam replied that his wife would be in to see him soon and suggested she stay and meet her.

After meeting Ann briefly, the therapist asked her to stop by her office before leaving.

Ann arrived at the office and sank gratefully into a chair, losing the bright, cheerful, and optimistic manner she had maintained while with her husband. Observing her concerned expression and slumped posture, the therapist inquired, "You are very concerned about your husband, aren't you?" Ann readily admitted that she was concerned but did not want her husband to know. When asked what specifically concerned her, she replied, "Sam's inability to accept any type of forced inactivity and his refusal to accept the possibility that he might have to change his hectic life-style. He can't *bear* the thought of being ill or being dependent on anyone or anything!"

The therapist explained that it is difficult for many patients to accept a passive, dependent role while ill and that it takes time for them to adjust to a changed life-style. She then explained to Ann that the physician had arranged for Sam to have therapy sessions for the next 6 weeks to help him through his crisis. Ann seemed relieved that someone else recognized the problems confronting her husband and would help him as he worked through his feelings about his illness and his unwanted but inevitable change in life-style.

The therapist suggested that Ann might also need some support, since she too had to adjust to Sam's illness. They agreed to meet for an hour each week so they could work together toward a resolution of the crisis. A convenient appointment time was arranged.

Sam's denial of the possibility that he might die like his father and one brother or that he might become an invalid, "useless and dependent," like his other brother was considered of prime importance. It was felt that the first goal of intervention was to help Sam to ventilate his feelings about his illness and hospitalization. A second goal was to help him to understand the situation realistically. A third goal established was that of giving support to Ann and assisting her in coping with the stress induced by her husband's hospitalization.

It was believed that Sam's high anxiety level would interfere with his ability to express his feelings about his illness and his hospitalization. In an attempt to reduce his anxiety, the therapist made two recommendations to his physician, which were accepted. The first recommendation was that Sam be moved out of the coronary care unit to a private room as soon as possible. The environmental surroundings in the coronary care unit, with its overwhelming and complex equipment, strange sounds, and constant activities of the staff, apparently increased Sam's anxiety. Because of his stress, he was not getting sufficient rest. After his move to a private room later that afternoon, he began to relax noticeably, became much less demanding of the staff, and began sleeping and eating better.

The second recommendation was that Sam be permitted to use the telephone for 30 minutes three times a day. Thus he was able to conduct some of his business from his bed. This apparently made him feel less dependent, and the increased mental activity relieved some of his anxiety about becoming a "helpless" invalid.

In the next sessions Sam began to discuss—hesitantly at first, and then more freely—his feelings about his illness and his reaction to hospitalization. He discussed his father's sudden death when he was in his teens and how lost he would have felt if his older brother had not stepped in and taken over. All three brothers were very close, and the death of the oldest one, while Sam was in college, reactivated the loss he had felt for his father. He was just beginning to accept this brother's death when, a year later, his other brother had a severe heart attack and was unable to continue in the family business. As Sam saw it, his brother was a helpless invalid. Sam, the youngest son, then became the major stockholder and president of the corporation.

He stated that although he certainly didn't *want* to die, he was less afraid of dying than he was of becoming useless, helpless, and a burden to his family.

Through discussion and verbal feedback, it was possible to get Sam to view his illness and the changes it would make in his life in a realistic manner. No, he was *not* an invalid. Yes, he *would* be able to work and live a *normal* life. No, he would *not* have to give up sailing, just have someone else do most of the crewing. Yes, he *would* be able to resume his activities but at a more leisurely pace, for instance, instead of scheduling sixteen things to do in one day, he might schedule eight. Gradually he became more accepting as he began to realize that the impending myocardial infarction was a warning he should heed; with proper care and some diminishing of his usual hectic pace he could continue a productive and useful life.

The therapist continued to meet with Ann to give her support and help with anticipatory planning for Sam's convalescence at home. They discussed Sam's strong need to feel independent and in control of all situations, and the therapist encouraged Ann to continue to let her husband make decisions for the family. She assured Ann that he would be able to continue a relatively normal life and that she did not need to protect and coddle him, something he would greatly resent! When asked how their children were reacting to Sam's hospitalization, Ann replied, "At first they were terribly concerned and silent; now they are beginning to ask when he is coming home and what they can do." It was obvious that Sam had strong situational support in his family!

Sam's recovery progressed fairly smoothly, and he began to ambulate and take care of his basic needs. Although more accepting of his need for some assistance, he still became upset and impatient if the staff intervened to assist him in routine care.

Sam was discharged after the fourth week, with instructions for his convalescence at home. The therapist continued to meet with Sam and Ann at their home during the fifth and sixth weeks to assist the family toward stabilization as Sam adjusted to his new regimen of reduced activity and to provide anticipatory planning for their future.

By the end of the fifth week, with the strong support of his family and the therapist, Sam was able to view his illness and his feelings about curtailing some of his hectic activities in a more accepting and realistic manner. His family still consulted him for advice and opinions about family decisions. This made him feel he was still an active, participating member of the family.

He was able to conduct a large part of his business from his home by having board meetings there and by having periodic telephone conversations with his office. His secretary came to his home 3 days a week to take dictation and secure his signature when needed on documents. Thus he remained in control of his business life, which contributed greatly to his self-esteem.

The children and Ann were encouraged to continue their usual daily activities so that Sam would not feel that his being at home was disrupting their lives. This also helped Ann to cope with her feelings and her desire to protect her husband from stress. Gradually she was able to realize that he was capable of coping with some stress and that he was not as fragile as she had believed him to be.

Before termination of therapy the therapist and Sam reviewed the adjustments he had made and the insights he had gained into his own behavior. He was able intellectually to understand his reasons for his denial and dependence-independence conflicts.

He was very optimistic about his future and believed that he could adjust to a reduced activity schedule. He still, rather wistfully, was hoping his physician would approve his entering the yacht race.

He was realistic about his physical condition and the possibility of another coronary attack, stating, "At least now I've learned to relax and roll with the punches."

Ann and the children thought that they would be able to cope with Sam's occasional bouts of frustration and temper flare-ups. They were now aware of how difficult it was for him to make the many adjustments necessary to his new way of life.

Summary

Sam's fear of becoming a "cardiac cripple" like his brother distorted his understanding of the event. He was unable to relax and be dependent in the coronary care unit. His anxiety and tension made him unable to accept the fact that he had had a myocardial infarction. His family and his colleagues—his usual situational supports—were unable to be with him because of hospital rules and his restricted activity. He used denial excessively because he was unable to accept the fact that he might have to change his life-style. Since this was his first hospitalization and the first time he had to be in a dependent role, his anxiety increased considerably.

Addendum

Several months later the physician informed the therapist that he had permitted Sam to enter the yacht race, as a passenger, not as crew, and that his yacht had finished third.

Mastectomy

Body image is one's constantly changing total of conscious and unconscious thoughts, feelings, and perception about one's body. It changes over time as society's standards—about what is acceptable in physical appearance—change. Body image is basic to identity. There is considerable agreement that one's body image functions as a standard, or frame of reference, which influences the ways in which a person sees himself and his ability to perform.

In illness and in health a wide variety of messages about the body are being constantly fed into the system, either for integration into the self or for rejection and revision. The infant responds to inner and outer experiences at the sensory level with screaming, raging, or cooing. Success in achieving comfort and relief from pain and anxiety prepares his body for the task of controlling the environment. Children from 2 to 4 years old are still uncertain of their body boundaries and may experience extreme anxiety about having their nails and hair cut.

After a sudden growth spurt, adolescents, not knowing how to manage their changed bodies, are very preoccupied with the changes in terms of cultural and social norms and attractiveness. They study their bodies and compare various aspects with those of their peers, questioning, "Am I too short?" "Too tall?" "Too skinny?" "Too fat?" and so forth. Older people defend themselves against the physical process of aging. More and more techniques have been developed for hiding wrinkles, maintaining hair color, disguising obesity, and generally trying to look younger.

Hospitalization may be very stressful if the patient is unable to maintain what he considers to be his proper body image. An individual's body image is normally disturbed following the loss of a body part. A classic example is the "phantom limb" of patients who have had a leg amputated. It is so real that patients often act as if they still had both legs and end up falling to the floor. Loss of any body part—hair, teeth, eye, nose, or breast—necessitates an adjustment of the individual's body image.

Because the body image provides a base for identity, almost any change in the body structure or function is experienced as a threat. This occurs even in normal growth; the maturing process may be welcome, but it also may be accompanied by the threat of new expectations and the threat of being inadequate. Surgery, although a "curative" procedure, is a strong threat to body image. Some patients feel that to sign a release for surgery is to sign away one's life. Others feel that to give permission for general anesthesia is to sign away control of their body and make themselves absolutely helpless. There is also the fear of being *cut,* being in *pain,* and being *mutilated.*

The patient experiencing alteration of body image goes through four phases: *impact, retreat, acknowledgment,* and *reconstruction.* During *impact* the patient may experience feelings of frustration, despair, or anger. Other behaviors may be discouragement or passive acceptance. The patient may project onto others the feelings of guilt and shame that he feels. This phase permits the patient to dissociate the body from the event.

In the *retreat* phase the patient is aware of the injury, loss, or disfigurement.

With the sudden realization of the problem *after* the shock subsides, the first reaction is to run; however, the immobilization does not permit this. So the patient emotionally retreats from the problem that must be eventually faced. When he looks at himself, he sees someone else's body, not his own. In this phase the patient is not able to mourn the loss and to reorganize his body image in an attempt to acknowledge the loss. Some patients retreat into denial.

The *acknowledgment* phase brings about a period of mourning the loss. The patient realizes that he can no longer hide or retreat. Patients begin to discuss the details or events that led to hospitalization. They discuss the altered body part in an attempt to integrate the event with the eventual alteration.

During the *reconstruction* phase the patient attempts to adapt to the changes in his body image. The patient is encouraged to try new approaches to life. In this phase patients usually begin to feel a more positive attitude toward living. They usually feel as if they have been given a "second chance." The goal is to help patients achieve the highest level of reconstruction possible.

Cancer causes much suffering and many deaths. It is inevitable that cancer patients fear that they may suffer terrible pain, waste away, and die before their hopes and goals are realized. Even when the cancer has been removed successfully, the patient has to live with considerable uncertainty as to whether and when the cancer will recur. Therefore many cancer patients and their families experience great stress.

The treatments used to combat cancer may greatly intensify this stress because they often have unpleasant side effects. The treatment may include the removal of a part of the body which was crucial to the patient's body image and self-esteem. Radiotherapy and chemotherapy cause fatigue, depression, nausea, vomiting, and hair loss. These side effects can be so severe that patients and their families come to dread further treatments; they may even refuse them.

Some patients find the strain of living with cancer and the consequences of treatment too much for them and develop serious psychological problems. Recent studies have found that between 20% and 40% of women who undergo mastectomy for breast cancer develop a depressive illness, anxiety neurosis, or sexual problems within 12 months of surgery.

Cancer and bodily disfigurement are two frightening realities. The mastectomy patient faces both as she struggles for adjustment and survival. Breast cancer continues to be the main cause of death from cancer among women in the United States, with over 33,000 deaths each year. The discovery of a lump in the breast evokes anxiety connected with possible breast removal. Possibly no other health problem among women causes so much fear and pessimism. Mastectomy, with or without adjunctive therapies, continues to be the most frequently used method of treatment for cancer of the breast. Such loss, by its very nature, interferes with the female body image and will affect the way a woman sees herself.

Some physicians are now doing less radical surgery such as lumpectomy. More and more patients are requesting removal of the cancerous lump only. Other surgeons are doing breast implants immediately after the removal of a breast to lessen the change in body image.

When a woman discovers a lump in her breast, she faces tension-provoking questions and alternatives. Common misconceptions about cancer and breast surgery complicate the picture. Some women respond with denial—pretending the lump is not there or that it is getting smaller. Others see their physician and are told to consult a surgeon. While in a state of shock, they are told they need surgery, usually for a biopsy and possible mastectomy. Questions race through their minds as they are faced with a deadly illness and the loss of a breast: "Is this physician any good?" "Should I get another opinion?" "What alternatives do I have?" "What if I do *nothing?*" The surgery itself is often carried out in an atmosphere of crisis. The patient usually is depressed on awakening and discovering that she has lost a breast and therefore has *cancer.* That terrifying word—*cancer!*

CASE STUDY: NAOMI

Naomi was in her fourth postoperative day at a medical center recovering from a radical mastectomy (removal of lymph nodes and breast). Her surgeon requested a consultation with a therapist because of Naomi's "inappropriate response" to his recommendation for chemotherapy. Dr. Maxwell said to the therapist, "She refuses even to discuss it—damn it, she is only 32! Will you see what *you* can do?" The therapist said that she would try, "but don't expect miracles."

The therapist read Naomi's chart and went to her room. She introduced herself, told Naomi that Dr. Maxwell had requested the consultation, and asked whether she had any objections. Naomi smiled and said, "No, of course not, please sit down." Naomi was a very attractive brunette with long wavy hair and expressive gray eyes.

The therapist sat down and said, "Dr. Maxwell is apparently having difficulty trying to convince you that you should have chemotherapy, is that correct?" Naomi replied, "Yes, the poor dear man, he just *can't* understand! He probably thought you could convince me because you are a woman." The therapist smiled and said, "Could be, he is feeling *very* frustrated with you. Naomi, tell me about yourself and why you don't want to have chemotherapy."

Naomi related her history very calmly and objectively. She said she was 32, divorced, and the mother of two sons who lived with her former husband. She was an executive secretary for the president of a large manufacturing company and traveled a great deal on business. She continued by saying this was the reason the children lived with their father and his "new" wife. "They have a more 'normal' home with them. I see them on weekends when I am in town." She stated that she had a very good friend, Roger, "but we are just good friends—not lovers." She continued, "I make very good money; I enjoy my work and traveling; I don't *need* a man in my life except as a friend. Roger has accepted this and we see each other for dinner or to go to a concert or a play."

Naomi was asked by the therapist when she found a lump in her breast. She took a deep breath and said, "I will tell you; I haven't told any of the doctors. Last year—10 months ago—I was on a business trip and as I was getting dressed, I touched my breast and felt a lump. I went numb! I decided it was because it was right before my menstrual period and that it would go away after my period. I went out to dinner and forgot about it.

After my period, I checked my breast again; it was still there. I believed—I *wanted* to believe—that it was just a cyst. I was able to ignore it for a while—a *long* while—and then I couldn't. I could feel the pressure in my breast; it was growing! Ten days ago I went to my gynecologist. He was shocked and insisted I see Dr. Maxwell, a very well known surgeon, immediately." She continued, saying that she saw Dr. Maxwell the next afternoon and he recommended that she enter the medical center as soon as possible for a biopsy and in all probability a radical mastectomy. Naomi said, "I did not want to believe it, but I knew I had cancer." The therapist asked, "Why did you think it was cancer?" Naomi replied, "I have *never* told a doctor this; I was afraid they would keep probing until they found it one day. I thought if I didn't tell them, they would treat me like any other patient."

The therapist asked, "Tell them *what,* Naomi?" She looked up with tears in her eyes and replied, "I have seen *too* much of it in my family. My mother had *two* mastectomies; she died a horrible death. Her two sisters died of *it* too! I don't care what anyone says, I know it is hereditary!" The therapist responded, "Naomi, there may be a *tendency* toward certain types of cancer, but it hasn't been proven that it is inherited. *Men*—a small percentage it's true—*also* have breast cancer."

Naomi appeared thoughtful and said, "I didn't know that men could get breast cancer, but it really doesn't matter. I didn't think I would get it so young." The therapist asked, "How old were your mother and your aunts when they got breast cancer?"

Naomi sighed and stated, "My mother was 46, Aunt Marge was 44, and Aunt Ruth was 42. I saw them go through *hell* with radiation and chemotherapy. I have always said that when I get it, I will *not* have any treatment whatsoever! I don't even know why I let Dr. Maxwell do a mastectomy. I should have refused—I feel so mutilated."

The therapist replied, "I know, Naomi, it is truly a shock seeing your body change so drastically, and I do understand. I realize how terrible it was for you to see members of your family suffer, but *you* are younger, and there are new cancer-fighting drugs that may not be as toxic as you remember." Naomi replied bitterly, "I know I *may* live longer, but it really isn't *living*—it would be nothing but *hell,* a living hell, physically and mentally."

The therapist asked, "What do you plan to do?" Naomi responded, "As soon as I am discharged from the hospital, I am going to take one day at a time, and *live* it the best I can. I want to see more of my sons, travel as much as I can, work, and *live* until I die. And *no one* is going to talk me into having chemotherapy! I don't know how long I have, but I will *die* the way I want to, without being sick and bald."

The therapist responded, "Is that what you want me to tell Dr. Maxwell?" She replied, "Yes, *please* try to make him understand. Tell my history. Tell him it is *my* life, not *his,* and this is what *I* want." The therapist said, "Naomi, why don't you think about it for awhile? You don't have to make a decision today." Naomi said firmly, "I don't need any more time; I *made* my decision a long time ago. Thank you for listening. Please tell Dr. Maxwell that I understand his position, but thanks—no thanks. *No* chemotherapy."

The therapist stood up and said, "I will let Dr. Maxwell know of your decision—and why— but he is very dedicated, so don't expect him to take this calmly." She left and dictated her consultation report and then called Dr. Maxwell to let him know of Naomi's reasons for not wanting further treatment. Dr. Maxwell responded sadly, "But she is only 32."

Summary

Early diagnosis of breast cancer is becoming more prevalent. Women are increasingly urged to become more inquisitive and assertive about their own bodies. They are provided information about breast cancer by the media to the saturation level. It is hoped that the increase in factual knowledge might help to decrease the fears and worries about treatment and the subsequent healing process.

CHRONIC PSYCHIATRIC PATIENT

Crisis intervention has gained recognition as a viable therapy modality to assist individuals through acute traumatic life situations. As large psychiatric facilities are beginning to shorten the length of hospitalization (slowly or rapidly, according to individual state laws and money restrictions), the chronic psychiatric patient is returning to the community, where care must be continued. The following questions must be asked and answered: (1) Does crisis intervention work successfully with chronic psychiatric patients? (2) If not, what other methods must be used to keep this patient functioning in the community?

With a chronic psychiatric patient, as with any patient, the causal event, the patient's symptoms, the patient's understanding of the event, his available situational supports, and his usual coping mechanisms are crucial factors in resolving his crisis.

Situational supports are those persons in the environment who can lend support to the individual. If a patient is living with his family or friends, are they concerned enough—and do they care enough—to give him help? The patient's situational supports can serve as "assistants" to the therapist and the patient. They are with him daily and are encouraged to have frequent communication with the therapist. Usually situational supports are included in some part of the therapy sessions. This provides them with the knowledge and information they need to help the "identified" patient.

If the patient is living in a board-and-care facility, are any of its members concerned and willing to work with the therapist to help the individual through the stressful period? If so, the therapist will make visits to the facility and conduct collateral or group therapy with the patient and other members to get and keep them involved in helping to resolve the crisis.

Occasionally a patient has *no* situational supports. He may be a social isolate; he may have no family and may have acquaintances but no real friends with whom he can talk about his problems. Usually an individual such as this has many difficulties in interpersonal relationships—at work, at school, and in all social encounters. For such a patient it is the therapist's role to provide situational support during therapy.

Experience has verified that crisis intervention can be effective with chronic psychiatric patients. When a psychiatric patient with a history of repeated hospitalization returns to the community and his family, his reentry creates many stresses. Although much has been accomplished to remove the stigma of mental illness, people are still wary and hypervigilant when they learn that a "former mental patient" has returned to the community.

In his absence the family and community have, consciously or unconsciously, eliminated him from their usual life patterns and activities. Thus they have to readjust to his presence and include him in activities and decision making. If for any reason he does not conform to their expectations, they want him removed so that they can continue their lives without his possible disruptive behavior.

The first area for the therapist to explore is to determine who is in crisis: the patient or his family. In many cases the family is overreacting because of anxiety and is seeking some means of getting the "identified" patient back into the hospital. The patient is usually brought to the center by a family member because his original psychotic symptoms have begun to reemerge. Questioning the patient or his family about medication he received from the hospital and determining whether he is taking it as prescribed are essential. If the patient is unable to communicate with the therapist about what has happened or what has changed in his life, the family is questioned as to what might have caused his return to his former psychotic behavior.

There is usually a cause-and-effect relationship between a change or antici- pated change in the life-style or family constellation and the beginning of abnormal overt behavior in the identified patient. Often families do not tell a former psychiatric patient when they are contemplating a change such as moving or changing jobs because "he wouldn't understand." This is taken by the patient as exclusion or rejection by the family and creates stress that he is unable to cope with; thus he retreats to his previous psychotic behavior. Such cases are frequent and can be dealt with through the theoretical framework of crisis intervention methods.

Family-focused crisis intervention usually brings about the resolution of the patient's crisis without hospitalization, and family crisis intervention can also be a viable alternative to rehospitalization. The emphasis is placed on the period immediately after the patient's release from the hospital. It is suggested that conjoint family therapy begin in the hospital before the patient's release and then continue in an outpatient clinic after his release. This approach has also served to develop the concept that a family can and should share responsibility for the patient's treatment.

The following brief case study illustrates the use of the crisis model in working with a chronic psychiatric patient in a community mental health center.

CASE STUDY: JIM

Jim, a man in his late thirties, was brought to a crisis center by his sister because, as she stated, "He was beginning to act crazy again." Jim had many prior hospitalizations, with a diagnosis of paranoid schizophrenia. The only thing Jim would say was, "I *don't* want to go back to the hospital." He was told that the therapist would help him stay out of the hospital if possible. A medical consultation was arranged to determine whether his medication should be increased or changed.

Information was then obtained from his sister to determine what had happened, when his symptoms had started and, specifically, what she meant by his "acting crazy again." His sister stated that he was "talking to the television set, muttering things that made no sense, staring into space, prowling around the apartment at night," and that this behavior had started about 3 days before. When questioned about anything that was different in their lives before the start of his disruptive behavior, she denied any change. When asked about any changes that were contemplated in the near future, she replied that she was planning to be married in 2 months but that Jim did not know about it because she had not told him yet. When asked why she had not told him, she reluctantly answered that she wanted to wait until all the arrangements had been made. She was asked whether there was any way Jim could have discovered her plans. She remembered that she had discussed them on the telephone with a girlfriend the week before.

Asked about her plans for Jim after she married, she said that her boyfriend had agreed, rather reluctantly, to let Jim live with them.

Since her boyfriend was reluctant about having Jim live with them, other alternatives were explored. She said that they had cousins living in a nearby suburb but that she did not know whether they would want Jim to live with them.

It was suggested that Jim's sister call her cousins, tell them of her plans to be married and her concerns about Jim, and find out their feelings about his living with them. The call was placed. Fortunately, their response was a positive one. They had recently bought a fairly large apartment building and were having difficulty getting reliable help to take care of the yard work and minor repairs. They thought that Jim would be able to manage this, and they would let him live in a small apartment above the garage.

Jim was asked to come back into the office so that his sister could tell him of her plans to marry and the arrangements she had made for him with their cousins. He listened but had difficulty understanding the information. He just kept saying, "I *don't* want to go back to the hospital."

He was asked if he had heard his sister talking about her wedding plans. He admitted that he had and that he knew her boyfriend would not want him around; he thought they would probably put him back in the hospital. As the session ended, he still had not internalized the information he had heard. He was asked to continue therapy for 5 more weeks and to take his medication as prescribed. He agreed to do so.

By the end of the sixth week he had visited his cousins, seen the apartment where he would be living, and discussed his new "job." His disruptive behavior had ceased, and he was again functioning at his precrisis level.

Since Jim had had many previous hospitalizations and did not want to be rehospitalized, time was spent discussing how this could be avoided in the future. He was given the name, address, and telephone number of a crisis center in his new community and told to visit the center when he moved. He was assured that the center could supervise his medication and that someone there would talk to him if he felt he again needed help.

Summary

Jim's sister had neglected to tell him about her impending marriage, which he took as rejection. Because of his numerous hospitalizations, he feared that his sister would have him rehospitalized "to get rid of him." Unable to verbalize his fears, he retreated from reality and experienced a return of his psychotic symptoms.

The therapist adhered to the crisis model by focusing the therapy sessions on the patient's immediate problems, *not* on his chronic psychopathology.

DIVORCE

In Western society, divorce has become a common rather than a rare occurrence. Much has been written and hypothesized about the causes and effects of divorce on individuals and family members. According to the *Los*

Angeles Times, April 2, 1980, the divorce rate in the United States increased 96% in the last decade. This trend appears to be leveling off, according to the Bureau of the Census. A national survey in March 1979 found that there had been 92 divorces for every 1,000 marriages in the previous year, compared with 47 divorces for every 1,000 marriages in 1970. Since divorce rates are so high and many marriages are centers of friction and unhappiness, something must be lacking in the preparation for marriage. No event of equal importance is viewed with so little realism, and many people marry with little or no preparation.

Marriage and its demands on individuals can be stressful, and failure to sustain a marriage can precipitate a crisis. Stress is most common in the following three phases: engagement, honeymoon, and early marriage (first 3 months). Engaged couples confront major tasks on two levels—intrapersonal and interpersonal. The intrapersonal task is review of readiness for marriage on a conscious, preconscious, or unconscious level of psychological maturity. This readiness is affected by the person's individual needs and perceived subcultural norms. The interpersonal tasks are concerned with developing an interpersonal adjustment or accommodation that will be satisfactory in the marital relationship. The engagement period involves a process of separation from previous life patterns and of commitment of the couple to one another. The honeymoon period is a time for establishing a basic sense of harmony. The early marriage phase involves establishing a system of authority, decision-making patterns, and patterns of the sexual relationship.

Couples do not always accomplish these necessary tasks in the first few months of marriage. For some these tasks may extend into the first few years of marriage. Additional stress factors may occur in this period to create even greater disequilibrium.

The largest proportion of divorces occurs in the early years of marriage among childless couples. The peak period of divorces is in the second year of marriage, after which the rate drops rapidly. A number of factors other than those previously mentioned are precipitating causes of divorce. Among these are urban background, early marriage (15 to 19 years of age), short courtship, short engagement, mixed racial or religious marriages, disapproval of friends and relatives, dissimilar backgrounds, and unhappy parental marriages.

Today there is greater acceptance of the possibility of divorce; because of this acceptance, divorced persons have lost some of the feelings of failure and guilt that were formerly associated with it. The higher divorce rate may reflect new values placed on marriage. Marriage is no longer accepted as an "endurance race" that is doggedly maintained "for the sake of the children." The current demands are for a "good marriage"—one that meets the needs of the individuals involved. In certain circumstances, if the children are not used as pawns by the separating parents, divorce may even create fewer psychological problems for the children, who seemingly pay the highest price for marital failure.

The rate of remarriage after divorce is high, and in cases where both parties had been divorced two or more times it is even higher. Divorce is a repetitive phenomenon. Any unresolved neurotic pattern carried over from one marriage to another would tend to reinforce the individual's failure pattern in the subsequent marriage.

The following case study concerns a 23-year-old woman who sought help from a crisis center on the advice of her attorney because of an impending divorce. Neither Margie nor her husband had attained the psychological maturity or readiness necessary for marriage. Margie's impulsive marriages after brief courtships indicated her unrealistic expectations and attitudes toward marriage. Clues given indicated that she believed herself a failure as a woman. These guilt feelings and lack of her usual situational supports caused a crisis. Intervention was planned to help her to cope with her feelings of failure and guilt and to view her divorce in more realistic terms.

CASE STUDY: MARGIE

Margie, an extremely attractive young woman in the process of divorce from her third husband, was referred to a crisis center for help because of severe depression and anxiety manifested by insomnia, lack of appetite, tremulousness, inability to concentrate, and frequent crying spells. These symptoms had begun 3 weeks earlier, when she was notified of the date of the divorce proceedings. She had lost her job because she was unable to control her crying spells and had subsequently developed bursitis in her shoulder, which further limited her ability to work. Her symptoms had intensified so much in the past 3 days that she felt she was losing complete control over her emotions and needed help.

During the initial session Margie stated that she did not want a divorce and that she still loved her husband even though he did not love her. When questioned about the increased intensity of symptoms that had occurred 3 days ago, she stated that at that time she had been informed by her attorney that she could receive alimony only if she countersued for divorce.

In Margie's two previous divorces she had remained a passive participant; her husbands had sued her for divorce. She had not contested the action. Now, for the first time, owing to her inability to work, she was forced to become an active participant in a divorce she did not want. She stated frequently, "Something must be wrong with me if I can't hold a husband," and later commented, "I don't feel this is a good marriage—but I hate to fail again." This ambivalence and her expressed guilt feelings were believed to be part of the crisis, as was the necessity of being forced to take an active part in a divorce she did not want.

The therapist thought that, although Margie was depressed and expressed feelings of worthlessness, she was not suicidal and did not constitute a threat to others.

Margie had almost totally withdrawn from her social and family contacts. Her mother came occasionally to give her money for rent and bring her food. Beyond this social contact, she remained isolated in the apartment she had shared with her husband, weeping at intervals, staring at her husband's picture, and unable to decide whether to contest the divorce.

Since she had not made active decisions in her previous divorces, she had no coping experiences in this situation. When questioned about her previous methods of coping with stress, she stated that usually she had no problems because she remained involved in her work and its many social contacts, usually bowling and going to bars with friends.

Her present inability to work eliminated these sources of social support, distractions from the problem, and her previous successful coping mechanisms could not be used.

The goal of intervention was to help Margie to recognize and cope with her ambivalence and guilt. Unrecognized feelings about her marriage and the impending divorce were also to be explored.

In the next 3 weeks, through direct questioning and reflection of verbal and nonverbal clues to Margie, it became possible for her to view the present crisis and its effect on her in relationship to her previous marriages and divorces.

Margie wanted desperately to marry in order to become a housewife and mother. Her usual social contacts, her patterns of meeting men (at bowling alleys and bars), her impulsive marriages (Las Vegas, three times), and her reasons for marriage ("I thought I could help him; he needed me") were not meeting this need. The men she had met and married, and who later divorced her, were men who did not want to settle down with a wife and children. Instead, they wanted a happy, attractive companion to show off to their friends. Margie always hoped that they would change after marriage. However, they remained unchanged and divorced Margie when she persistently suggested "starting a family." With each marriage and subsequent divorce, her guilt feelings about her ability to be a good wife magnified. With the loss of her previous patterns of coping, the third divorce caused this crisis.

After the third session Margie's depression and symptoms had lessened as she recognized the possibility that the failure of her marriages may not have been caused by her inability to be a good wife but by differences between what she wanted and expected from a marriage and what the men she had married wanted and expected.

Exploration with Margie of her usual modes of social contact and her impulsive marriages (usually after only 3 or 4 weeks' courtship) assisted her in viewing her current divorce in more realistic terms. This was an important phase in anticipatory planning.

By the fourth week Margie had made significant changes in her patterns of living. She moved from the apartment she had shared with her husband to a small house near her mother. She also signed the papers to contest the divorce and found a new job.

Margie was granted the divorce and was apparently able to view her past experience as a traumatic but valuable learning experience.

In discussion and review of her future plans, Margie was cautious but realistic. She was enjoying her new job and new friends, and going to movies and occasionally to dinner with girlfriends. She stated that she was not accepting dates from men yet, "although I've been asked," and that if she married again, "it would not be in Las Vegas!"

Before termination of the therapy Margie and the therapist reviewed and assessed the adjustments she had made in coping with the crisis, the insight she had gained into her own feelings, and her needs regarding future plans.

At termination Margie was reassured that she could obtain assistance in any future crisis that might occur.

Summary

Margie's inability to cope with a third divorce was caused by the lack of her usual situational supports, that is, her involvement and social contacts at work. This was also the first time Margie was forced into the role of an active participant in the divorce process, and she had no previous coping skills. Her inability to work as a result of illness further isolated her from her usual contacts, and she began to introspect about her previous divorces, seeing herself as a failure as a woman. As her doubts increased, her feelings of guilt and failure magnified until she feared complete loss of emotional control.

Intervention was focused on encouraging Margie to bring her feelings of failure and guilt into the open. By direct questioning and reflecting the information back to Margie, the therapist helped her to view her current divorce and its effect on her in more realistic terms. She was given support by the therapist as she began to explore what she wanted and expected from marriage in the future.

SUICIDE

Each year suicide accounts for more than 13.3 deaths per 100,000 population in the United States, which makes it a leading cause of death. It ranks second as a cause of death for adolescents and college students. Although this death rate has remained relatively stable during the past decade, suicide attempts, suicide threats, drug overdoses, and other forms of self-destructive behavior have increased dramatically. At large general hospitals a night rarely goes by without at least one admission for attempted suicide.

The most common form of attempted suicide is the ingestion of a sedative or hypnotic drug. Other methods include hanging, wrist cutting or other body mutilation, gas inhalation, gunshot wounds, and jumping from high places.

In addition, persons may be referred or brought to hospitals or mental health centers because they have *threatened* suicide or because they have demonstrated some form of *self-destructive behavior* such as running into highway traffic or threatening to jump from a bridge or freeway overpass.

Regardless of how suicidal behavior is manifested, the basic question remains, "Why suicide?" There is no single answer to this question. The complex motivations, weaknesses, and strengths that determine all types of human behavior apply also to suicide. Consequently, there are many roads that individuals may take in reaching a decision to commit suicide. Usually the process is long, and often it is complicated by other physical and emotional symptoms of distress. Despite the multiplicity of causes and patterns, suicidal behavior can usually be related to three primary motivations: loss of communication, ambivalence about life and death, and the effects of suicidal behavior on significant others.

Communication

Suicidal reactions are usually associated with feelings of hopelessness and helplessness, often related to the separation from or loss of a significant or valued person. Suicidal behavior can best be understood as an expression of intense feelings when other forms of expression have failed. The expression of feelings can range from sad cries for help to statements of despair. A person is driven to suicide because he feels unable to cope with a problem and believes that others are not responding to his need. The suicidal behavior becomes a claim for the attention the person feels he has lost. Suicidal thoughts may be expressed verbally or by actions. Either directly or indirectly, the communication is frequently aimed at a specific person—the significant other. Indirect communication poses the problem of recognizing the intent of the disguised message and understanding its real content.

Ambivalence

Only a small percentage of people who threaten or attempt suicide actually succeed. The general explanation for an incomplete or partially effective suicidal act is that the individual is filled with contradictory feelings about living and dying. This state is termed *ambivalence.* Ambivalence is a universal human trait. We all have it at times, and it is not a weakness. Everyone experiences ambivalence over decisions at one time or another, such as when choosing a career, a spouse, or a place to live. The choice of a place and time to die is no exception. In the decision of whether to live or die, one would expect to find even more than the normal amount of ambivalence. This psychological characteristic accounts for the sometimes puzzling fact that a person will take a lethal or near-lethal action and then counterbalance it with some provision for rescue. The very fact that every person is divided within himself over decisions provides the chance for successful intervention with a suicidal patient. If one makes use of the patient's wish to live, his cry for help, suicide may be averted. The myth that if a person talks about suicide, he will not do it is actually that—a myth. Every statement or ideation of the wish to die should be taken seriously and explored with the individual.

Effect on others

Suicidal behavior can further be understood in terms of its effect on those receiving the communication. A suicidal attempt may arouse sympathy, anxiety, anger, or hostility on the part of the individual's family or friends and therefore serve to manipulate relationships. Already feeling *helpless and lost,* the suicidal person who perceives excessive anxiety from his family may lose hope of being helped and may bluntly say so.

Suicidal potential

Death is a process that is a part of life and living. The moment one is born, the process toward death begins. Unfortunately, Western cultures have surrounded death with many powerful taboos. The feelings that these taboos can arouse may interfere in the therapist's and the family's interactions with the suicidal patient. Each must be sensitive to his own thoughts about death and suicide but, regardless of personal attitudes, must avoid moralistic judgments about the patient's suicide attempt. The professional point of view is that death must be prevented if possible. A therapist will often be placed in the position of actually debating life and death questions with upset people. Although he must recognize the existence and merits of other viewpoints, his role is to represent life and to assist distressed, helpless people.

From the first conversation with a suicidal individual, a therapist assumes some responsibility for preventing the suicide. In working out some plan for prevention, the therapist must first determine the individual's suicidal potential, that is, the degree of probability that the person will try to kill himself in the immediate or near future. In some individuals the suicidal potential is minimum, whereas in others it is immediate and great. The therapist must determine the degree of risk for each patient.

The prediction of suicide is by no means an exact science. Certain criteria allow suicidal potential to be evaluated with some assurance. Assessment of suicidal potential depends on obtaining detailed information about the patient in each of the following categories.

Age and sex. Statistics indicate that women attempt suicide more often than men, but that men succeed more often than women. Currently this trend is changing, as women are beginning to feel the same stresses in their "equal opportunity" position as men feel. Women are also beginning to use more lethal methods in their suicide attempts. The rate for completed suicide rises with increasing age. Consequently, an older man presents the greatest threat of actual suicide, a young woman, the least. Thus age and sex offer a general, although by no means clear-cut, basis for evaluating suicidal potential. One must remember that young women and young men do kill themselves, even though their original aim may have been to manipulate other people. Each case requires individual appraisal.

Suicidal plan. How an individual plans to take his life is one of the most significant criteria in assessing suicidal potentiality. One must consider the following three elements:

1. Is it a relatively lethal method? An individual who intends to commit suicide with a gun, by jumping from a tall building or bridge, or by hanging is at far greater risk than someone who plans to take pills or cut his wrists. Since the latter two methods are amenable to treatment or resuscitation, they are less lethal than the irrevocable consequences of putting a gun to one's head.

2. Does the individual have the means available? Is the method of suicide being considered in fact available to the person? A threat to use a gun is obviously more serious coming from a person who owns a gun than from someone without a gun.

3. Is the suicide plan specific? Can the individual tell exactly when he plans to do it (for example, after his wife goes to work)? If he has spent time thinking out details and specific preparations for his death, his suicidal risk is greatly increased. Changing a will, writing notes, collecting pills, buying a gun, and setting a time and place for suicide suggest a high risk. When a patient's plan is obviously confused or unrealistic, one should consider the possibility of an underlying psychiatric problem. A psychotic person with the idea of suicide is at particularly high risk because he may make a bizarre attempt based on his distorted thoughts. Always find out whether the patient has a history of any emotional disorder and whether he has ever been hospitalized or received other mental health care.

Stress. One should find out about any stressful event that may have caused the suicidal behavior. The most common stresses are losses: the death of a loved one; divorce or separation; loss of a job, money, prestige, or status; loss of health through illness, surgery, or accident; and loss of esteem or prestige because of possible prosecution or criminal involvement. Not all stresses are the result of bereavement. Sometimes increased anxiety and tension are a result of success, such as a promotion with increased responsibilities. Any sudden change in the individual's life situation should be investigated.

It is important to evaluate stress from the individual's point of view rather than from society's point of view. What for you may be minimal stress could be perceived by the patient as severe stress. The relationship between stress and symptoms is useful in evaluating prognosis.

Symptoms. The most common and most important suicidal symptoms relate to depression. Typical symptoms of severe depression include loss of appetite, weight loss, inability to sleep, loss of interest, social withdrawal, apathy and despondency, severe feelings of hopelessness and helplessness, and a general attitude of physical and emotional exhaustion. Some persons exhibit agitation through such symptoms as tension, anxiety, guilt, shame, poor impulse control, or feelings of rage, anger, hostility, or revenge. Alcoholics, homosexuals, and all substance abusers tend to have high suicidal risks.

The patient who is both agitated and depressed is particularly at high risk. Unable to tolerate the pressure of his feelings, the individual in a state of agitated depression shows marked tension, fearfulness, restlessness, and pressure of speech. He eventually reaches a point where he must act in some direction to relieve his feelings. Often he chooses suicide.

Suicidal symptoms may also occur with psychotic states. The patient may have delusions, hallucinations, distorted sensory impressions, loss of contact with reality, disorientation, or highly unusual ideas and experiences. As a baseline for assessing psychotic behavior, use your own sense of what is real and appropriate.

Resources. The patient's environmental resources are often crucial in deciding how to manage the immediate problem. Who are his situational supports? Who can support him through this traumatic time: family, relatives, close friends, employers, physicians, or clergymen? To whom does he feel close? If the patient is already under the care of a therapist, this therapist should be contacted.

The choice of various resources is sometimes affected by the fact that the patient and the family may try to keep the suicidal situation a secret, even to the point of denying its existence. As a general rule, any attempt at secrecy and denial must be counteracted by dealing with the suicidal situation openly and frankly. It is usually better if the responsibility for a suicidal patient is shared by as many people as possible. This combined effort provides the patient with a feeling that he lacks—that others are interested in him, care for him, and are ready to help him.

When there are no apparent sources of help or support, the therapist may be the person's only situational support, his one link to survival. This is also true if available resources have been exhausted or family and friends have turned away from the individual. In most cases, however, people will respond to the situation and provide help and support if given the opportunity.

Life-style. How has the person functioned in the past under stress? First, has his life-style been stable or unstable? Second, is the suicidal behavior acute or chronic?

The stable individual will describe a consistent work record, sound marital and family relationship, and no history of previous suicidal behavior. The unstable individual may have had severe character disorders, borderline psychotic behavior, and repeated difficulties with major situations such as interpersonal relationships or employment.

A suicidal person responding to acute stress such as the death or loss of someone he loves, bad news, or loss of a job, which has pushed him into an unwanted and unfamiliar status, presents a special concern. The risk of early suicide among this group is high; however, the opportunity for successful intervention is great. If the suicidal danger can be averted for a relatively short time, individuals tend to emerge without great danger of recurrence.

By contrast, individuals with a history of repeated attempts of self-destruction may be helped through one emergency, but the suicidal danger can be expected to return at a later date. In general, if an individual has made serious attempts in the past, his current suicidal situation should be considered more dangerous. Although individuals with chronic suicidal behavior benefit temporarily from intervention, the emphasis should fall more on continuity of care and the maintenance of relationships.

Acute suicidal behavior may be found in either a stable or an unstable personality; however, chronic suicidal behavior occurs only in an unstable person. In dealing with a stable person in a suicidal situation, one should be highly responsive and active. With an unstable person one needs to be slower and more thoughtful, reminding the patient that he has withstood similar stresses in the past. The main goals will be to help him through this period and assist him in reconstituting an interpersonal relationship with a stable person or resource.

Communication. The communication aspects of suicidal behavior have great importance in the evaluation and assessment process. The most important question is whether communication still exists between the suicidal individual and his significant others. When communication with the suicidal patient has been completely severed, it indicates that he has lost hope of any possibility of rescue.

The form of communication may be either verbal or nonverbal, and its content may be direct or indirect. The suicidal person who communicates nonverbally and indirectly makes it difficult for the recipient of the communication to recognize or understand the suicidal intent of these communications. Also, this type of communication in itself implies a lack of clarity in the interchange between the suicidal person and others. At the same time, it raises a danger that the individual may act out his suicidal impulses. The primary goal is to open up and clarify communication among everyone involved in the situation.

The patient's communication may be directed toward one or more significant persons in his environment. He may express hostility, accuse or blame others, or demand (openly or subtly) that others change their behavior and feelings. His communication may express feelings of guilt, inadequacy, and worthlessness or indicate strong anxiety and tension.

Significant other. When the communication is directed to a specific person, the reaction of the recipient becomes an important factor in evaluating suicidal danger. One must decide whether the significant other can be an important resource for rescue, whether he is best regarded as nonhelpful, and whether he might even be injurious to the patient.

The nonhelpful significant other either rejects the patient or denies the suicidal behavior by withdrawing, both psychologically and physically, from continued communication. Sometimes this other person resents the patient's increased demands, insistence on gratification of dependency needs, or demands to change his own behavior. In other situations the significant other may act helpless, indecisive, or ambivalent, indicating that he does not know what the next step is and has given up. The significant other's reaction of hopelessness gives the suicidal individual a feeling that aid is not available from a previously dependable source. This can increase the patient's own hopelessness.

By contrast, a helpful reaction from the significant other is one in which the other person recognizes the communication, is aware of the problem, and seeks help for the individual. This indicates to the patient that his communications are being heard and that someone is doing something to provide help.

CASE STUDY: CAROL

Carol was referred to a crisis center for help by a physician in the emergency room of a nearby small suburban hospital. The night before she had attempted suicide by severely slashing her left wrist repeatedly with a large kitchen knife, and she had severed a tendon as a result.

When she was first seen by the therapist at the center, her left wrist and arm were heavily bandaged and splinted. She appeared tense, disheveled, very pale, and tremulous. She described her symptoms of insomnia, poor appetite, recent inability to concentrate, and overwhelming feelings of hopelessness and helplessness.

Carol was a 30-year-old single woman who lived alone. She moved to a large Midwestern city about 4 years before, immediately after graduating with a master's degree in business administration from an Eastern university. Within a few weeks she obtained a management trainee position with a large manufacturing distributor company. In the next 3 years she advanced rapidly to her current position as manager of the main branch office. She stated that her co-workers considered her to be highly qualified for the position. She denied any on-the-job problems other than "the usual things that anyone in my position has to expect to deal with on a day-to-day basis." As a result of her rapid rise in the company, however, she had not allowed herself much leisure time to develop close social relationships with either sex.

About a year ago Carol met John, a 40-year-old widower who had a position similar to hers with another company. His office was on the same floor as hers. Within a few weeks they were spending almost all their leisure time together, though still maintaining separate apartments.

Carol's symptoms began about 2 weeks ago, when John was offered a promotion to a new job in his company, which he accepted without mentioning it to her first. It meant that he would be transferred to an office in the suburbs, about 30 miles away. She stated that she did feel upset "for just a few minutes" after he told her of his decision: "I guess that was just because he hadn't even mentioned anything about it to me first."

They went out that evening for dinner and dancing to celebrate the occasion. Before dinner was over, John had to take her home because she "suddenly became dizzy, nauseated, and chilled" with what she described as "all of the worst symptoms of stomach flu."

Carol remained at home in bed for the next 3 days, not allowing John to visit her because she thought she was contagious. After she returned to work, she continued to feel very lethargic, had difficulty concentrating, could not regain her appetite, "and felt quite depressed and tearful for no reason at all."

Convincing herself that she had not yet fully recovered from the "flu," she cancelled several dates with John so that she could get more rest. She described him as being very understanding about this, even encouraging her to try to get some time off from work to take a short trip by herself and really rest and relax.

During this time John began to spend more time at his new office. Their coffee-break meetings at work became infrequent. Within the next week he expected to be moved completely.

The night before Carol came to the crisis center she had come home from work expecting to meet John there for dinner; instead she found a note under her door written by her neighbor. It said that John had telephoned him earlier in the day and left word for her that he had suddenly been called out of town, was not sure when he would be back, but would get in touch with her later.

She told the therapist, "Suddenly I felt empty, that everything was over between us. It was just too much for me to handle. He was never going to see me again and was too damned chicken to tell me so to my face! I went numb all over. I just wanted to die." She paused a few minutes, head down and sobbing, then took a deep breath and went on, "I really don't remember doing it, but the next thing I was aware of was the telephone ringing. When I reached out to answer it, I suddenly realized I had a butcher knife in my right hand and my left wrist was cut and bleeding terribly! I dropped the knife on the floor and grabbed the phone. It was John calling me from the airport to tell me why he had to go out of town so suddenly—his father was critically ill."

Through sobs she told him what she had just done to herself. He told her to take a kitchen towel and wrap it tightly around her wrist. After she had done that, he told her to unlock the front door and wait there, that he would get help to her.

He immediately called her neighbors, who went to her apartment and found her with blood-soaked towels around her wrist and sitting on the floor beside the door. They took her to the hospital, and John continued his trip. After being treated in the emergency room, Carol went home to spend the night with her neighbors. They drove her to the crisis center the next morning.

During her initial session Carol told the therapist that she had no close relatives. Her father and mother had died within a few months of each other during her last year in college. Soon after that she had fallen in love with another graduate student, and at his suggestion they had moved into an apartment together. She had believed that they would marry as soon as they both graduated and had jobs.

Just before graduation, however, her boyfriend informed her that he had accepted a postdoctoral fellowship in France and would be leaving within the month. They went out for dinner "to celebrate" that night; she said, "I couldn't help but be happy for him—it was quite an honor; I just couldn't tell him how hurt I felt."

She stated that the next morning after he left for classes she "suddenly realized I would never see him again after graduation, that he had never intended to marry me, and I was helpless to do anything about it." She took some masking tape and sealed the kitchen window shut, closed the door and put towels along the bottom, and turned on all of the stove gas jets.

About an hour later a neighbor smelled the gas fumes and called the fire department. The firemen broke into the apartment, found her lying unconscious on the floor, and rushed her to the hospital. She was in a coma for 2 days and remained in the hospital for a week. Her boyfriend came only once to see her. When she returned to the apartment, she found that he had moved out, leaving her a note saying that he had gone home to see his family before taking off for France. He never contacted her again. A month later Carol moved to the Midwest.

For the first few months after meeting John, Carol was very ambivalent about her feelings toward him. She frequently felt anxious and fearful that she was "setting myself up for another rejection." Even when John talked of marriage, she found herself unable to consider it seriously and told him that they should wait a while longer "to be sure that they both wanted it." Continuing, she stated, "Until about 2 days ago I had never felt so secure in my life. I'd begun to seriously consider proposing to him! Then suddenly the bottom began to fall out of everything."

When John accepted the new job without telling her first, Carol saw this as the beginning of another rejection by someone highly significant in her life. As her anxiety increased, she withdrew from communication with John "because of her flu." John's well-intentioned agreement to cancel several dates so that she could get more rest further cut off her opportunities to communicate her feelings to him. His suggestion that she take a trip alone compounded her already strong fear of imminent rejection by him.

Finding the neighbor's note under the door was, for her, "the last straw," final proof that he was leaving her, "just like my boyfriend did in college."

Unable to cope with overwhelming feelings of loss and anger toward herself for "letting it happen to me again," she impulsively attempted to commit suicide.

Carol's two suicide attempts, except for the method used, were quite similar. Both were precipitated by the threat of the loss of someone highly significant in her life; both were impulsive, inappropriate attempts to cope with intense feelings of depression, hopelessness, and helplessness; and both demonstrated an inability to communicate her feelings in stressful situations.

When asked by the therapist how she usually coped with anxiety in the past, Carol said that she would keep herself so busy at work that she did not have much time to worry about personal problems. This had been her method for coping with anxiety at school, too, until her first suicide attempt. Since she had been too ill to work full time the past 2 weeks, her previous successful coping mechanisms could not be effectively used.

The goal of intervention was to help Carol gain an intellectual understanding of the relationship between her crisis and her inability to communicate her intense feelings of depression and anxiety caused by the threat of the loss of John.

Before the end of the first session the therapist's assessment was that Carol was no longer acutely suicidal. However, because of her continuing feelings of depression, a medical consultation was arranged and an antidepressant prescribed. A verbal contract was agreed on; Carol was to call the therapist if she felt suicidal again. Carol agreed to the suggestion that she have a friend move into her apartment to help her until her arm was less painful. Before leaving, she assured the therapist that she would call him immediately if she began to feel overwhelmed by anxiety before her next appointment.

When Carol returned for her next session, she was markedly less depressed. She told the therapist that John had called her soon after she came home from the center the week before. Although he had expressed great concern for her, she had been unable to tell him exactly why she had attempted suicide. "I just couldn't tell him that I thought he had left me for good—he'd think that I was trying to blame him. After all, I've been telling him for months that we should both keep our independence!" However, she said she felt much more reassured of his love for her. John expected to be back in about 2 weeks.

During this and the next few sessions the therapist explored with Carol why she found it difficult to communicate her feelings to someone so significant in her life. Carol was reluctant at first to admit that this was a problem that could have contributed to her recent crisis. She perceived herself as someone who was completely self-sufficient and denied any dependency needs on John. As a child she had been expected to control her emotions and to appear "ladylike" and composed at all times. Efforts on her part to communicate her feelings as she passed through the normal developmental stresses of childhood and adolescence were met with rejecting behavior from those most significant in her life—her parents. Slowly she began to gain insight into the inappropriate methods she had learned to cope with stress, such as withdrawing from contact with others whenever she felt threatened by a stressful situation and by somatizing her anxiety rather than admit it was more than she could handle. By the end of the third session she reported that she had been able to communicate her feelings to John more openly and honestly than she had ever done in the past. She appeared to be surprised and pleased that John had responded so positively to her. When asked what she would have done if he had not responded this way, she paused thoughtfully, then answered, "It was a risk I had to take. I just had to find out for sure if I could handle it this time." She added that although she had been very anxious while talking to him, she at no time felt that she could not go on living if things had turned out differently.

By the end of the fourth session John had returned to the city and Carol had returned to her job full time. She no longer felt depressed, and her wrist was slowly regaining its functioning. They were seeing each other frequently despite the distance between their offices, and Carol now said that she felt much more comfortable talking things out with him.

Because Carol had attempted suicide once before under much the same stressful situation, she continued in therapy for the full 6 weeks. The purpose was to ensure that she could depend on situational support from the therapist while adjusting to the fact that she would no longer be seeing John every day. She was encouraged to telephone the therapist at any time she began to feel a recurrence of her earlier symptoms and felt unable to communicate these feelings to John.

Because she now seemed to have a better understanding of the relationship between her suicide attempts and the causal events, she said that she felt more secure in being able to cope with stressful situations in a more positive manner.

Summary

Carol's feelings of rejection by John were compounded by her previous experience of losing someone highly significant in her life. Because she was unable to communicate her feelings directly to John, her anxiety and depression increased. Lacking adequate coping mechanisms and situational support, she became overwhelmed with feelings of hopelessness and helplessness. Anticipating another rejection and entering a state of crisis, Carol impulsively attempted suicide. Intervention was focused on getting her to understand why she was unable to communicate and cope with her intense feelings of inadequacy in interpersonal relations.

DEATH AND THE GRIEF PROCESS

To all who are living, death is certain. This universal phenomenon has ominous presence in that it is realistic and inescapable. Since every human being will at some time be subject to death, death is extremely significant. Much is unknown of the process of death, and human beings are noted for their fear of the unknown. It might be said that this is a basic fear, and throughout the ages human beings have sought self-preservation. Advances in medical science as well as in allied areas support this contention.

The critical question is not the sham dichotomy of life and death, but the way in which each person relates to the knowledge that death is certain. The fear of death may be the prototype of human anxiety. Throughout history death has posed an external mystery that is the core of religious and philosophical systems of thought. Anxiety relates to the fact that each person is powerless; he may postpone death, may lessen its physical pain, may rationalize it away or deny its very existence, but there is no escape from it, and so the fight for self-preservation is inevitably lost.

The attitudes of the persons involved in the situation are basic to the process of dying. Concepts, philosophies, and attitudes about death evolve from centuries of conflicting ideas and thought.

Traditionally, the attitude of a society toward death has been a function of its religious beliefs. Religion denies the finality of death and affirms the continuation of the human personality either in its psychophysical totality or as a soul. The medical and social sciences, by challenging these traditional beliefs, have indirectly caused alienation and a serious mental health problem.

Family reaction to the death of a member passes through stages that vary in time. The death of a loved one produces an active expression of feeling in the normal course of events. Omission of such a reaction is to be considered as much a variation from the normal as is an excess in time and intensity of the reaction. Unmanifested grief will be found expressed in some way or another; each new loss can cause grief for the current loss as well as reactivate the grieving process of previous losses.

Three phases of mourning follow the loss.

Phase I: shock and disbelief

There is a focus on the original object with symptoms of somatic distress occurring in waves, lasting from 20 minutes to an hour at a time, a feeling of tightness in the throat, choking with shortness of breath, need for sighing, an empty feeling in the abdomen, and lack of muscular power. There is commonly a slight sense of unreality, a feeling of increased emotional distance from other people, and an intense preoccupation with the image of the deceased.

There is a strong preoccupation with feelings of guilt, and the bereaved searches the time before death for evidence of failure to do right by the lost one, accusing himself of negligence and exaggerating minor omissions.

Phase II: developing awareness

Disorganization of personality accompanied by pain and despair because of the persistent and insatiable nature of yearning for the lost object occurs in the second phase. There is weeping and a feeling of helplessness and possible identification with the deceased.

Phase III: resolution of the loss

Resolution of the loss completes the work of mourning. A reorganization takes place with emancipation from the image of the lost object, and new object relationships are formed.

The clearest evidence that mourning or grieving has been successfully completed is the ability to remember *completely* and *realistically* the pleasures *and* disappointments of the lost relationship.

In this phase one must also consider pathological mourning, in which there is an inability to express overtly the urges to recover the lost object. When all reactions are repressed, they will influence behavior in a strange and distorted way; for example, a schizophrenic person's reaction to the death of a significant individual may be laughter. There may be a delayed reaction or an excessive reaction, or the grief reaction may take the form of a straight agitated depression with accompanying tension, agitation, insomnia, feelings of worthlessness, bitter self-accusation, and obvious need for punishment. Individuals reacting in this way may be dangerously suicidal.

Proper management of grief reactions may prevent prolonged and serious alterations in an individual's social adjustment. The essential task is that of sharing and understanding the individual's grief work. Comfort alone does not provide adequate assistance. The person has to accept the pain of the bereavement. He has to review his relationships with the deceased. He has to express his sorrow and sense of loss. He must accept the destruction of a part of his personality before he can organize it afresh toward a new object or goal. Although they are unwelcome, such phases are a necessary part of life.

The following case study concerns a retired widower who is threatened by a second loss before he has completed grief work from the recent death of his wife. Initial assessment of the crisis situation indicated that he was probably in the last phase of mourning and became overwhelmed by the threat of losing another highly cathected object, his son. The goal of intervention was to assist

Peter in reentering his social world and in gaining an intellectual understanding of the grief process as it related to his symptoms.

CASE STUDY: PETER

Peter, 67 years old and recently widowed, came for help to a crisis center on the advice of his family physician because of severe depression and anxiety. He described his symptoms as loss of appetite, inability to concentrate, restlessness, insomnia, and loss of energy. These symptoms had been first manifested a month earlier, following the death of his wife, Joan. He thought that they had been subsiding, but they suddenly increased to an intolerable level and he feared loss of emotional control. He denied any suicidal ideas, stating, "I don't want to die, it's just that I've lost all interest in life and no longer care what happens to me."

During the initial visit Peter was at first unable to determine any specific event that might have caused the sudden and acute rise in his symptoms. His wife's death was not unexpected, and he had felt "well prepared" for a future life without her. He viewed himself as realistic in his attitudes and planning before she died and as having experienced a "normal amount of grief" afterward.

Since mandatory age retirement when he was 65, he had devoted most of his time in helping to care for his wife, a semi-invalid with severe coronary disease. "I think I was really glad when I retired because I'd had so little time for myself in those last few years, working all day and then going home and trying to catch up with things I had to do there." Having little time for social activities with his business friends, he had felt little sense of their loss when he left his job.

He had one son, married and living nearby. The son and his wife had had close relationships with Peter and Joan, helping them out with household activities and with the care of Joan. Peter had made tentative plans to move into an apartment after his wife's death, feeling fully able to care for his own needs. However, just after she died, his son and daughter-in-law brought up the idea of their moving into his house with him. It was a large home, much larger than their rented one, and they would pay him monthly amounts toward eventually buying it from him. He said that he was quite pleased with the idea, preferring to remain in his home but unable to justify to himself any reason for staying there alone. They moved in 2 weeks ago, and he felt an immediate lessening in his grief reaction to his wife's death.

A week ago Peter's son had received an unexpected offer of a better job in another state. Peter related that he felt very proud of the offer to his son and had strongly urged him to accept it. The decision had to be made within the month. Since Peter had previously begun plans to live alone, he did not feel too concerned for himself if his son and daughter-in-law did decide to leave.

The night of the son's job offer Peter had suddenly awakened, feeling nauseous, tense, anxious, and very depressed, and sleep had become increasingly difficult as these symptoms had increased in the past few days. Although he no longer experienced nausea, there was a loss of appetite, insomnia, and a feeling of total exhaustion. He summed up his feelings by saying, "Maybe I'm not as happy about my son's leaving as I told him I was."

The therapist thought that Peter's recovery from the grief at the loss of his wife had evolved through the stage of shock and disbelief. He had anticipated her death realistically and had accepted it as inevitable. He had begun to overcome his feelings of guilt and sense of failure, as well as his persistent longing for the lost object (his wife). Peter was probably in the last phase of mourning, that of emancipation from the image of the lost object and initial formation of new object relationships. At this stage, before final resolution of his grief, he was unexpectedly threatened with another loss, that of his son.

Peter had few social contacts because of his total involvement with the care of his wife during the past few years. His son and daughter-in-law had been providing situational support before and during this period of mourning, and this support was now in jeopardy. He had unrecognized ambivalence with regard to the job offer made to his son. Although intellectualizing plans to move into an apartment by himself, he lacked skills that would be necessary to repeople his social world. The anxiety generated by his unresolved grief and his ambivalence about his personal future were compounded by the unexpected threat of a new loss.

When asked how he had coped with stress in the past, Peter said he had always been able to keep busy caring for his wife and the housework. He had also been able to talk things over with his son. He now felt unable to talk to his son about his present feelings "for fear he might think he'd have to give up the job offer and stay here with me."

The goal of intervention was to help Peter gain an intellectual understanding of his crisis in order to recognize the relationship between the threatened loss of his son and his present severe discomfort. His unrecognized ambivalence between his needs for independence as opposed to dependency was explored.

During the next 2 weeks it became possible for him to see the present crisis and its accompanying symptoms in relation to his reactions to the loss of his wife and the threatened loss of his son.

During Joan's illness he had narrowed his own life-style to conform to hers. In failing to acknowledge his lack of the interpersonal skills necessary to maintain a social life of his own, he justified his action as "what would be expected of any husband in a similar situation." Joan had been the dominant member of the marriage. Even when bedridden, she had guided the decision making that he thought was independent on his part. The additional support and assistance of his son and daughter-in-law served to increase his dependency on others for decision making.

At times during the past few years he had thought of "all the things we could have done if I'd retired when my wife had not been so ill." He had deflected these thoughts into overt sympathy for her rather than for himself and what he was missing. As her death became imminent and inevitable, his wife began to make plans with him for his future. She told him to sell the home and to move into an apartment, even selecting which furniture he should keep and which he should give away.

When she died, he was finally faced with the reality of his inability to cope with the changes. Crisis at this time was circumvented by the offer of his son to move into his home. He was able to continue in much the same life pattern that had previously existed for him, with the son and daughter-in-law assuming the leadership role. With their strong situational support, the work of grief had not become overwhelming.

The sudden threat of their loss had caused the crisis. Unrecognized feelings of inadequacy and dependency had come into painful focus. He feared both the physical loss of his son and the loss of his son's love if the job were turned down "because he'd think I couldn't take care of myself if he left me here alone."

By the third session, through discussion and clarification with the therapist, Peter was able to recognize his ambivalent feelings and relate them to his own needs for dependency. He saw the disparity between his concept of what he thought others expected of him and what he could actually achieve alone. His acceptance of this enabled him to reestablish meaningful communication with his son and to gain his support in making more realistic plans.

Peter's exploration of his feelings related to his loss and subsequent grief helped him to gain an intellectual understanding of the process of mourning. His recognition of his symptoms as part of the process helped to reduce his anxiety and enabled him to better perceive the reality of the situation and to use his existing coping skills. Realization was gained that he himself was withdrawing from available situational support because of his concept that his role was to be "an independent person." He was able to accept the fact that this might not be true, and as a result he felt better about communicating his fears to his son and enlisting his assistance in planning.

By the third week his son had decided to accept the position and move out of the state in another month. Through joint efforts they located an apartment-hotel for Peter, where he would have the independence to "come and go as I'd always planned for in my retirement." The hotel preferred its guests to be in the retirement age group, and there were programs established for the guests' interests and social needs.

Peter moved into the hotel 3 weeks before his son left town. The period of transition was facilitated with minimum rise in his anxiety. There was a gradual removal of his son's situational support, which was being replaced by the support gained in new social contacts. Although he felt grief when his son and daughter-in-law left town, Peter could recognize and relate his symptoms to the event and so was able to cope with them.

In discussion and review of his future plans, Peter was optimistic about his ability to live independently within the framework of his new environment. He was slowly entering new activities and making new friends, although he admitted "being a bit rusty about how to do it."

Before termination of therapy Peter and the therapist reviewed the adjustments that he had made as well as his new insights into his own feelings. He thought that the crisis situation, although being very painful to him at the time, had provided him with a "good idea of how to face up to things in the future." His future plans were also reviewed, and he was reassured by the therapist that he could always return for help should the need arise.

Summary

Peter had failed to recognize any relationship between his feelings of increased anxiety and the death of his wife. His inexperience with independent decision making made him inadequate to cope with the stressful event alone. Intervention with strong situational support by his son and daughter-in-law helped him to begin to work through the grief process.

The unexpected threat of his son's and daughter-in-law's departure and his inability to communicate his fears resulted in their loss to him as situational supports. These factors were compounded by incomplete grief work and failure to see any connection between his severe anxiety and his reaction to a second loss.

The therapist kept focus on the areas of stress to determine the adequacy of his past coping skills with bereavement. Intervention was directed toward helping him to explore and ventilate his feelings of dependency. Anticipatory planning was directed toward providing him with situational supports when his son moved from town.

BURN-OUT SYNDROME

In this book *burn-out* refers to a progressive loss of idealism, energy, and purpose experienced by people in the helping professions as a result of the conditions of their work. These conditions may include insufficient training, too many hours, too little pay, inadequate funding, too little appreciation, bureaucratic or political constraints, and the gap between aspiration and accomplishment.

There are four stages of disillusionment: (1) enthusiasm, (2) stagnation, (3) frustration, and (4) apathy. Hopelessness may be an important factor in the last three stages. The four stages, hopelessness, and some intervention techniques will be discussed briefly.

Stages of disillusionment

Enthusiasm. Enthusiasm is the initial period of high hopes, high energy, and unrealistic expectations. During this period the person does not need anything but the job because the job promises to be everything. Overidentification with clients and excessive and inefficient expenditure of one's own energy are the major hazards of this stage.

Individuals go into the human services to make a living but not to make money. Although the full extent of the inequities in salaries between publicly funded service positions and jobs in the private sector may become apparent only after an individual has invested years of training and work in a helping profession, there is a general awareness that such professions do not pay especially well. Thus motivation to enter such a profession is usually the desire to help people. Most individuals become helpers because they really enjoy working with people and they want to make a difference in people's lives. Those who are genuinely involved far outnumber those who are cynical and self-seeking.

An important factor in bringing people into the human services is the example of others. People want to be like the people who have helped them. This is especially common in teaching and medicine, since every young person is exposed to teachers and physicians, some of whom are inspiring models.

A person in the stage of enthusiasm commonly believes that the job is his whole life and that all gratifications are coming from the job. This unbalanced existence comes about by a kind of vicious cycle. On the one hand, an inflated conception of the job tends to obliterate personal needs and concerns. But the reverse may also be true: glorification of work may itself arise from deficiencies in one's personal life. The cycle of overcommitment is self-fulfilling because the longer one's personal life is neglected, the more it deteriorates. One is thus left in a highly vulnerable position when the job ceases to furnish the rewards it once did.

The problem facing those who are dedicated to human services is to be realistic enough to cope with discouraging conditions without suffering a total loss of idealism and concern. This is the area where intervention is the most crucial, especially when one reflects that an initial lack of realism leaves one most vulnerable to eventual disillusionment.

Stagnation. Stagnation refers to the process of becoming stalled after an initial burst of enthusiasm. It is the loss of the momentum of hope and desire that brought the person into the helping professions. No sharp distinction can be drawn between stagnation and frustration, or between any two successive stages of burn-out. The progression through the stages is not something that can be traced in precise chronological sequence in any given instance.

When accomplishments are reduced to a human scale, minor annoyances such as low pay and long hours begin to be noticed. The frustrations that occur at this point are not enough to cause the person to question doing the job, but they are enough to cause him to question doing nothing but the job.

In stagnation one is still doing the job, but the job can no longer make up for the fact that personal needs—to earn a decent living, to be respected on and off the job, to have satisfying family and social relationships, and to have some leisure time in which to enjoy them—are not being met. If those needs remain unmet, one will not be able to keep on doing the job for very long.

Stagnation often begins with the discovery that it is not as easy as anticipated to see, let alone assess, the results of one's labors. Initially it is experienced not as a source of active discontent but as a kind of bewilderment that leaves one wondering why the job is not quite what it appeared to be. At the heart of stagnation lies the feeling that one's career is at a dead end.

Frustration. In the stage of frustration, individuals who have set out to give others what they need find that they themselves are not getting what they want. They are not doing the job they set out to do. In essence, they are not really "helping." Besides the low pay, long hours, and low status, there is a more basic frustration in the helping professions. It is extremely difficult to change people—and it is even more difficult under current prevalent working conditions.

The sensation of powerlessness is experienced at many levels by people in the helping professions. Most obvious is the powerlessness felt by front-line workers who occupy the lowest positions in the decision-making hierarchy, for example, the therapist who has no way to compel his crisis patients to keep their appointments with him. Powerlessness is relative to one's position. A frequent complaint of supervisors is that their subordinates credit them with more power than they actually have.

The feeling of powerlessness is universal; it goes beyond hierarchical status. Its broader implications are the inability to change the system and the inability to control patients, subordinates, superiors, or the agency. This is the frustration that leads directly to burn-out.

Notwithstanding the idealism that motivates people to enter the helping professions, the issues of power and control are central to the helping relationship. Some people complain that they have too little power, whereas others complain that they have too much power. The unresponsiveness of the system to the people working in it is experienced as a lack of appreciation. Individuals who are not given responsibility, are not consulted about decisions, and are generally overlooked by the bureaucratic system believe they are not appreciated by their supervisor or by the organization as a whole.

Appreciation from clients is what enables the individual to go on despite lack of institutional support. One can take the stress from the supervisor when one is appreciated and receives positive feedback from patients. When patients, too, are unappreciative, one questions the whole purpose in being there. Helping people is what it is all about.

The effects of frustration and stagnation on the quality of services rendered to individuals are all too evident. Implicit and explicit in the accounts of overwork, inadequate funding, staff polarization, bureaucratic sluggishness, and other sources of discouragement and demoralization among staff members is the almost inevitable conclusion that the patient is the one who suffers.

The importance of frustration for burn-out lies in what one does with it. Reaction to frustration has a great deal to do with whether one will fall deeper into burn-out and, ultimately, whether one can stay in the field. One can respond to frustration in three ways: (1) use it as a source of negative energy, (2) use it as a source of positive energy, or (3) withdraw from the situation.

There is no doubt that frustration creates energy. When it is an energy of willful denial, a frenzy of activity aimed at evading the reality of frustration or doing away with the causes of frustration that are among the givens of the situation, then it is a self-destructive, negative energy. The energy of frustration can also be directed into a constructive effort. By taking responsibility, confronting issues, and taking actions that may bring about change, one can release some of the emotional tension created by frustration. Frustration can be a major turning point in the progression through the stages. An individual who misses this turn is likely to descend into apathy.

Probably the most common response to frustration is not to express it at all, but to internalize it and withdraw from the threatening situation. The helper avoids patients because he has come to dislike or resent them, despairs of being able to do anything for them, or is physically exhausted. Some individuals walk away from their jobs and from their idealism and concern. Then they may get angry, assert themselves, and get back into the center of things. Others drift into the fourth and last stage of burn-out—apathy.

Apathy. Apathy takes the form of a progressive emotional detachment in the face of frustration. The starting point is the enthusiasm, the idealism, the overidentification of the beginner. If one is to come down from the clouds and work effectively, some detachment is desirable and inevitable. But most individuals do not have ideal learning conditions and sympathetic guidance to help them reach an optimum level of detachment. Frustration comes, sometimes brutally, and the detachment that develops in its wake is less a poised emotional distancing than a kind of numbness. In turning off to frustrating experiences, one may well turn off to people's needs and to one's own caring. Apathy can be felt as boredom. The once idealistic helper can trace the erosion of the desire to help and the feeling of involvement with patients that he used to have. People who started out caring about others end up caring mainly about their own health, sanity, peace of mind, and survival.

The most severe, and saddest, form of apathy is that which is experienced when a person remains at a job for one reason only—because the job is needed for survival. The person has seen what is going on but has no inclination to try to change it. Certainly no risks will be taken when the individual just goes along, protecting his position while doing as little as possible. Security has become the prime concern.

Of all the stages of burn-out, apathy is the hardest to overcome and the one against which it is most difficult to intervene successfully. It is the most settled, the most deep-seated, the one that takes the longest to arrive at and lasts the longest. It stems from a decision, reached over a period of time and reinforced by one's peers, to stop caring. In the absence of a major personal upheaval, vastly changed conditions on the job, or a concerted intervention, it can last forever.

Hopelessness

Hopelessness is implicitly evident in stagnation, frustration, and apathy. Hopelessness is the ultimate product of unresolved conflicts. The hopeless person looks forward to an event or an occurrence with the deeply held belief that the desired will not occur.

When hope is lost, one may be in the stage of stagnation, frustration, or apathy. Hopelessness may fluctuate, diminishing at times and then returning full force to make the individual feel like giving up the role of helper. When one is experiencing hopelessness, there is a tendency to deny or to avoid revealing personal thoughts and feelings that could be considered "unprofessional" and to behave instead as if one were in control of the situation and doing well. Failing to share true feelings with others leads to the erroneous assumption on the helper's part that he is the only one experiencing such problems. This error is further enhanced by the fact that the individual who believes he is alone in having these feelings will be especially careful not to reveal this response to others and will maintain the facade of professionalism.

Intervention

Intervention may be self-initiated or may occur in response to an immediate frustration or threat. It may be fueled in part by one's own strength and in part by support and guidance from peers, supervisors, family and friends, or other important people in one's life. It may be a temporary stop-gap or a real change.

Intervention can occur at any of the stages of disillusionment. It should occur as soon as the disillusionment is recognized. One of the major tasks of supervisors should be to help staff members experience the stages with greater awareness and thus be less subject to violent swings of emotion. In reality, though, intervention most often takes place at the stage of frustration, when it is almost too late. In the stage of enthusiasm people are having too good a time to see any need for intervention. Stagnation does not usually provide the energy required to change course, though interventions in the areas of further education, skill development, and career advancement are sometimes initiated at this stage. As for apathy, that stage is already a long way down into disillusionment, and the road back up is a long, hard one that some individuals negotiate successfully but many never attempt.

More often it is frustration that moves a person off center and impels change. Frustration can get people angry enough to break out of a bad situation instead of becoming apathetic.

Nothing is more important in handling burn-out than knowing what responsibilities the individual does and does not have. The professional is not responsible for patients or for the institution but is responsible for himself. This does not mean that the professional should not become involved with patients or try to change the way the institution is run. It simply means he is responsible for his own actions, not those of others, and remains responsible for his actions regardless of what others do or do not do.

When other systems in life are strengthened, the individual gains strength for coping with work as well. The things people do to strengthen their outside lives and enlarge their horizons vary from individual to individual. An important first step is to make a clear separation between work and other areas of life by limiting off-hours socializing with co-workers and others in the same field and by controlling the tendency toward extracurricular preoccupation with job-related issues. The number of hours required at work is usually set, but the rest of the day is controlled by the individual. The professional can refuse to give friends and relatives free professional assistance with their personal problems.

Probably the most important way of enlarging one's world is through close personal and family relationships. Developing and maintaining these relationships requires, and in turn creates, time commitments and emotional commitments that keep one from being devoured by the job. It may take a lot of work to negotiate with family and close friends the space needed for commitment to the job and the space all concerned need to be together and to be away from constant reminders of the job. But it is by making this effort that an identity independent of the job is created. There are, of course, many other reasons for wanting to have a fulfilling personal life. With regard to burn-out, however, the importance of close personal ties is clear and crucial. When one is loved and appreciated by the family, it is no longer a life-or-death matter whether one is loved and appreciated by patients or supervisors. When deep and constant support of family and friends is enjoyed, one's whole self is not put on the line every morning.

Other interventions could include the technique of planned, temporary social isolation. At a minimum, professionals need times when they can get away from those who are often the direct source of job stress—the recipients and, in some cases, the administrators. This can be accomplished through physical and psychological withdrawals and long vacations.

Another alternative is a "decompression routine" between leaving work and arriving home, some solitary activity, usually physical and noncognitive, that helps one unwind and relax. After being alone for a while, one is more ready to be with people again, especially with people who are close to him.

Some helping professionals deliberately use some off-duty hours to engage in activities with people who are "normal," healthy, and well functioning. By having pleasant and successful interactions with these people, professionals can counteract the development of negative attitudes about patients and about their ability to work well with patients.

CASE STUDY: PATRICIA

Patricia came to the crisis center and told the intake worker that she had "so many problems I don't know which ones to put down." The intake worker told her not to worry but just to "put them down in any order."

The therapist came to the reception room, introduced herself, and asked Patricia to come to her office. Patricia was a tall, attractive, and poised 26-year-old registered nurse. The therapist asked what brought her to the center. Patricia answered, "I don't know where to begin. I have so *many* problems." The therapist asked, "Has anything in your life changed in the past 24 hours?" Patricia hesitated and then stated firmly, "Yes, I am seriously thinking of running away from home." The therapist responded, "Oh? Any specific place in mind, or just to get away?" Patricia answered, "Quite frankly, I just want to get away!" The therapist said, "Why don't you just tell what is bothering you?"

Patricia appeared to be trying desperately to remain in control of her emotions. She maintained her composure and stated in a cold, objective tone, "I can *list* my problems for you. *One,* my husband, Ross; *two,* my job in the intensive care unit at the medical center; *three,* my son Scott, 4 years old; *four,* my son Wesley, 3 years old; and *fifth,* my daughter Rachel, 26 months old. Does this give you some idea of *why* I want to run away from home?" The therapist replied, "You obviously feel that you have five major problems. Why don't we take them one at a time. First, what is your problem with your husband, Ross?"

Patricia, apparently sensing that she was indeed being taken seriously, relaxed slightly and began to talk about her problem. Patricia related that she and her husband met 5 years ago, when she was a "starry-eyed, idealistic" student nurse and Ross was a new intern. She continued, saying, "It was love at first sight." She added that they were married 2 days after she took her state boards. Both she and Ross wanted a large family, "at least four children. However, I didn't expect to get pregnant on my honeymoon! Ross was delighted when I told him I thought I was pregnant. Because *he* was so happy, it made me happy. Scott was born 9 months and 3 weeks after we were married." She continued, "Ross and I do not approve of birth control pills; they may have too many side effects." Patricia stated that she continued working full time until the eighth month of her pregnancy and went back to work when Scott was 3 months old. She continued, "I always have very smooth pregnancies. I feel good, and I never have any complications."

The therapist refocused on the problem by asking Patricia, "What problem are you having with your husband?" Patricia said, "Once I start talking about *any* of my children, I get carried away." She sighed and began to discuss her problem with Ross. "He is really a very good husband and father—when he is there. The problem is that he is never home."

She went on to say that when Ross had finished his internship, he continued in his residency at the medical center in orthopedic surgery. "Quite a coup, there are always so many applicants. Everyone wants to study with the famous Dr. Brick, an internationally known orthopedic surgeon. Dr. Brick was so impressed with Ross that he is going to take him in his office as a junior partner when he finishes his residency in 3 months." She continued, "We have no time together, he is either working or with Dr. Brick, helping him entertain his famous colleagues! I am not even certain that the children *know* that he is their father! Yesterday in the store, Rachel called a strange man Daddy. I waited up for Ross until 1:00 AM to tell him about it, and he just laughed. I was furious! So we had a nasty argument."

The therapist assured Patricia that all children go through a phase of calling strange men Daddy simply because they are men—like Daddy. The therapist asked, "What is it you want Ross to do?" She replied, "I really don't know. I am happy that he will be working with Dr. Brick. I just wish he would spend more time with us. I work too, *plus* take care of the house and the children when I am off duty. I am so exhausted sometimes I just can't think."

The therapist asked, "Who takes care of the children when you work?" She replied, "My sister. She has a 2-year-old, so I take my children to her house every morning and pick them up in the afternoon." She was asked, "Do you really need to work full time?" She replied, "Not really. I *do* love my work, but it is very stressful—the pace in intensive care is horrendous! It seems like we never stop running."

The therapist asked, "Patricia, what do you really want to do with your life?" She was silent for a moment and then replied, "Establish priorities." She was asked to explain further. She continued, "I want to see more of Ross." She was asked, "How could *you* manage that?" She said, "I think I could sit down and tell him how I feel, maybe he could give up some of his social life with Dr. Brick. I could work part-time, maybe 2 or 3 days a week, then I wouldn't be so tired all the time. It would also give me more time with the children and maybe I could go out with Ross, occasionally, when he is entertaining all those VIPs. I must admit I have been a *little* jealous. As a nurse, I know they are very famous physicians. I would like to meet them too. I also must admit I have been feeling a little guilty about the children being at my sister's every day. I am usually so tired when I get home, I am *not* the most patient mother in the world."

The therapist asked if she might consider "a nursery school for Scott and Wesley, so she could spend more time with Rachel." She said, "I have thought of that. I think it would be very good for them, and heaven knows Rachel needs more attention now." The therapist asked, "You said you had problems with your children, what are they?" Patricia replied, "As we have been discussing how I could change my life, I realized *they* are no problem, the problem is *me!*"

Patricia smiled and said, "I *really* overreacted last night—what a stupid argument. Ross is really great. I just have not taken the time or the effort to let him know how I feel. I realize now that I am the one who can make the changes to make our family life better." She stood up and said, "Thank you for helping me clarify my multitude of problems. Now I want to get home and start making those changes!" She hugged the therapist and left, apparently quite happy with *her* decisions.

Summary

Patricia could have been in any stage of burn-out. She was physically tired from working in a stressful job (an intensive care unit), taking care of three small children when she was home, and caring for the house. She was resentful because her husband was "never" home to be with her and the children. The therapist, by listening objectively and letting her ventilate her feelings, assisted Patricia in reaching her own decisions.

CASE STUDY: ROGER

Roger was a 23-year-old police officer who came to the crisis center as a "walk-in" (with no referral) and asked for help with a problem. He was seen by the intake worker, but he refused to discuss his problem with anyone but a therapist. He appeared to be extremely upset and was assigned immediately to a therapist.

The therapist read his record, went to the reception room, introduced herself, and asked him to come to her office. Once in the office, Roger lit a cigarette and asked cautiously if everything he said would be kept confidential. He was assured by the therapist that they would have a confidential relationship similar to that of an attorney and a client. The therapist explained that the only thing she was required by law to reveal was whether he was planning to kill someone and, if so, who, how, and when, if she could find out. She asked him if he was planning to kill someone. Roger shook his head and said, "No, of course not." He appeared to relax slightly, but continued puffing nervously on his cigarette.

Roger was asked by the therapist to tell her more about himself, since there were few details in his record. Roger said that he had graduated from the police academy with top honors 6 months ago. He added that he had always wanted to be a police officer "just like my dad." He said that he was married and that he and his wife, Paula, had a 9-month-old son named Roger, Junior. He smiled and said that they call him J.R. for Junior. He stated that he loved his wife and son very much but added ruefully, "I don't think I am a very good husband or father; I am never home."

Roger was asked, "What is bothering you? You seem very upset." Roger hesitated and softly replied, "I almost killed someone last night—for no reason." He was asked to elaborate on the details. He stated that when he reported for duty 6 months ago, he was put on patrol duty and then almost immediately was promoted to the Narcotics Unit. "I look younger than I am, the 'new kid on the block' and a new face for the 'buy programs.' " He stated that at first he had been thrilled and excited "working Narc"—he thought it was where the action was, "real cloak and dagger." He stated that he was soon disillusioned, adding, "I *hate* working with the Narcotics Unit."

Roger continued to chain smoke and exclaimed, "You have no idea what it's like out there—it's crazy, full of junkies, pushers, you name it. The *only* way I have managed to survive 6 months on the streets is because those of us working Narcotics arrange to meet when we get off duty, have a few beers, and talk for hours, to get it out of our systems. I don't like to drink, but I've learned how to nurse a beer for a long time since I've been on Narc. It's just that I *have* to be with the rest of the guys because they know what it's like out there."

Roger continued to chain smoke and to talk. He said that he knew he could be a good police officer and that it was the only thing that he wanted to do, but he just could not "take working the Narcotics Unit." Asked why he did not request a different assignment, he replied, "I don't want to. It would look bad on my record." He went on to say, "You don't know how frustrating it is. We arrest them, they go to jail, and they are back on the streets the next night! It's a vicious cycle that *never* ends—every night. The *same* damned junkies, the *same* damned pushers! Last night . . . " He stopped abruptly, jumped out of his chair, and walked rapidly to the window. The therapist got up and walked over to him; he was trembling, his fists were clenched, and he appeared to be fighting to stay in control of his emotions. She put her hand lightly on his shoulder and said, "Roger, it's all right. Maybe if you tell me about last night, I can help." He looked down at her with tears in his eyes and said, "Please help me—I am so afraid." The therapist replied, "I know. Let's sit down and you can tell me about it."

They sat down, and he was given some tissues to wipe his eyes. He said, "I feel so stupid, crying like a baby. I haven't cried since my father was killed." The therapist said,

"Don't worry, tears are not a sign of weakness. They can be a great emotional release." She sat quietly as he continued to cry. After approximately 10 minutes he wiped his eyes and said, "Thank God none of my buddies are here to see me making a fool of myself." The therapist replied, "You aren't making a fool of yourself. Do you think you can tell me about last night?" He took a deep breath and began to talk about what had happened.

Roger stated that he had worked as usual and then gone to the apartment of one of his friends in the Narcotics Unit. He had a couple of beers, and they talked for about 2 hours. He said, "I was tired, so I told him I would see him later and I left. I walked to my car. When I got close to it, I saw a figure. It looked like a man near the front door. I pulled my gun, took the safety off, and told him to freeze. The man looked over his shoulder at me and I recognized him! It was a junkie I had arrested the night before! It was unreal. I remembered that my father had been killed when he was going to his car. It was like a nightmare. I had the strangest feeling. I could feel my finger tightening on the trigger. I *wanted* to kill him! I *never* want to feel that way again. I could have killed him!" The therapist said, "But you *didn't*, Roger." He replied, "No, thank God. But I am afraid of the next time."

The therapist asked Roger how he had been sleeping. He replied, "Terrible. I have nightmares, I wake up in a cold sweat, and Paula says I have been talking in my sleep! I used to sleep like a baby. I don't understand what is happening to me." The therapist explained that the stress he was encountering in his work was not being reduced completely by his drinking and trying to "decompress" by talking with other members of the Narcotics Unit. What he needed was a transfer out of the unit and several nights and days of rest.

The therapist asked Roger, "Doesn't your department have therapists available to you—at no cost?" He replied, "Yes, they do, but I didn't want anyone in the department to know." The therapist answered, "Roger, just because you don't *like* working on the Narcotics Unit doesn't mean there is something *wrong* with you. Many officers don't like it. It takes a certain kind of person to feel comfortable working that detail. If you ask to be reassigned, it doesn't have to be a negative report. It can be a positive one. You tell me that you are a good police officer, and I believe you. You just may not be suited to work on the Narcotics Unit." She continued, "Roger, I truly think you should ask to be reassigned back to Patrol and talk to one of the therapists in your department. Everyone, at some time or other, has a problem he may need help with; yours just came early in your career."

Roger thought for a moment and then said, "I know you are right. I just wasn't thinking clearly last night, I guess I panicked." He continued, "I *am* tired. I have 3 days off. I'll get some rest and talk to Paula. I know *she* will be glad if I change assignments. I'll also talk with my sergeant, Sergeant Goldberg. He warned me that Narcotics could be tough; I know he will understand. I think I'll be all right. I can't thank you enough for listening to me."

The therapist said that she was glad she was there to help him and to let her know what happened. Roger assured her that he would. Approximately a month later Roger called to say that he "had been reassigned to Patrol," was seeing a "shrink" at the department, and that everything was going great!

Summary

Roger, a new police officer, was apparently in the stage of frustration. By letting him ventilate his fears and feelings, the therapist was able to provide Roger with the necessary information for him to get help with his problem—to seek a reassignment.

CASE STUDY: NELDA

Nelda was a 42-year-old elementary school teacher in a large metropolitan city. She was divorced and had a daughter, Rebecca, aged 17. She was referred to the crisis center by the principal of her school following an incident with the parents of one of her pupils at an open house (information from the record).

Nelda looked much older than her stated age, her posture was poor, and her hair, sprinkled with gray, was tucked behind her ears in a most unbecoming fashion. She was wearing a pair of slacks and a shirt; both needed mending and fit poorly. She had on a pair of "scruffy-looking" boots that needed polishing and new heels.

The therapist introduced herself and asked Nelda to come into her office. Nelda slouched into the office, sank wearily into a chair, and started picking at her fingernails. She was asked, "Why did you come to the center today?" She avoided eye contact with the therapist and replied, "I was told to come." Asked "By whom?" and "Why?" she reluctantly answered, "The principal of my school said he would place me on suspension if I didn't get some help." The therapist asked, "What happened that made him say that?" She sighed and said, "I had a disagreement with some parents last night at the open house." She was asked what the disagreement was about. Nelda hesitated and then began to tell what had happened and why it had happened.

Nelda stated that she had been a fourth grade teacher for 20 years and that she has always been considered an *excellent* teacher, by both her peers and her students. She said, "I *used* to love teaching; it was so exciting and rewarding." She was asked to continue; she did so and stated, "It is so different now!" When asked how it was different, she elaborated by telling how her responsibilities had changed.

She stated, "*Now*, I don't have time to teach! There is *too* much paperwork, *too* many legal requirements, *too* many different court decisions about busing, and *too* little cooperation between the school and the home! In essence, *too* much bureaucracy! I love teaching, and my fourth grade class is now 50% minority children. I love them, it is such a challenge, but I don't have *time* to teach them as I want to! Last night at open house I was talking with the parents of one of my pupils, Susie, who has been very lackadaisical about her homework and is doing poorly in class. I casually tried to suggest to her parents that she may need to have more responsibility. Naturally, they took offense. To them, Susie is perfect. They reported me to the principal, and he called me to his office and said I had better get some help. Help? All I need is *less* paperwork and more *time* to be a creative teacher!"

The therapist said to Nelda, "You seem very disillusioned by teaching now." She responded, "I am, and so are most of us. We get no rewards for being good teachers, just for keeping all the records straight. I would give it up in a minute, but I love teaching, and it's the only thing I know how to do." The therapist commented, "I noted in your record that you are divorced and have a daughter, Rebecca. Do you receive any alimony or support from your ex-husband?" Nelda replied, bitterly, "I have neither seen nor heard from him since Rebecca was 3 years old." The therapist asked Nelda to tell her about Rebecca.

Nelda's face softened as she talked about her daughter. She stated, with pride, that Rebecca graduated from high school at 16, received a scholarship at a local teacher's college, and was doing beautifully. Nelda continued by saying, "I have tried to discourage her from becoming a teacher, but she won't listen. She is too young, enthusiastic, and idealistic." The therapist smiled and said, "As you were once?" Nelda laughed and said, "Yes, exactly as I was once." The therapist added, "You must have been a good role model for her." Nelda replied, "Yes, unfortunately! I have tried to tell her that teaching has changed, but she won't listen." The therapist asked, "Would *you* have listened to your mother at 16?" Nelda's reply was, "Probably not."

The therapist asked Nelda what she did in the summer when school was out. She replied, "I am busy taking education courses, so I can get a pay raise." She was then asked, "What do you do for relaxation or fun?" She looked surprised and answered,

"*Nothing!* I am so exhausted when I come home, I just collapse and worry about whether or not I got all the paperwork completed." Nelda was asked if she had family or friends that she felt close to. "Not really, just Rebecca, and she has her own friends and things to do. I have just felt too tired and frustrated to go out. I haven't seen some of my friends for 2 years."

The therapist explored other alternatives with Nelda by asking, "What about taking some courses just for fun? Have you considered leaving the public school system and teaching in a parochial or private school? Have you considered taking the summer off to rest and regain some of your energy and enthusiasm?"

Nelda listened and was very quiet as she considered the alternatives. She said, "Do you think I'm sick? Do you think I am losing my mind? What do you think is wrong with me?" The therapist smiled and said, "No, Nelda, I do *not* think you are sick *or* losing your mind. I *do* think you are very tired and need to gain a new perspective on your teaching responsibilities."

Nelda listened and then said, "You know, I think you are right. I *am* tired; I think I *have* blown everything out of proportion. Now, what do I do?" The therapist replied, "This is May. You have only a few more weeks to teach. I think you should take the summer off, rest and enjoy it. You should renew some of your friendships, get out and meet people, and do things. Stop isolating yourself from the rest of the world."

Nelda replied, saying, "I know I could get better organized at school *and* keep the records straight *and* be a good teacher. I think I have been too busy feeling sorry for myself." The therapist smiled and agreed with her.

Nelda continued in therapy for 4 more weeks (until the end of the school year). Each week improvement was noted, not only in her attitude but in her physical appearance as well. She had her hair cut and colored in a becoming shade, her clothes were much more attractive, her posture improved, and she spoke with much more animation. She had also begun to renew some of her friendships and was going out occasionally. She stated, "I am more organized at school now. I get the paperwork done, at least *most* of it, and still have time to enjoy teaching."

Summary

Nelda was apparently fluctuating between the second and third stages of burn-out, stagnation and frustration. Through direct questioning and confrontation, the therapist was able to redirect Nelda to appropriate methods of coping with her stress.

Developmental crises

Our life-style is continually subject to change in the course of maturational development, shifting situations within our environments, or a combination of both. Potential crisis areas occur during the periods of great social, physical, and psychological change that we all experience in the normal growth process. These changes could occur during concomitant biological and social role transitions such as birth, puberty, young adulthood, marriage, illness or death of a family member, the climacteric, and old age.

Developmental crises have been described as normal processes of growth and development. They usually evolve over an extended time, such as the transition into adolescence, and they frequently require us to make many characterological changes. We may be aware of increased feelings of disequilibrium, but our intellectual understanding of their relationship to normal developmental changes may be quite limited.

Hazardous situations that occur in daily life may compound normal developmental crises. When we feel a need for help at these times, it is necessary to determine what part of our symptoms is due to transitional developmental stages and what is due to a stressful event in our current daily lives.

For the sake of clarity the developmental crises discussed in this chapter are in the generally familiar phases: infancy and early childhood, preschool age, prepuberty, adolescence, young adulthood, adulthood, late adulthood, and old age.

The case studies that are presented will illustrate some common developmental crises. It must be emphasized that seldom are hazardous events and developmental crises this clearly defined.

INFANCY AND EARLY CHILDHOOD

The first year of life is one of almost total helplessness and dependency. The infant must learn to trust the maternal figure and become able to allow her out of his sight without fear or rage. He must also be able to develop confidence in the sameness and continuity of his environment and to internalize it through his developing touching (tactile), hearing (auditory), smelling (olfactory), and seeing (visual) senses. Limitations in any one or a combination of these senses could lead to the learning of maladaptive ways to cope with expected life situations. This could affect the child's future biological, emotional, and social development.

During this stage the mutually dependent (symbiotic) relationship that develops between the infant and the mother figure forms a foundation for later personality development. This relationship goes beyond mutual dependency for biological survival; in the psychosocial development of the infant it implies that the mother is willing and ready to assume responsibility for the infant, who in turn accepts her care passively without reciprocating.

During infancy the mouth is the primary source for gratification and exploration; feeding becomes an important aspect of meeting needs. This is controlled by someone else, usually the mother, and her consistency in meeting her infant's needs for oral gratification is the beginning of his development of trust in his environment.

As a result of the varied experiences that he and his mother share, the infant develops confidence that his needs will be met. Through her own dependability the mother structures these situations to provide a basis for a mutual sense of confidence. For example, if the infant is fed regularly at times when he has come to expect a feeding, his sense of trust is encouraged. But, if the feedings become sporadic, he will become uncertain and anxious about his environment, a sense of mistrust will begin to appear, and his fretful, anxious behavior may inspire further inadequate mothering. Another essential component of a healthy, mutually dependent relationship is the comfort brought by the mother; if she creates discomfort, any continued trust can be destroyed.

Environmental consistency and stimulation are important for development and growth of the infant's awareness and understanding of his world. He usually becomes aware of his mother as a person by 9 months; however, absence of *mothering* can provoke symptoms of insecurity by the age of 4 weeks, such as crying and rocking, followed by withdrawal, depression, and even death.

During the first year the automatic behavior patterns with which the infant was born are repeated and strengthened with practice. As a newborn he is capable of grasping, sucking, and responding to and trying to follow sounds and objects in his environment and other repetitive behavior patterns. After being activated a number of times, these responses become spontaneous without further external stimulation. For example, at birth the infant is able to suck at the breast; continued practice improves his coordination and the ease with which he does it until this ability becomes well adapted to the goal of taking nourishment.

These primary reflex actions become coordinated into new actions. For example, the hand accidentally comes in contact with the mouth and initiates sucking movements that may lead to more coordinated actions and to thumbsucking as an established form of behavior. Later actions become oriented toward people and things in the environment that stimulate his seeing and hearing, and intentional behavior emerges as he seeks to repeat these actions. He learns to begin meaningful actions in sequence and to explore new objects within his reach, thus developing goal-oriented activity. In this way, what begins as physical activity patterns develops into mental activity patterns of response.

By the end of the first year the stage of purposeful behavior is reached and the next stage is begun. By the age of 2 years a child can truly imitate such behavior as eating, sleeping, washing himself, and walking.

If the child does not develop the beginnings of trust, in later life he may have a sense of chronic mistrust, dependency, depressive trends, withdrawal, and shallow interpersonal relationships.

During the second year the child begins a struggle for self-direction. He shifts from dependency on others toward independent actions of his own. As his musculature matures, it is necessary for him to develop coordination abilities such as "holding on" and "letting go." Since these are highly opposing patterns, conflict may occur; one example is the conflict arising over bowel and bladder control. A power struggle may develop between the child and his parents, since elimination is completely under *his* control; approval or disapproval become strong influences because of his parents' attitudes toward his bowel and bladder control habits. The child is expected to abandon his self-centered needs and substitute ones that meet the demands of his parents, representing the later demands of society.

In this stage the child begins to use words and simple phrases. He begins to manipulate objects and will look for hidden items. He recognizes differences between "I" and "me," "mine," and "you" and "yours." He also begins to manipulate others by such words as *no* and, a few years later, *why?*

This developmental phase continues through the age of 7. One of its characteristics is the child's preoccupation with having his own needs met and his inability to accept the viewpoint or opinions of another person (egocentrism). At the end of this phase, such *self*-centered behaviors are replaced by *other*-centered, or social, interactions. The child has now formed rather concrete concepts, thing to thing—for example, sharp object relates to hurt finger, sugar to sweet "good" taste, lemon to sour "bad" taste; certain actions will be rewarded and certain actions, if not avoided, will be punished. What he perceives dominates what he decides to do; he operates on what he can see, hear, feel, smell, or taste in his "here and now" world.

This is an important time for the child to establish an acceptable balance between love and hate, cooperation and willfulness, and the sense of freedom to be his own person and its suppression. Failure to achieve these things at this stage in childhood leaves a child feeling shame and self-doubt and he becomes very conforming and ritualized in his activities. In later adulthood this can be seen in the person who is a "compulsive character," one who has an abnormal need for conformity and the approval of others.

PRESCHOOL AGE

It is believed that in the preschool stage the child discovers what kind of person he is going to be. He learns to move around freely and has a wide variety of goals. His language skills broaden, and he will ask many questions. His skill in using words is not matched by his skill in understanding them, so he is faced with the dangers of misinterpretation and misunderstanding. His increasing skills allow him to expand his imagination over such a broad spectrum that he can easily frighten himself with dreams and thoughts.

Initiative becomes governed by a firmly established conscience. The child feels shame not only when he is found out but also when he fears being found out; he feels guilt for thoughts as well as deeds. In this stage, anxiety is controlled by play, by fantasy, and by pride in the attainment of new skills.

He is ready to learn quickly and to share and work with others toward a given goal; he begins to identify with people other than his parents and will develop a feeling of equality with others despite differences in functions and age.

At 4½ to 5 years of age the shift from infantile to juvenile body build is rapid, and the beginning of hand-eye coordination as well as an intellectual growth spurt occurs. The social base of gender role is firmly laid down by the end of the fifth year. If this stage is successfully accomplished, the child develops the false belief that he can become whomever he chooses to be when he grows older; but if the child is excessively guilt-ridden, he develops false belief that he is so unworthy that he should not dream of such goals. The desired self-concept at the end of this stage is that the child is not afraid to try new things, even if he is still small.

PREPUBERTY

During prepuberty years the child is in his learning stage. He wants to be shown how to do things alone and with others. He wants to know not only "what is," but also "why is is." He becomes easily dissatisfied if he does not feel that the things he is doing are useful. He wants to be able to make things and to make them perfectly. He wants to win recognition for what he has accomplished and takes great pleasure when this happens. He not only learns to master skills in handling objects in his environment, but also in handling the thinking, attitudes, and beliefs of his culture.

By the end of this phase the child has the ability for simple deductive reasoning and has learned the rules and basic living skills of his culture. This reinforces his sense of belonging in his environment.

His self-esteem is derived from his sense of adequacy and the beginning of "best" friendships and sharing with peers. This also marks the beginning of friendships and loves outside his family as he begins to learn the complexities, pleasures, and difficulties of adjusting himself and his drives, aggressive and erotic, to those of his peers. By learning and adjusting he begins to take his place as a member of their group and social life. In making this adjustment he seeks the company of his own sex and forms groups and secret societies. The gangs and groups, especially of boys, fight each other in games, baseball, and cops and robbers, working off much hostility and aggression in a socially approved manner.

Feelings of inadequacy and inferiority may begin if the child does not develop a sense of adequacy. Family life may not have prepared him for school, or the school itself may fail to help him develop the necessary skills for competency. As a result he may feel that he will never be good at anything he attempts.

In general, children are better able to cope with stress when normal familial supports are available. Any real or imagined threat of separation from a close family member could drastically reduce their abilities to cope with new or changing psychosocial demands. They are particularly vulnerable to such crisis-causing situations as the loss of a parent through death. Equally stressful are recurring partial losses of a parent from the child's usual environment. Examples of the latter are repeated episodes of a parent's hospitalization or the frequent, extended absences from home by one or both parents.

An increasingly common source of emotional distress for children of this age group is the entry, or re-entry, of the "homemaker" parent into the work field. Any major change in the parenting role demands reciprocal changes in the child's role. For some children imposed demands to assume increased independence and responsibility for self may be more than the child is mature enough to cope with. Not yet able to assume the level of expected independence, the child may actually perceive a form of rejection by the parent.

A common symbol of this role change is the house key that is bestowed on the child, much like a rite of passage and with the accompaniment of new social rules and regulations. In general, such rules and regulations focus on protection of the child and the home, with the child given much responsibility for ensuring that neither is violated in the parent's absence.

The following case study is about Billy, an 8-year-old boy to whom the house key symbolized only rejection by his mother.

CASE STUDY: BILLY

Billy, 8 years old, was referred with his mother to the school counseling psychologist by his homeroom teacher. In the past few weeks, the teacher reported, Billy's usual cheerful, outgoing, alert behavior had changed to moodiness and apparent preoccupation. He was falling behind in his schoolwork, and twice during the past week he had failed to return to his classes after the lunch hour. The first time that he had done this, the school had contacted his mother at her place of work. She told them that Billy had already telephoned her from home. He told her that his stomach was upset, so he had decided to go home and call her from there. She was planning to go right home when the call came from the school.

Yesterday, the counselor was told, Billy again failed to return to his classes after the lunch hour. This time he did not call his mother and he did not go home. After being notified by the school, his mother had telephoned home. She thought that Billy would be there as before. Failing to get an answer, she went directly home from her work to begin looking for him around the neighborhood.

About an hour later, while making his routine security rounds, the apartment house custodian heard muffled sounds coming from a basement stairway and went to investigate. He found Billy crouched and sobbing on the top steps, his head on his knees. He was taken immediately to his mother. When questioned, he denied having been threatened by anyone or being injured, and he showed no signs of physical abuse. He refused to say why he had left school early again or why he had not gone directly home.

His mother immediately called the school and told them that Billy had been located and was safe. She was asked, and agreed, to come to school the next day with Billy to meet with his homeroom teacher. At her request during the meeting the following day, a referral was made for Billy and herself to meet with the counseling psychologist.

Billy was seen initially without his mother present. He was of average height and weight, appeared physically healthy, though pale, and spoke hesitantly. He slouched in his chair, his eyes downcast, and appeared rather depressed. When asked why he had left school without permission twice that week, he muttered, "I don't know what everyone is so excited about. I can take care of myself—ask my mother. I can go home alone because I have the house key and can get in when my mother isn't home."

He stated that he had always liked school, received A's and B's, and that he particularly enjoyed gym and outdoor sports such as soccer and football. Until a week ago he had attended an after-school boys' sport group with many of his friends. This, however, had been suddenly cancelled when the group director had resigned and moved to another city. He also said that his parents had been divorced when he was "a little kid" (4 years old) and that he now lived with his mother. He had frequently visited with his father, who lived nearby, until about 4 months ago. At that time his father had remarried and, a month later, his father's company had transferred him out of state.

After seeing Billy alone, the counselor talked to Billy's mother to verify and to clarify this information and to assess her feelings about his problems and her ability to cope with them.

His mother was a tall, attractive, well-dressed woman who gave the impression that she was deeply concerned about the recent changes in Billy's behavior. She stated that Billy, an only child, had always been considered "well adjusted," got along well with his friends, and, until recently, could always be depended on to keep up with his schoolwork. She went on to say that she and the boy's father had been particularly concerned about what effect their divorce might have on him. They had met regularly with a family therapist during that period to help Billy through their separation and eventual divorce.

She had met her husband in college, and they had married right after graduation. He was an electronic engineer, and she had majored in business administration. During the 3 years before Billy was born she had advanced to a well-paying position as administrative assistant to the director of a large advertising company. When she learned that she was pregnant, she arranged to take a 6-month leave of absence after the baby's birth.

However, as she described it to the counselor, Billy was not a healthy baby and seemed to have one medical problem after another for more than 2 years.

She described Billy's father as very possessive and domineering regarding decisions about Billy's care. "In fact," she said, "when the time came that I could safely leave Billy with a sitter and go back to work, it became clear to me that our marriage was in for a lot of rocky days ahead." After many days of arguing and eventual compromise, it was agreed that she would return to work on a part-time basis, and this only if they were both satisfied that the baby-sitter was giving Billy the best of care. Furthermore, the father completely refused the idea of a day nursery and insisted that they get a sitter to come to their home, stating, "It's his home as much as it is ours, and he is entitled to be here—not in some stranger's house where I can't check up on things whenever I want."

By the time Billy was 3 years old, his mother reported, both parents realized that he was being emotionally "ping-ponged" between them and that her returning to work, even for a day, would always be a point of conflict with her husband. He had grown up in a very patriarchal family with his mother never daring even to dream of any other role than that of "Kinder, Kirche, und Kuche" (children, church, and kitchen). It was difficult for him to consider any other role for his wife now that they had a family.

On the other hand, Billy's mother had grown up in a family that encouraged equal rights for women. Her mother was a practicing attorney while rearing four children and her father had managed a produce company. She just could not understand why she and her husband were having so many conflicts with only *one* child.

By the time Billy was 4 years old, they had separated, and they were eventually divorced when he was 5. The final decree provided Billy's father with ample visitation rights, and the parents shared equal responsibility for child support funds.

Until 4 months ago Billy's mother had been able to manage on part-time work and was able to be home each day when he returned from school. However, at the time Billy's father had transferred out of state 4 months ago, he was over 6 months delinquent in payments for his share of child support. Being, as she put it, "a very realistic person," she decided that she could no longer depend on Billy's father for regular payments. Three months ago she asked her boss to reassign her to full-time work as soon as possible.

She stated that Billy had never expressed any particularly negative feelings about his father remarrying and moving away, only that he would miss seeing him as often as he had in the past. She had taken particular care in planning with Billy for her return to full-time work. She knew, for example, that she would not be able to be home before he got back from school at the end of the day, so they planned for him to join an after-school supervised sport group. This was one that would pick him up at the school and return him to his home by supper time each day. "By that time," she said, "I would be home and he wouldn't come home to an empty apartment." This, she felt, also took care of her worry about his playing in the neighborhood without her there to "keep an eye on things."

Three weeks ago she had started her full-time work and for 2 weeks managed to get home before Billy returned from the sports group. It seemed to her that there were going to be no really major changes for either of them to adjust to. One week ago, however, the director of the sports group suddenly resigned without notice. A replacement had not been found yet, and the group had been temporarily cancelled. As the only interim choice that she could think of, Billy's mother decided to give him his own key to the apartment.

Worried about all the real and imagined things that might happen to him before she came home, she accompanied the key with many admonitions about coming home from school, checking in with the apartment manager when he got there, and being sure to keep the door locked until she got home. She said that Billy did not seem to object to this at all. In fact, he had purchased a key chain to hook on his belt just like one that the building manager wore.

When the school called her the first time Billy cut classes and went home, she had counseled him to remain at school the next time he felt ill and told him she would pick him up there. She told him that he must "never go home alone again without first telling me or someone at the school. I don't like the idea of your being alone and sick. You know I would worry about you." She had also reminded him that they had planned this together and that they both had certain responsibilities to each other in working out this new living schedule. "Neither of us had much choice in this, you know," she told the counselor. "I'm making the best of things that I know how, and Billy is just going to have to cooperate. I just don't know why he is acting this way now."

The sudden, rapid changes in Billy's life during the past few months had forced him into assuming a degree of independence and self-responsibility beyond his maturational level of skills. Not yet accepting the loss of his father and perceiving it as a rejection of himself, he was forced to full dependence on his mother for a sense of security and all decision making. The timely entrance into the after-school sports group had provided him with opportunities to express his feelings of anger and hostility about the situation through the competitive, aggressive sports activities with his peers. Unfortunately, the group was cancelled about the same time his mother started her new job, and he lost his normal outlet for expressing such feelings. Not only did he lose situational support of his peers when he most needed it, he had the further situational loss of his mother from her familiar roles. He could no longer depend on her being at home when he might need her during the day. His anxiety increased as he perceived this to be another sign of rejection from a parent figure. Billy had no coping mechanisms in his repertoire with which to handle these feelings of added anxiety and depression. At the particular time when he needed to use his usually successful coping behaviors, the opportunity was not available because of the demand by his mother that he "come home directly after school—you can't play in the neighborhood after school with your friends."

It was believed that his mother needed assistance in gaining a realistic, intellectual understanding of the situation as it related to Billy's current behaviors. Increasingly anxious about the added responsibility that had been placed on her during the past few months, she was projecting her own feelings of insecurity into overprotective behaviors toward Billy such as, "It is Billy, not *I*, who should not be out alone and unprotected. Something terrible might happen to *him* when there is no longer a strong, dependable person nearby to help keep an eye on things."

Billy would need to explore his perceptions and feelings about the psychosocial losses of both parents from the family roles that they had occupied in his life. He needed to be helped to express his feelings constructively and to make a positive adaptation to the new role demands made of him.

During the first session the counselor focused on identifying with Billy's mother the many critical changes that had occurred in Billy's life during the past few months and their impact on his level of maturational skills development. The goal was to provide her with insight into how Billy might be perceiving such events at his level of comprehension and concrete thinking. Old enough to be fully aware of the events, he was still too young to deal with them abstractly. When, for example, his father had remarried and then moved away soon after, Billy most likely had perceived these actions as signs of complete rejection by his father and blamed himself in some way. He may have wondered, "Why else would my father marry someone else and then move away, abandoning both me and my mother?"

It was also suggested to Billy's mother that her comments at the time such as, "If I don't go back to full-time work, we won't have a roof over our heads or food to eat," were probably taken literally by Billy. So, also, was her later admonishment to him always to come straight home from school, implying that he was one more source of problems for her.

In the next two sessions, through the use of direct questioning and reflection of verbal and nonverbal clues with her, it became possible for her to express feelings about the recent chain of events in her life and to begin to relate them to Billy's behavioral changes. It was suggested that she try to find some alternative supervised peer-group activities for Billy after school. The purpose was to reinstate the opportunity for some normal, acceptable outlets for the angry, hostile feelings that he must be still having from the recent losses in his life.

The counselor met with Billy at the beginning of each session to discuss with him how he was doing in school classes and what things he was doing to occupy his time after school before his mother got home from work. Billy's feelings of rejection and insecurity were dealt with during this time.

The remaining time was spent with his mother. She was encouraged to continue to provide Billy with as much independence as feasible, yet not expect him to assume any more than he could comfortably cope with at this time. The importance of providing Billy with every opportunity to learn new social skills and to develop strong feelings of competency and self-adequacy was emphasized. The fact that closing off his access to usual after-school activities with his peers would greatly limit his chances for new learning experiences was discussed. It might also precipitate his return to the same maladaptive coping behaviors that he had been demonstrating during the past few weeks.

Billy's mother was not able to locate another supervised activity group for her son to attend after school. However, she did make arrangements with a retired gentleman who lived in the same apartment house to "keep an eye" on Billy and to be a contact for him when he came home and played in the neighborhood with his friends after school.

An important focus of anticipatory planning was to review with Billy's mother the developmental changes that she could expect in Billy over the next few years. The need for her to continue to allow him normal opportunities for growth and development was stressed. The fact that Billy was now a member of a single-parent family should not create any particular peer group problems, since this situation was increasingly common among children his age. However, potential stressful situations were identified with her and discussed in terms of how she might approach coping with them as they arose, both for herself and in her dealings with Billy.

Billy was encouraged to be more direct in questions to his mother and in letting her know when he felt confused or angry about things that were happening to him. He understood that he could stop in and talk to the counselor whenever the need arose, but that he would also be expected to keep in close touch with his mother about his feelings in the future.

Summary

Billy had perceived his father's remarriage and move out of state as a rejection of himself. Unable to express his feelings to his mother, he coped by acting out his anger and hostility in competitive, aggressive sports activities with his peers. Despite his mother's assumptions to the contrary, planning with Billy for her return to full-time work had served to reactivate his fears of another rejection. No longer having his sports activities available to him as before, his anxiety increased. Lacking any other available coping skills, he became overwhelmed.

Intervention focused on helping Billy explore his feelings of loss and rejection. Time was spent with his mother, helping her understand the level of maturational skills and the need to better recognize when her demands or expectations of him might exceed his abilities to meet them.

ADOLESCENCE

The adolescent has a strong need to find and confirm his identity. There is rapid body growth equaling that of early childhood but compounded by the addition of physical-genital maturity. Faced with the physiological revolution within himself, the adolescent is also concerned with consolidating his social roles. He is preoccupied with the difference between what he appears to be in the eyes of others and what he believes himself to be; in searching for a new sense of continuity, some adolescents might refight crises left unresolved in previous years.

Changes that occur as secondary sex characteristics make the adolescent self-conscious and uncomfortable with himself and with his friends. Body image changes, and the adolescent constantly seeks validation that these physiological changes are "normal" because he feels different and is dissatisfied with how he thinks he looks. If sudden spurts of growth occur, he concludes he will be too tall; conversely, if growth does not occur as expected, he thinks he will be too short, or too thin, or too fat. In this period of fluctuation, half-child and half-adult, the adolescent reacts with childish rebellion one day and with adult maturity the next.

The adolescent is as unpredictable to himself as he is to parents and other adults. On the one hand, he seeks freedom and rebels against authority; on the other, he does not trust his own sense of emerging maturity and covertly seeks guidelines from adults. In his struggle for an identity he turns to his peers and adopts their mode of dress, mannerisms, vocabulary, and code of behavior, often to the distress of adult society. There is a desperate need to belong and to feel accepted, loved, and wanted.

This is the age for cliques and gangs. The "in group" can be extremely clannish and intolerant of those who do not belong. Banding together against the adult world, its members seek to internalize their identity, but because of different and often rebellious behavior they are frequently incorrectly labeled as "delinquent."

Having achieved a sense of security and acceptance from peers, the adolescent begins to seek involvement with the opposite sex. This occurs first at group-oriented social events such as dances, parties, and football games. As comfort and confidence increase, the adolescent progresses to more meaningful and deeper emotional involvements in one-to-one relationships. Because of conflict between sexual drives, desires, and the established norms of his society, this stage can be extremely stressful, and again the individual is faced with indecision and confusion.

Occupational identify also becomes a concern at this time. There are continual questions by parents and school authorities about career plans for the future. Uncertainties are compounded when a definite choice cannot be made because he cannot fully identify with the adult world of work. Having only observed or participated in fragments of work situations, most adolescents find it difficult to commit to the reality of full-time employment and its inherent responsibilities. It is easier and more realistic to state what is *not* wanted rather than what *is* wanted as a career.

At this time the goal is independence. In midadolescence acceptance of the idea that it is possible to love and at the same time to be angry with someone is one problem that should be solved. If this stage is successfully negotiated, the capacity for self-responsibility is developed; failure may lead to a sense of inadequacy in controlling and competing.

Because of the number and wide variety of stimuli and rapid changes to which he is exposed, the adolescent is in a hazardous situation. A crisis situation may be compounded by the normal amount of changes characteristic of adolescent development.

The following case study illustrates some of the conflicts that adolescents face while trying to find their identity, strive for independence, and win acceptance from their peer group. It also points out the need for understanding and patience on the part of parents as their adolescents grow up.

CASE STUDY: MARY

Mary, a 14-year-old high school sophomore, was referred to a crisis center with her parents by a school nurse. During the past few weeks she had shown signs of increased anxiety, cried easily, and lost interest in school activities. That morning, for no apparent reason, she had suddenly left the classroom in tears. The teacher followed and found her crouched in a nearby utility closet, crying uncontrollably. Mary seemed unable to give a reason for her loss of control and was very anxious. When her mother came in response to a call from the school nurse, she agreed to follow the school's advice and seek family therapy.

During the first session the therapist saw Mary and her parents together in order to assess their interaction and communication patterns and to determine Mary's problems.

Mary's mother was quiet and left most of the conversation up to her husband and Mary. When she attempted to add anything to what was being said, she was quickly silenced by Mary's father's hard, cold stare or by Mary exclaiming in an exasperated tone, "Oh, Mother!" Mary's father spoke in a controlled, stilted manner, saying that he had no idea what was wrong with his daughter, and Mary's mother responded hesitantly that it must be something at school.

Mary was particularly well developed for her age, a fact that was apparent despite the rather shapeless shift she was wearing. She might have been very attractive if she had paid more attention to her posture and general appearance.

When questioned, Mary said that she had not been sleeping well for weeks, had no appetite, and could not concentrate on her school work. She did not know why she felt this way, and her uncontrolled outburst of tears frightened and embarrassed her. She was also afraid of what she might do next, adding that her crying that morning was probably because she had not slept well for the past two nights. At first she tried to brush this off as final exam jitters.

She evaded answering repeated questions about sudden changes in her life in the past few days. When the therapist asked if she would be more comfortable talking alone, without her parents, she gave her father a quick glance and replied that she would. Her parents were asked if they objected to Mary's talking to the therapist alone. Both agreed that it might be a good idea and went to the waiting room.

For a time Mary continued to respond evasively. It was obvious that she had strongly mixed feelings about how to relate to the male therapist: should it be "woman to man" or "child to adult"? Throughout this and the following sessions she alternated between her child and adult roles. The therapist recognized the role ambivalence of adolescence and adjusted his role relationship, using whichever was most effective in focusing on the problem areas and making Mary more comfortable.

Mary eventually relaxed and began to talk freely about her relationship with her family, her activities at school, and some of the feelings that were troubling her. She said that she had two older brothers. The younger of the two, Kirk, was 16 years old and a senior in high school. She felt closer to him because "he understands and I can talk to him." Mary said that she had "as good a childhood" as the rest of her friends. However, she did think that her father kept a closer eye on her activities than did the parents of most of her friends. He still called her his "baby" and "my little girl" and lately had begun to place more restrictions on her friendships and activities than usual.

She related that during the past year she had gone through a sudden spurt of body growth and development. She was keenly aware of these differences in her appearance and sensed the changing attitudes of her father and her friends. She felt her father was worried about her growing "up and out so fast." He was the one who insisted that she wear the almost shapeless shifts. She said she knew "it wasn't really because I outgrow things so fast right now—he thinks I look too sexy for my age!"

About 3 weeks ago she had been invited to the junior-senior prom by a friend of her brother Kirk. She liked the boy and wanted to go, but was not sure Kirk would approve because he would be at the prom too. Another problem was getting her parents' permission to go and to buy the necessary formal clothes. She had looked at dresses and knew exactly the one she wanted but knew her father would not let her have it.

Mary was asked whether she would be able to tell her parents the things that were bothering her if the therapist were present to give her support. She thought that she would if he would "sort of prepare them first" and explain how important it was for her to go dressed like the rest of her girlfriends. He suggested that Mary discuss the situation with Kirk to see how he felt about her going to the prom with his friend, and she agreed to do this before the next session. The therapist assured her that he would spend the first part of the next session with her parents to discuss and explore their feelings about this.

It was apparent that Mary needed support to assist her in convincing her parents to allow her to grow up. Her parents needed to gain an intellectual understanding of some of the problems that adolescent girls face as they search for an identity, seek independence, and feel the need to be like their peers. Mary's mother would have to be encouraged to give support and guidance to Mary and help to resist her husband's attempts to keep Mary as the baby of the family.

At the next session the therapist went to the waiting room to get Mary's parents and saw that Mary had brought her brother Kirk with her. Mary asked whether Kirk could come in with them at the last half of the session when the family would be together. The therapist agreed, realizing that Mary had brought additional support and that apparently Kirk had approved of her going to the prom.

During the first part of the session the therapist and Mary's parents discussed the general problems of most adolescents, as well as the reasons behind their often erratic and unusual behavior. Both parents seemed willing to accept this new knowledge, although her father said that he had not noticed any of this with the boys. Her mother said, "No, but you treated them differently, you were glad they were becoming men." The therapist supported her and said that this was one of Mary's specific problems. He then repeated to the parents what Mary had said about the things that were bothering her. Both parents seemed slightly embarrassed, and the father's voice and manner became quite angry as he tried to explain why he wanted to "protect" Mary: "She's so young, so innocent; someone may take advantage of her," and so on.

Discussion then focused on Mary's anxiety and the tension she felt because her father had made her feel different from her friends. Compromise between the parents and Mary was explored when Mary and Kirk joined them for the last half of the session. Mary was more verbal with Kirk present to support her, and Kirk told his father, "You are too old-fashioned. Mary's a good kid; you don't have to worry about her. You make her dress like a 10-year-old," and so on. The father was silent for a while and then said, "You may be right, Kirk, I don't know." He then asked Kirk, "Do you think I should let her go to the prom?" Kirk answered, "Yes, Dad, I'll be there; she can even double with me and my girl." Her father agreed, adding that Mary's mother should go with her to pick out a "fairly decent dress." Mary began to cry, and her father in great consternation asked, "What's wrong now?" She replied, "Daddy, I'm so happy, don't you know women cry when they are happy, too?"

The next few sessions were spent in supporting the family members in their changing attitudes toward each other. Anticipatory planning was directed toward establishing open communication between the parents and Mary to avoid another buildup of tensions and misunderstandings. Mary was encouraged to use Kirk as a situational support in the future, since he and his father were not in conflict.

The parents were told they could return for help with future crises if necessary and were assured that they had accomplished a great deal toward mutual understanding.

Summary

Mary had suffered acute symptoms of anxiety because she had to ask her father for permission to go to a dance. She wanted to be a member of her peer group but felt uncomfortable because she was not allowed to dress as they did. She wanted independence but was inexperienced and afraid to make a decision that would oppose her father. Because the situation involved possible conflict with her brother, she did not feel comfortable in talking with him about her problem.

Intervention was based on exploring areas of difficulty with the family and helping them to recognize, understand, and support Mary's adolescent behavior, her bid for independence, and her need to become a member of her peer group.

YOUNG ADULTHOOD

Young adulthood is the time in which childhood and youth come to an end and adulthood begins. It involves studying for a specific career or seeking employment, as well as sociability with the opposite sex and sexual behavior. Socioeconomic developments make it difficult to determine the exact time of change from adolescence to adulthood. Originally this was determined by the young adult maintaining an independent job, having the capacity for marrying, and forming a new family unit. Today the young unemployed tend to live at home with their families in a dependent relationship that has some of the characteristics of adolescence and some of the independence of adulthood. The young adult can no longer look forward confidently to gainful employment; without technical or professional education, he may have to be satisfied with unskilled temporary jobs. The more time he spends in technological or professional training, the longer he remains financially dependent on his family, and changes and uncertainties in modern socioeconomic situations may extend the period of dependence into the middle or late twenties. If the preceding stages of development have been successfully negotiated, the young adult will have confidence in himself and his ability for decision making, and as a result will be able to establish and maintain real intimacy with the opposite sex.

Adult society demands that young adults not deviate from the established norms: they are expected to remain in school if studying for a career, or to be consistent and productive in a job while maintaining an active social life.

The young adult explores and exploits or denies cultural and familial heritage and clarifies "who" he is and his social role. The psychosexual task is one of separating self from family without completely withdrawing from the family.

Unsuccessful transition at this stage or lack of inner resources may lead to confusion when decisions are made regarding future goals. There is an inability to establish a true and mutual psychological intimacy with another person; there is also a tendency toward self-isolation and the maintenance of only highly stereotyped and formal interpersonal relationships, characterized by a lack of spontaneity, warmth, and an honest exchange of emotional development.

In the next case study a young adult is faced with the problem of deciding whether to conform to society's norms for choosing a vocation and marriage or remain self-absorbed in his own immature interests.

CASE STUDY: BOB

Bob, 18 years old, came for help from his pastor, who had special training in crisis intervention techniques. He stated he was "feeling bad." When he was asked to be more specific, he said he was not sleeping, was nervous, and that things seemed unreal to him. When asked who referred him to the pastor, he replied a friend who had come there when he had been in trouble.

Bob was short, slim, with a shaggy black beard, neatly dressed in Levis, sport shirt, and cowboy boots. During the initial session Bob appeared overtly nervous and depressed. He sometimes spoke in short, rapid bursts, usually after a period of silence, but more often he spoke in a slow, hesitant manner. He would neither establish nor maintain eye contact with the pastor, continually looking down at the floor.

When asked about events occurring before the onset of his symptoms, Bob said that "during the past 10 days so many things have happened it's difficult to remember what happened first." He began to recite events. After he had worked on his car for 6 months, "it blew up" the first time he drove it. This was also the first time he had been able to drive in 6 months because his driver's license had been revoked for speeding. This precipitated a quarrel with his girlfriend, Lauri, because he had promised to take her out when the driver's license was reinstated and his car was fixed. He had recently received a promotion to foreman at work, but he was ambivalent—pleased with the promotion although uncertain of his readiness to accept the responsibility of a permanent job. Last, his best friend, a member of his motorcycle club, was out of town, and he felt that he had no one with whom to talk about his problems.

Further exploration with Bob revealed that his usual pattern of coping with stress was to ride his motorcycle with his friend "as fast and as far as we can go." They would stop someplace and "talk it out." He felt that this relieved his tension; things became clearer, and he could usually solve the problem.

Bob also expressed ambivalence in his relationship with Lauri. He loved her and wanted to marry her but was concerned because he thought that they had conflicting values; she was from a middle-class family with values that emphasized the importance of a steady job, conformity, and so forth, whereas he felt he belonged in the motorcycle club and liked its philosophy—as he stated it, "to be free, take what you want, don't work." He was afraid that marriage to Lauri would inhibit his freedom and that to please her family he would have to give up riding with his friends and working on his car and would have to trim his beard.

Because of the many problems presented, it was necessary for the pastor to sift through extraneous data and concentrate on major areas of difficulty. He decided at this time to assume the role of available situational support until other support could be found. This would give Bob the opportunity to use his prior successful coping device of "talking it out." As tension decreased, other support would be provided for his attempts to solve his problems.

The goal of intervention was established by the pastor to assist Bob to recognize and cope with his feelings of ambivalence toward his job and Lauri and with the implications of making a choice. The areas of difficulty were determined to be a conflict of values and Bob's need to feel that he belonged to something or someone.

In the next two sessions, while the pastor acted as a situational support, Bob's symptoms diminished. He was able to discuss and explore his feelings about Lauri and his job; he also began discussing his fears of "giving up so much" if they married. Because Bob's relationship with Lauri appeared to be a major problem area, the pastor suggested that she be included in the sessions.

In the subsequent sessions, which Lauri did attend, they began discussing areas of mutual concern and conflict. Lauri said that she did not expect him to give up riding his motorcycle. "He can do it on weekends, and I'll go along." Bob became angry, saying he did not want her along because she "was too nice for that crowd." He then admitted he was not certain he would continue with them anyway, *but* he wanted it understood that he could go riding with his friends occasionally if he wanted. Bob added that if they *were* married, he might not need them because he would have her (to satisfy his need to belong).

When Bob spoke of her parents' comments about his shaggy beard, Lauri said that she liked his beard and that he was marrying her, not her family.

She insisted, however, that Bob spent too much time working on his car and not enough with her. Bob replied that the car was his hobby and said that he probably spent less time on his hobby than her father did on his golf.

In the concluding sessions Bob apparently resolved his conflicts and stated firmly that he thought he would be gaining more than he might lose if he married Lauri and kept his job. At the last session they made tentative plans to be married.

Summary

The most important phase in anticipatory planning occurred when Bob agreed that Lauri be included in the therapy sessions. The necessity of choosing between present modes of behavior and gratifications and future expectations in his life led Bob to weigh the consequences involved. His decision to include Lauri in planning indicated an orientation toward reality. In certain phases of life it is necessary to give up certain pleasures of youth that appear to be consistent with freedom. An orientation toward the future, where maturity of decisions reflects not only an inner freedom but also a sense of self-fulfillment and a recognition of one's own strength, is consistent with a strong ego-identity.

Bob was forced to seek help because of increased symptoms of tension and anxiety. So many stressful events occurring in rapid succession had made it impossible for him to decide which problem should be solved first. His usual situational support, the friend from the motorcycle club, was out of town, and his normal method of coping with stress was unavailable.

Ambivalent feelings about his job situation and his girlfriend Lauri increased his feelings of tension; he became immobile and unable to make decisions or to solve his problems.

Intervention focused on providing Bob with the situational support of the pastor, and Lauri was included as an active participant in the later sessions. When Bob was encouraged to ventilate his feelings, his anxiety decreased and he was able to perceive relationships between the stressful events and his crisis situation more realistically. Previous successful coping skills were reintroduced and proved adequate in helping him to solve his problem. Major focus of the last sessions was anticipatory planning to help him cope with future areas of stress as he made the transition to increased maturity.

ADULTHOOD

Adulthood is the period of life when the responsibilities of parenthood are usually assumed, involving the abilities of a man and woman to accept the strengths and weaknesses of one another and to combine their energies toward mutual goals. It is a crucial time for reconciliation with practical reality.

Maturity is always relative and is usually considered to develop in adulthood. Many adults who marry and have children never do achieve psychological maturity, whereas others who choose not to marry may show a greater degree of mature responsibility than many of their married peers.

Adult normality, like maturity, is also relative. Normality requires that a person achieve and maintain a reasonably effective balance, both personal and interpersonal. The normal adult must be able to control and channel his emotional drives without losing his initiative and vigor. He should be able to cope with ordinary personal upheavals and the frustrations and disappointments in life with only temporary disequilibrium and be able to participate enthusiastically in adult work and adult play, as well as have the capacity to give and to experience adequate sexual gratifications in a stable relationship. He should be able to express a reasonable amount of aggression, anger, joy, and affection without undue effort or unnecessary guilt.

In actuality, it is unreasonable to expect to find perfect normalcy in any adult. Absolute perfection of physique and physiology is rare, and an adult with a perfect emotional equilibrium is equally exceptional.

The following case study concerns a young woman whose lack of psychosocial maturity created problems when she was faced with the responsibility of motherhood. Her husband's competence and pleasure in caring for their baby increased her feelings of inadequacy and rejection.

CASE STUDY: MYRA AND JOHN

Myra and John, a young married couple, were referred by Myra's obstetrician to a crisis center because of her symptoms of depression. Myra said she was experiencing difficulty in sleeping, was constantly tired, and would begin to cry for no apparent reason.

Myra was an attractive but fragile blonde of 22 years whose looks and manners gave her the appearance of a 16-year-old. John, 28 years old, had a calm and mature demeanor. They had been married a year and a half and were the parents of a 3-month-old son, John, Jr.

John was an engineer with a large corporation. Myra had been a liberal arts major when they met and married. John was the oldest of four children and was from a stable family of modest circumstances; Myra, on the other hand, was an only child who had been indulged by wealthy parents.

When questioned by the therapist specifically about the onset of her symptoms, Myra stated that they had begun after the baby was born, with crying spells and repeated assertions that she "wasn't a good mother" and that taking care of the baby made her nervous. She said she felt inadequate and that even John was better with the baby than she. John attempted to reassure her by telling her she was an excellent mother and that he realized she was nervous about caring for the baby. He suggested that he get someone to help her, but Myra said she did not want anyone because it was *her* baby. She could not understand why she felt as she did.

When questioned about her pregnancy and the birth of the child, she said there had been no complications, but added hesitantly that it had not been a planned pregnancy. When asked to explain further, she replied that she and John had decided to wait until they had been married about 3 years before starting a family. She went on to explain that she did not think she and John had had enough time to enjoy their life together before the baby was born.

After she had recovered from the shock of knowing that she was pregnant, she became thrilled at the thought of having a baby and enjoyed her pregnancy and shopping for the nursery. Toward the end of her pregnancy she had difficulty sleeping and was troubled by nightmares. She began to feel uncertain of her ability to be a good mother and was frightened because she had not been around babies before.

When she and John brought the baby home, they engaged a nurse for 2 weeks to take care of the child and to teach Myra baby care. She thought that basically she knew how, but it upset her if the baby did not stop crying when she picked him up. When he was at home, John usually took care of the baby, and his competency made her feel more inadequate. The crisis-causing event was thought to have occurred the week before when John had arrived home from work to find Myra walking the floor with the baby, who was crying loudly. Myra told him she had taken the baby to the pediatrician for an immunization shot that morning. After they returned home, he became irritable, cried continuously, and repeatedly refused his bottle. When Myra said she did not know what to do, John told her the baby felt feverish. After they took the baby's temperature and discovered it was 102° F, John called the pediatrician, who recommended a medication to reduce the temperature and discomfort; John got the medication and gave it to the baby; he also gave the baby his bottle. The baby went to sleep, but Myra went to their bedroom crying and upset.

The therapist decided that Myra's mixed feelings toward the baby should be explored in addition to her feelings of inadequacy in caring for him. She apparently resented the responsibility of the parental role, which she was not ready to assume. Unable to express her hostility and feelings of rejection toward the baby, she turned them inward on herself, with the resulting overt symptoms of depression. Bringing these feelings into the open would be a goal. Myra also needed reassurance that her feelings of inadequacy were normal because of her lack of contact and experience with infants and also because most new parents feel inadequate in varying degrees. John obviously was comfortable and knowledgeable in the situation because of his experience with a younger brother and sisters; he should be used as a strong situational support.

The therapist, believing that a mild antidepressant would help to relieve Myra's symptoms, arranged a medical consultation. It was not thought that she was a threat to herself or to others, and intervention was instituted.

Myra's mention in the initial session that she and John had not had enough time to enjoy each other before the baby was born was considered to be an initial reference to her negative feelings regarding her pregnancy and the baby. In subsequent sessions, through direct questioning and the reflection of verbal and nonverbal clues by the therapist, Myra was able to express some of her feelings about their life as a family with a baby in contrast to her feelings when there had been just herself and John.

Their life pattern revealed much social activity before the birth of the baby and almost none afterward. Myra said that although this had not bothered her too much at first, recently she had felt as if the walls were closing in on her. John appeared surprised to hear this and asked why she had not mentioned it to him. Myra replied with some anger that it apparently did not seem to bother him, because it was obvious that he enjoyed playing with the baby after he came home from work. The possibility of reinstating some manner of social life for Myra and John was considered to be essential at this point. John told her that his mother would enjoy the chance to babysit with her new grandson and that he and Myra should plan some evenings out alone or with friends. Myra brightened considerably at this and seemed pleased at John's concern.

The therapist also explored their feelings about the responsibilities of parenthood and Myra's feelings of inadequacy in caring for the baby. Myra could communicate to John and the therapist her feelings that the baby received more of John's attention than she and that she resented "playing second fiddle." John explained than he had originally assumed care of the baby so that she could get some rest and that he enjoyed being with her more than with the baby. He told her that he loved her and that she would always come first with him.

Myra eventually was able to see that she was being childish in resenting the baby and competing for John's attention. As her social life expanded, her negative feelings toward the baby lessened and she became more comfortable in caring for him. After the fourth session the medication was discontinued and Myra's symptoms continued to decrease.

Because of John's maturity, it was thought important that he be made aware of the possibility that Myra could occasionally have a recurrence of feelings of rejection. If the original symptoms returned, he would recognize them by their pattern and would be able to intercede by exploring what was happening, discussing this openly with Myra. When the progress and adjustments they had made in learning to cope with the situation were reviewed with them, both expressed satisfaction with the changes that had occurred. They were told that they could return for further help if another crisis situation developed.

Summary

Myra was an only child and rarely had to accept responsibility for others before her marriage. Because she had planned to wait 3 years before having a child, she experienced strong mixed feelings about the responsibilities of motherhood before that time and felt unprepared. Her husband's adequacy in caring for the baby when she failed reinforced her mixed feelings. Loss of the social life shared with her husband, combined with the diversion of his attention from her to the baby, reinforced her strong feelings of rejection.

Because she was unable to recognize and accept her feelings of ambivalence and was also unable to tell her husband of her anger and frustration, she turned these feelings inward. Lack of previous experience in caring for infants made her unable to cope with the situation, increased her frustration and anger, and resulted in severe symptoms of depression and anxiety.

LATE ADULTHOOD

In late adulthood if an individual has successfully negotiated the preceding stages, he should be mature enough to accept responsibility for his life-style without regrets.

To the average person, reaching late adulthood implies that life patterns have been fairly well set and no longer are open to choices for change. Anxiety results if a man or woman has not demonstrated some capacity for success in either family or career roles. Symptoms of this are frequently noted in such forms as excessive use of alcohol, psychosomatic symptoms, feelings of persecution, and depression.

Our culture seems unable to place any firm boundary lines on phases of the aging process. The general tendency is to view life as uphill from infancy and over the hill and decline after the peak middle years. With cultural emphasis on youthfulness, it is not unusual for a person of 50 years to view his future with regret for things left unaccomplished. This is the period of life when one is confronted with the reality that the unfulfilled goals of youth may remain just that—unfulfilled. It is a period when one may have to make many emotional and social adjustments to maintain a state of emotional equilibrium.

Family life changes as children grow up and become involved with school, careers, and marriage. For parents it is a time when specific tasks of parenthood are over and they must return to the family unit of two, making reciprocal changes in role status in relation to their children and to the community. New values and goals must be developed in the marriage to replace those values no longer realistic in the present; failure to recognize this need can open the way to frustration and despair. The wife and mother now has freedom from parental responsibility, but if her entire life-style was centered around the parental role, she may lack interests, skills, and abilities with which to make the role change when her children leave home.

Menopausal changes occur in women at this time. Usually around the age of 45 years the activity of the sexual glands decreases relatively rapidly, over a period of 2 to 3 years. Sometimes this is accompanied by a syndrome of psychophysiological symptoms such as hot flashes, dizziness, cold shivers, and anxiety attacks. It is thought that personality plays a larger part of these symptoms than the cessation of glandular activity. Many women go through this phase without any stressful symptoms; others become panicky and afraid of a loss of sexual identity.

There is no definite evidence that sexual gland activity in the male undergoes similar rapid decline and cessation; however, men can experience symptoms similar to those of women at the same age period. Some consider these syndromes to be neuroses rather than a result of changes in sexual gland activity. The unmarried individual with thoughts of eventual marriage and a family is now faced with the reality of advancing years. This is a particularly critical time for the woman. If her reliance for social status and emotional security has been strongly dependent on physical attractiveness, she faces the inevitability of physical decline. Like the man, she can continue her career interests, but she too may be confronted with limitations for further career advancements.

The following case study concerns a 42-year-old wife and mother who was faced with the loss of one major role in her life and felt threatened with the loss of another.

CASE STUDY: ELIZABETH

Elizabeth, a 42-year-old youthful appearing mother of three daughters (twins, aged 17 years, and another, aged 22 years) was referred to a crisis center by her physician because of severe anxiety and depression, loss of appetite, insomnia, and crying spells. Her symptoms, which had started 2 weeks ago, had increased so much in the past 2 days that now she feared a complete loss of emotional control. During the past month her oldest daughter had been married and the twins had left home to attend college in another state.

When asked what had occurred within the last 2 days to increase her symptoms, she said that her husband had come home 2 nights ago and found her "looking a mess" and crying. For the second time that week she was not dressed and ready to go to a scheduled business dinner. He angrily told her that he no longer knew what to do to make her happy and said, "Pull yourself together and find someone to help you, because *I've* tried and *I* can't!" Then he left home, alone, for the dinner. Early the next morning he left town on a business trip after getting her to promise to see their physician.

Elizabeth described herself to the therapist as someone who had always taken a lot of interest in her children's activities and in the business and entertaining activities of her husband, Ben, who was senior salesman for a nationwide women's clothing firm. Ben's work required him to make frequent trips out of town and to do much business entertaining while at home. She stated that she had seldom gone on any of her husband's trips because the girls were growing up and, "of course, they needed me to be at home with them." However, she had always been deeply involved with planning and hostessing all his in-town business entertaining. She had always enjoyed doing this because it made her feel that she was helping his business. Until recently she had always been confident of her ability to do well.

Ben was also 42. He was socially adept, and her women friends frequently told her that they thought he was "so charming and handsome." He was aggressive in business and had rapidly advanced in his company. She said that they had always been sexually compatible, shared mutual interests, and had respect for each other.

When they entertained any of Ben's clients, one of her roles as his wife was to act as the "unofficial model" for his company's clothing. She thought that Ben always took a lot of pride in any compliments she received, so she always tried to look her best.

Gradually, during the past few weeks, she had begun to feel less sure of herself in this role. She felt that Ben was becoming increasingly indifferent to her because he recently had begun to spend more time than usual away from home on his business trips. It seemed to her that, just when she needed his help the most, he deliberately stayed away from home. Their oldest daughter had married 2 weeks ago, and the twins had left home for college a week ago. There had been so many decisions left for her to make, so many things to do, and so little time to get everything done.

One evening 3 weeks ago Elizabeth was alone at home. Ben had gone on another trip, and her daughters were out for dinner with their friends. She said that the three girls had kept her so busy that week with their shopping and other wedding preparations that she really had looked forward to an evening alone at home.

Soon after her daughters had gone out, Elizabeth prepared some dinner, set up a TV table in the living room, and turned on one of her favorite TV programs. As she later described it, "At first the peace and quiet felt great! I felt so relaxed as I began to eat my dinner and watch TV. But, all of a sudden I had this terrible feeling of being all alone. The house had never seemed so quiet or so empty. I began to think about what it would be like after all my daughters had left home. Then, I realized that *this was it*, that I would have evenings like this to face for the rest of my life. I suddenly felt *so* alone, useless, and not needed by anyone anymore." About that time her husband telephoned to tell her he had finished up his business deal several days sooner than expected. When she began crying and told him how lonely she felt, he said that he would catch an earlier plane home the next morning. She said that she had felt much better for a little while after talking to Ben, but later that night her stomach became upset, she felt "tied up in knots," and she had trouble sleeping. She still felt depressed the next morning but decided that it was probably because she was so tired from all the recent rushing about helping her daughters prepare to leave home.

For years Elizabeth had looked forward to the time she could go along with Ben on some of his trips. He had agreed that he would like to have her accompany him on the longer trips that kept him from home several weeks. Now that their daughters were leaving home, there was no longer a need for her to remain home. Now she was becoming fearful that Ben no longer would see any need for her to travel with him. Her plans seemed to be falling apart. The event that caused her crisis was overwhelming fear of losing both her mother role and her wife role. She was not seen as a suicidal risk or as a threat to others even though she was severely depressed and expressed feelings of worthlessness. Despite a high level of anxiety, she was able to maintain some semblance of control over her emotions.

Elizabeth's goal to make the role change away from that of busy motherhood to emphasis on her wife role with her husband was threatened. The loss of her daughters left a great void in her daily life, and she had no coping experiences for this particular situation.

Previous methods of coping were investigated with her. She said that in the past she had always kept so busy with her children that she either would soon forget a problem or she could talk it out later with her husband. Now she found it difficult to communicate with him. Her inability to communicate her feelings and the loss of busy mother work since her children had moved away left her with no immediate situational supports. This prevented her from using previously successful coping mechanisms. The focus for intervention would be to help her to reach an intellectual understanding of the crisis.

It was soon apparent to the therapist that Elizabeth lacked insight into her feelings of loss and threat of loss. Unrecognized feelings about her relationship with her children and her husband would be explored. During the next two sessions, through the use of direct questioning and reflection of verbal and nonverbal clues from Elizabeth, it became possible for her to begin to see a connection between the present crisis and its effect on her and her past separations from her husband and her previously successful ways of coping.

Throughout the years that Ben had traveled alone, she had felt left out of a part of his life and had looked forward to the days when she could go with him. But she had always kept busy caring for their daughters, so she had never had to deal with feelings of absolute loneliness. Knowing that his business brought him in frequent contact with attractive women buyers and models, she regarded her own physical attractiveness as a prime requirement to "meet the competition." With Ben's frequent trips away from home, she had perceived her part in their relationship more on the sexual-social level than in terms of shared roles of parental responsibilities.

Elizabeth was given situational support to discuss her feelings about the recent weakening and eventual loss of her role as a mother and her feelings of insecurity about her marriage. She was encouraged to begin to review the recent past events in more realistic terms. Relationships between the crisis-causing events and her physical and emotional symptoms were explored—for example, how she felt that evening 3 weeks ago when she suddenly believed how alone she might be when her daughters left home, and how much better she felt, if only for a brief time, when she talked about it with her husband on the telephone.

It was explained to her that every parent has to make some emotional adjustments when any of his children leave home. It is a loss with accompanying feelings of grief and mourning, uselessness, and a sense of decreased self-worth. This is commonly known as the *empty nest syndrome*. The last "chick" has left the nest; the maternal role is no longer needed to help meet the children's basic dependency needs for survival.

Those who have focused most of their interests and energies into the development of the maternal role are likely to react to this sense of loss more strongly over a more prolonged period than those who have dispersed their interests and energies into developing many roles in their lives.

Elizabeth was the former type. Because of her husband's frequent absences from home, she had devoted an inordinant amount of energy into developing her two major life roles as she perceived them—mother and wife. As the time for loss of her mother role came closer to reality, her depression and anxiety increased. With her daughters and her husband otherwise occupied, she no longer had their immediate situational support for "keeping busy" or talking things out. As her anxiety increased, her perception of the situation became increasingly narrow, with reality more likely to be distorted.

She was encouraged to talk out her concerns about their marriage with Ben and to explore with him how he felt about their daughters leaving home. By the second week she had made significant progress in reestablishing communication with Ben. She reported that she was surprised to find out that he had been sad, too, about their daughters leaving home. "In fact," she reported, "he said that recently I had always seemed too busy with the girls to take time to talk to him. He really felt that we didn't need him at all to help in those final preparations. That's why he has been spending more time away from home on those business trips."

As this information was reflected back to her, Elizabeth began to see the extent to which increased stress and anxiety has caused distorted perceptions of reality for both her and her husband. By reinstating their previous coping method of talking problems out together, her level of anxiety was reduced, and she was able to resolve her problems.

Summary

Elizabeth had been unable to cope with the actual and threatened loss of major roles in her life. Her usual situational supports were not immediately available to assist her in using her usual method of coping. Increased feelings of loss, grief, and inadequacy resulted in symptoms of anxiety and depression, which led to a crisis level of emotional disequilibrium.

Initial intervention focused on providing Elizabeth with an intellectual understanding of the relationship between the recent events in her life and her feelings of emotional turmoil. She was encouraged to explore and ventilate her feelings about her relationship with her husband and the "loss" of her daughters. As her perception of the situation became more realistic, her coping skills were reinstated successfully.

OLD AGE

In human beings the aging process must not be viewed only in terms of chronological years, but also with regard for the complex interrelationships of biological, psychological, and sociological changes that occur during these years. There is no exact age of onset of a particular developmental period.

Generally, psychologists look on aging as a period of decline. The pace of physical decline is highly individual; it occurs throughout life, yet it is most commonly attributed to the period loosely called old age. "Old age with respect to what?" is a most significant question. It could be one of many things—organic, sensory, or structural changes—and the significance of each is not fully understood.

Personality changes have been substantially investigated, but problems of interpretation have arisen because studies have been directed toward segmentalized personality traits rather than the total organization or adaptiveness. Individual studies have found the aged to be "more set" in problem solving and to be "more stable" in their habits and tendencies than are younger subjects.

Abnormal behavior in the aged is difficult to diagnose because of the increase of organic damage with longevity. These abnormal patterns of experience and behavior develop along new lines with age and raise questions as to the exact nature of endogenous psychosis and what part is played by reactive ill humor or somatically based psychosis. Abnormal mental attitudes may develop as reactions to loss of influence, destroyed or unfulfilled life goals, onset of human isolation, and threats to economic security.

Our culture values mutual independence of the aged and their married children. Feelings of obligation on the part of adult children to support and care for their aging parents have declined with the establishment of social insurances of medical care and other community forces. An exaggerated premium is placed on the physical and psychological attributes of youth. When a culture assigns a role to the individual, his acceptance and performance of it depend greatly on his conception of the role as it relates to his own self-concept.

Like the first years of adolescence, the later years of life are characterized by physical, emotional, and social crises. The onset of physical infirmities may require that the aged person turn to his environment for a measure of care and security. The presence or absence of environmental resources, as well as the degree to which help from others is required for survival, becomes of prime importance. The elderly who are economically secure, alert, and outgoing may be able to rise above social attitudes and continue to influence the lives of others, whereas those who are not in this position may be forced to play the roles designated by society's attitudes.

Among the significant stresses of old age are the problems accompanying economic, social, and psychological losses. These include the loss of usual work and familial roles and status, which leads to feelings of uselessness and loneliness; loss of income; loss of significant others in the narrowing social environments; decreased cognitive functioning, which interferes with the ability to adapt to problems in daily living; and loss of physical functioning such as hearing, sight, and mobility.

Fear of death is not unique to the aged; its proximity is undeniably closer to some. This is verified as groups of contemporaries become smaller because of losses by death. The old *are* living longer. Various studies and observations have noted that feelings of anxiety about death are most commonly coped with by the mechanism of denial, but it is not unusual to hear the very aged speak of "welcoming death" or saying that they "have lived a full life and have no fear of death." The social taboos that our culture places on frank discussion about death may lead to suppression of fear, to increased anxiety, and to resulting disequilibrium.

The aged are also faced with the fear of invalidism or chronic debilitating illness that might lead to dependency on society for survival. This may lead to a regression to earlier childlike levels of thinking and behaving as a means of adjusting.

It has been suggested that as the aged become increasingly powerless and lose status, they also lose the respect of those who are younger. Youth becomes angry at this reversal in dependency roles, the loss of their child role to the parent, and the anxiety of desertion by death. In order to feel comfortable with these feelings, the young people project them. It is the aged who are evil, isolated, alienated, and to be denied equal participation in society for all the evils for which they become blamed.

Two critical events take place during old age: the loss of a spouse and retirement. Both represent conclusions of central tasks of adult life. The loss of a spouse is particularly traumatic for the aging person. For both the widow and the widower it represents the loss of someone for whom there has been a strong emotional attachment, feeling, and significance (cathexis), one that has been a primary source of need satisfaction. There is a loss of emotional security and a feeling of intense loneliness at a time when only the most resourceful may be able to find means to redistribute the cathexis. The surviving spouse loses those aspects of social identity which were dependent solely on a marital partner role. Both the widow and the widower must develop social identities of their own, based on their own interests, economic status, and social skills as old social systems become closed to them and they are faced with finding and integrating into new ones.

Retirement is a highly critical time in a person's life. It is one thing if this occurs of one's own volition and planning; it becomes more complex when mandated by another. Losses include status identity based on identification with a productive and functional role in society. The retiree is also faced with the loss of a peer group.

Some people do not move easily into the role of pure sociability. Their sociability has been directed toward their occupational peer group, and loss of this group through retirement leaves an emptiness with few purely social skills to fill it.

Role reversal caused by a debilitating illness of a spouse is also a fertile area for the development of a crisis. Rarely is either spouse prepared socially, psychologically, or physically to assume all the responsibilities of such a role change; the adjustments involved may be beyond the older individual's ability to cope and adapt.

Developmental stages are more difficult to define for the aged than for younger groups, since the processes of decline and growth occur concomitantly but not in equal balance. The process is highly individualized in all cases, and the variability of physiological, psychological, and sociological factors makes definite chronological relationships highly improbable.

When an elderly person is in a stressful situation and feels the need for help from others to solve problems, it is particularly important for him to be aware that other people may have the tendency to stereotype his problems as a "normal" part of aging. For this reason elderly people in particular should seek professional help with their physical, social, and psychological problems. Determining which of the crisis symptoms may be caused by physical changes is particularly important, since rapid onset of behavioral changes is not infrequently caused by cerebrovascular or other physical changes associated with longevity. A professional review of the current medical history of the individual must be a recognized part of the initial assessment phase.

Too often the individual, because of physical changes, cannot gain an intellectual understanding of the crisis or recognize his present feelings. It may also be that those who directed him to the therapist are *themselves* in crisis; if this is true, the therapist may first have to resolve the feelings of the referrers that have been projected toward the aged individual who is assumed to be in need of help. The ability to accept new value systems and to adapt to necessary changes in the achieved maturational development of earlier years without loss of achieved integrity may be a developmental task for the aged.

CASE STUDY: JOHN AND SARAH

Sarah was accompanied to the crisis center by her husband, John, a former client who, about 10 years ago, had come there for help when in crisis following the death of their only son.

Sarah was 69 years of age, 3 years younger than John. She was neatly dressed, appeared to be slightly apprehensive, and walked with obvious difficulty, supported by a Canadian crutch and her husband's arm. After being assisted into a chair in the therapist's office, she quickly asked that John be allowed to remain with her during the interview. She stated that it "had really been John's idea that we both come here today. I'm sure that he can explain the problem better than I."

After a slight pause and several hesitations, John began to speak. Sarah sat tensely forward on her chair, never taking her eyes from his face as he spoke.

According to John, their problem "probably first began" about 3 months ago, when Sarah had fallen in the house and fractured her hip. After a month in the hospital she had been sent home in his care. The plan was for her to continue physiotherapy as an outpatient. Despite all the therapy and exercises at home, she was apparently not making the progress they had expected. "Look at her—she still can't walk alone! She still needs someone to help her about or she might fall again—and God knows what would happen to us then! It's been a worry for both of us."

As John continued to speak, it became obvious that he was avoiding any direct references to himself. He described Sarah as having recent symptoms of insomnia, anxiety, and depression and expressed the fear that she might be going into the same crisis symptoms for which he had been treated at the center 10 years ago. "It was sheer hell to feel the way I did then; she doesn't deserve to go through what I did then if she can be helped now."

As he spoke, he was becoming obviously more agitated. He avoided eye contact with Sarah, kept moving about restlessly in his chair, became increasingly tense and tremulous, and chain smoked. His eyes frequently became tearful, and his voice broke on several occasions. In almost direct contrast to his behavior, Sarah had assumed a very supportive role, reaching out several times to pat his arm in a calming gesture and, finally, holding his hand tightly.

When it seemed he might begin to cry openly, he abruptly stood up and said, "OK, Sarah, I've told her all about the problem. Now I'm going to go take a walk for a while and let you do some of the talking, too." With that, he said he'd be back in about 20 minutes and left the office.

As soon as John had left, Sarah began to cry quietly. Then she gave several deep sighs and, for the first time, relaxed back into her chair. "Please," she asked the therapist, "can you help him again like you did the last time?" She stated that for the past week he had not slept more than an hour at a time during the night, paced constantly, cried easily—and often for no apparent reason, and had reached the point where he now seemed too anxious and too preoccupied to make even the simplest of decisions.

According to Sarah, she and John had been married for 42 years. They had had only one son, who had died, unmarried, 10 years ago. Although Sarah had never held a salaried job, she had always been very actively involved in both civic and church organizations in their community. After John's retirement from a federal service, she had withdrawn from several of these organizations to devote more time to activities that they could participate in together. They had developed many new social interests in common and maintained a fairly active social life. Sarah felt that the past 10 years had included some of the best times in their life together. They had always seemed to be planning something "for the future" and had acquired many new friends. Their home was completely paid for, they had planned wisely for financial security "in their old age," and, until her accident, they had had few health problems to worry about.

Even after her hip fracture they had apparently been able to provide each other with the situational support needed to cope adequately with the many new changes arising in their daily lives. "After all," Sarah said, "it wasn't as though our world was going to come to an end because of this, only that it might have to slow down a bit until we could catch up again."

After a month in the hospital Sarah went home and arranged to continue therapy as an outpatient. Despite regular visits to physiotherapy and John's rigidly imposed schedule of exercising at home, her recovery had been much slower than they had anticipated. Last week her physician, who was also not satisfied with the rate of her progress, recommended that she seriously consider admission as a full-time inpatient to a well known rehabilitation center in a nearby city. He was unable to guarantee how long she might have to remain, estimating only that it would be a minimum of a month.

She stated that at the time John seemed to be as much in agreement as she with the idea, although, she recollected, he had seemed a bit preoccupied on the drive home. He took her out to dinner that night to celebrate her improved chances for a full recovery.

That night she was awakened several times by John getting out of bed and pacing about the house. When she mentioned it to him in the morning, he quickly apologized for disturbing her and blamed it on "too much coffee and food" the night before. She noticed, however, that he seemed very preoccupied that day, even to the point of having to be reminded by her when it was time for her exercises. Several times he asked if she felt confident that they were making the right decision, or if they should try to find another physician for her who might suggest "better treatments."

His tension and anxiety continued to increase over the next few days. He seemed unusually concerned with how she felt about the decision, and no amount of reassurance from her could convince him that she really wanted to go to the hospital for treatment. Several times yesterday she found him looking at her sadly with tears running down his face. His only explanation was that he felt "so sorry for you—having to go to a strange place—and I might not be there when you need me!" Last night he had not gone to bed at all, but had sat chain smoking in the living room. She had not dared to sleep for fear he would drop a cigarette and start a fire.

Several times during the past few days she had suggested he contact the crisis center to speak to his former therapist. At first he ignored her, then finally yesterday he had countered with the proposal that they go together. "I'm sure," he told her, "that you must be feeling just as anxious as I am about all of this." She said that she agreed to this because she could think of no other way to convince him to go. "Of course, I'm upset about having to go back to a hospital," she told the therapist. "Anyone in my condition would like to have some sort of a guarantee that they are going to improve. But my greatest concern is what this all has done to John." After discussing her feelings a bit longer with her, the therapist determined that Sarah appeared to be coping adequately with the recent events in her life and, although anxious and concerned about them, was indeed not in crisis.

Finding that John had returned from his walk, the therapist arranged to have Sarah wait outside and called him back into the office. He still appeared very tense, yet when confronted with his evident symptoms of depression and anxiety, he at first denied their severity. Then, after several evasive responses, he began to describe openly just how frightened and overwhelmed he had been feeling for the past week. "I just don't know what's going to happen to us next. I don't think I'll be able to handle much more. I was so sure she'd be back walking by this time. We did everything that the doctors told us to do—I worked so hard with her to keep up with the exercises and all of the appointments, and they haven't helped. Now she has to go back to the hospital. I feel that some of this is all my fault—maybe I didn't work hard enough with her, or maybe I was doing the exercises the wrong way. She hates being crippled like this. Sometimes I think she must hate me because she has to be so dependent on me for doing everything."

After Sarah had come home from the hospital 2 months ago, John had been kept very busy and involved in driving her to appointments, arranging the household schedules, and helping her exercise at home. He found many rewards in this role, feeling that he was contributing greatly toward her eventual recovery. However, as the weeks and months passed without much apparent improvement in her condition, he was disturbed to find himself angry toward her, even at times blaming her for not trying harder. Lately he had been finding it increasingly difficult to hide these feelings from her and found himself wishing that he could just get away from the situation for a while, to take a trip like they used to—even if it meant going off without her!

Now, because of her decision to go into the rehabilitation center for treatment, he was being given the opportunity to "get away from it all" for a while, to turn the responsibility for her daily exercises and care completely over to others, and he felt very guilty. Perhaps he had not really tried hard enough to help her walk; maybe he should have found ways to encourage her more. The more he ruminated on these thoughts, the more he convinced himself that her lack of progress was entirely his fault. Therefore it was his fault that she had to go back to a hospital, and it would be completely his fault if she were never able to return home again!

The goals of intervention were to help John obtain a realistic perception of the situation, to help him to ventilate his feelings about the effects of Sarah's disability on his life, and to provide him with situational support to help him cope with the pending loss of Sarah, albeit temporary at this time. Before the next session and with his consent, his personal physician was contacted to determine whether there were any organic bases for his behavioral changes. The physician's report was negative.

During the next two sessions, through questioning and reflection, John was helped to ventilate his feelings about his fears that Sarah might never recover beyond her present level of functioning. With situational support supplied by the therapist, he was able to begin to discuss openly the anger that he had felt toward Sarah for "threatening the security of their future" by her accident. All the careful planning they had made for their "old age" seemed to be falling apart more each day. "It wasn't just the financial security," he said, "we have enough insurance to take care of our illnesses. Our plans were all made for the *two* of us, *together*—not for just *one* of us, *alone!*" His fears of losing her had been displaced into anger against her for being the cause of his unpleasant feelings.

It became apparent during the first session that John did not have any clear idea as to the nature of Sarah's injury. To him, a broken bone was just that, regardless of which one. It broke; therefore it should heal! He had never sat down with the orthopedic surgeon to ask questions, leaving it to Sarah to keep him informed. He was advised to make an immediate appointment with the physician in order to get direct information about Sarah's expected progress rather than to continue to rely on his own uneducated conclusions. At the next session he reported that he had followed through, kept the appointment, and was relieved to learn that, although Sarah's progress was a bit slower than expected, the physician expected her to return to a fairly normal level of functioning. But, he was advised, it would take time, and he would be expected to help Sarah have patience. The recommendation that she enter the rehabilitation center in another city was made in an effort to speed up her progress and was not to be construed by him as a sign that she might never recover.

As John's anxiety and depression decreased, he began to perceive the events leading up to his crisis in a more realistic manner. He realized that his anger was a normal response to his situation with Sarah but that what he *did* with that anger was not normal. Rather than openly discussing his feelings with Sarah as he would have at any other time in their lives, he found himself "protecting" her from them, yet blaming her for all the misery they were causing him. Because he had no other available situational support, his anxiety and depression had increased, further distorting his perceptions of the event.

When the suggestion was made that Sarah enter a rehabilitation center for further therapy, John's anxiety level interfered with his ability to perceive this as anything other than the beginning of a final loss of Sarah from his life. As he later described it to the therapist, "I guess this is always in the back of a person's mind once they get around my age. When you're young, you go to a hospital and the odds are good that you come home again—but when you get to be Sarah's and my age, the odds *aren't* so good that you come home again! And she was asking me to help her make the decision to go to that hospital—*me*, who was already mixed up in my feelings about having to take care of her like this the rest of my life!"

By the end of the third session John's symptoms had lessened greatly, and he was able to help Sarah pack and move to the rehabilitation center without any increase in anxiety. He realized now that in overprotecting her from his true feelings, he had only created anxiety for her as well as a crisis for himself. He planned to visit her three times a week. They agreed that this would give her time to concentrate on "being able to walk at home," and he would begin to reestablish ties with their old friends so that he would not feel so lonely while she was away.

Exploration with John about his feelings concerning the possibility that Sarah might not improve beyond her current level of functioning helped prepare him for this eventuality. He was able to begin to consider alternative modes of life for the two of them. For example, he decided that they should seriously consider selling their two-story home. "After all," he said, "if it isn't her broken hip, sure enough it's going to be my arthritis in the next few years that is going to make those stairs seem like Mount Whitney!" Furthermore, John found himself faced with the realities of what he would have to be able to do for himself if Sarah ever left him forever. While Sarah was in the rehabilitation center, he knew that he would have to begin learning how to plan a life for himself. Granted that she might outlive him, he recognized that this time without her was a sample, for him, of what life "might be for him—and only a complete idiot would not recognize that I had better learn what to do and learn damned fast!"

Summary

Because he was unprepared to assume his new role in caring for Sarah, John's increased anxiety distorted his perceptions of their stressful situation. When Sarah failed to make the progress that he had expected, he became frustrated and angry and perceived himself as a failure in his new role. Unable to communicate these feelings appropriately, he displaced his anger on Sarah. When asked to help her decide about reentering a hospital, he felt threatened by a permanent role reversal and the eventuality of her loss. He lacked adequate coping mechanisms to deal with the increasing stresses of the situation; he became immobile and unable to make any decisions for their future.

Intervention focused on helping John to ventilate his feelings and to obtain a realistic perception of the event. As his anxiety and depression decreased, he became able to anticipate and plan for their future. The major focus of the last session was to help him recognize that with increasing age there could be future threats to his biopsychosocial integrity and that he should learn to seek help as problems arose and not try to assume all the responsibility himself.

Two months later the therapist received a telephone call from John. Sarah had come home from the rehabilitation center about 2 weeks before. Her progress, unfortunately, was not what they had expected. However, according to John, she was at least able to stand in the kitchen and make the "best damned dinner I have eaten in a month" and that was "good enough for me!" They had already put their home up for sale and were looking for a large mobile home into which they could move and begin traveling around the country to begin living the retirement they had planned.

Suggested readings

Adler, G.: Helplessness in the helpers, Br. J. Med. Psychol. **45**:315, 1972.

Aguilera, D.C.: Review of psychiatric nursing, St. Louis, 1977, The C.V. Mosby Co.

Albronda, H.F., Dean, R.L., and Starkweather, J.A.: Social class and psychotherapy, Arch. Gen. Psychiatry **10**:276, 1964.

Alexander, F.: Psychoanalysis and psychotherapy, New York, 1956, W.W. Norton & Co., Inc.

Alexander, F., Eisenstein, S., and Grotjohn, M., editors: Psychoanalytic pioneers, New York, 1966, Basic Books, Inc., Publishers.

Alexander, F., and French, T.M.: Psychoanalytic therapy, New York, 1946, The Ronald Press Co.

Allport, G.W.: Pattern and growth in personality, New York, 1961, Holt, Rinehart & Winston.

Amir, M.: Patterns in forcible rape, Chicago, 1971, University of Chicago Press.

Asch, G.: Effects of group pressure upon the modification and distortion of judgment. In Guetzkow, H., editor: Groups, leadership and men, Pittsburgh, 1951, Carnegie Press.

Bandura, A., and others: Cognitive processes mediating behavioral change, J. Pers. Soc. Psychol. **35**(3):125, 1977.

Bellak, L.: A general hospital as a focus of community psychiatry, J.A.M.A. **174**:2214, 1960.

Bellak, L., editor: Handbook of community psychiatry and community mental health, New York, 1964, Grune & Stratton, Inc.

Bellak, L., and Small, L.: Emergency psychotherapy and brief psychotherapy, New York, 1965, Grune & Stratton, Inc.

Benedict, R.: Anthropology and the abnormal, J. Gen. Psychol. **10**:59, 1934.

Bernstein, R.: Are we still stereotyping the unmarried mother? Soc. Work **5**:22, 1960.

Bierer, J.: The Marlborough experiment. In Bellak, L., editor: Handbook of community psychiatry and community mental health, New York, 1964, Grune & Stratton, Inc.

Black, M.: Critical thinking: an introduction to logic and scientific method, Englewood Cliffs, N.J., 1946, Prentice-Hall, Inc.

Bloch, H.S.: An open-ended crisis-oriented group for the poor who are sick, Arch. Gen. Psychiatry **18**:178, Feb. 1968.

Bourne, R., and Newberger, E.H., editors: Critical perspectives on child abuse, Lexington, Mass., 1979, Lexington Books.

Bowlby, J.: Separation anxiety, Int. J. Psychoanal. **41**:89, 1960.

Brill, N.Q., and Storrow, H.A.: Social class and psychiatric treatment, Arch. Gen. Psychiatry **3**:340, 1960.

Brown, H.F., Burditt, V.B., and Lidell, W.W.: The crisis of relocation. In Parad, H.J., editor: Crisis intervention, New York, 1965, Family Service Association of America.

Burgess, A.W., and Holmstrom, L.L.: The rape victim in the emergency ward, Am. J. Nurs. **73**(10):1741, 1973.

Burgess, A.W., and Holmstrom, L.L.: Rape trauma syndrome, Am. J. Psychiatry, **131**:982, Sept. 1974.

Cameron, N.: Personality development and psychopathology, Boston, 1963, Houghton Mifflin Co.

Cannon, W.B.: Bodily changes in pain, hunger, fear, and rage, New York, 1929, D. Appleton & Co.

Cannon, W.B.: This wisdom of the body, ed. 2, New York, 1939, W.W. Norton & Co., Inc.

Caplan, G.: A public health approach to child psychiatry, Ment. Health **35:**235, 1951.

Caplan, G.: An approach to community mental health, New York, 1961, Grune & Stratton, Inc.

Caplan, G.: Principles of preventive psychiatry, New York, 1964, Basic Books, Inc., Publishers.

Chown, S.M., editor: Human aging, New York, 1972, Penguin Books, Inc.

Christmas, J.J., Wallace, H., and Edwards, J.: New careers and new mental health services: fantasy or future? Am. J. Psychiatry **126:**1480, April 1970.

Claridge, G.: Drugs and human behavior, Middlesex, England, 1972, Penguin Books, Ltd.

Clark, T., and Jaffe, D.T.: Change within youth crisis centers, Am. J. Orthopsychiatry **42:**675, July 1972.

Coleman, J.C.: Abnormal psychology and modern life, Chicago, 1950, Scott, Foresman & Co.

Collins, J.A.: The paraprofessional. I. Manpower issues in the mental health field, Hosp. Community Psychiatry **22:**362, Dec. 1971.

Collins, J.A., and Cavanaugh, M.: The paraprofessional. II. Brief mental health training for the community health worker, Hosp. Community Psychiatry **22:**367, Dec. 1971.

Comstock, B.S., and McDermott, M.: Group therapy for patients who attempt suicide, Int. J. Group Psychother. **25**(1):44, 1975.

Corsini, R.J., and Rosenberg, B.: Mechanisms of group psychotherapy, J. Abnorm. Soc. Psychol. **51:**406, 1955.

Croog, S.H., Levine, S., and Lurie, Z.: The heart patient and the recovery process, Soc. Sci. Med. **2:**111, 1968.

Cropley, A., and Field, T.: Achievement in science and intellectual style, J. Appl. Psychol. **53:**132, 1969.

Cumming, E., and Henry, W.E.: Growing old, New York, 1961, Basic Books, Inc., Publishers.

Decker, J.B., and Stubblebine, J.M.: Crisis intervention and prevention of psychiatric disability: a follow-up study, Am. J. Psychiatry **129:**101, Dec. 1972.

Decker, J.B., and Stubblebine, J.M.: Crisis intervention and prevention of psychiatric disability: a follow-up study, Am. J. Psychiatry **129**(6):725, 1972.

Demarest, M.: Cocaine: middle class high, Time, July 6, 1981.

De Smit, N.W.: Crisis intervention and crisis centers: their possible relevance for community psychiatry and mental health care, Psychiatr. Neurol. Neurochir. **75**(4):299, 1972.

Dewey, J.: How we think, Boston, 1910, Heath Co.

Dunbar, F., and Dunbar, F.: A study of centenarians. Quoted in Solomon, J.C.: A synthesis of human behavior, New York, 1954, Grune & Stratton, Inc.

Dzhagarov, M.A.: Experience in organizing a day hospital for mental patients, Neurapathologia Psikhiatria **6:**147, 1937. (Translated by G. Wachbrit.)

Eastman, K., Coates, D., and Allodi, F.: The concepts of crisis: an expository review, Can. Psychiatr. Assoc. J. **15:**463, 1970.

Edelwich, J., and Brodsky, S.: Burn-out: stages of disillusionment in the helping professions, New York, 1980, Human Sciences Press.

Ellison, K.W., and Geng, J.L.: The police officer as burned-out Samaritan, FBI Law Enforcement Bulletin, March 1978.

Engel, G.L.: Grief and grieving, Am. J. Nurs. **64:**93, Sept. 1964.

English, O.S., and Pearson, G.H.J.: Emotional problems of living, New York, 1955, W.W. Norton & Co., Inc.

Erikson, E.H.: Growth and crises of the health personality. In Senn, M.J.E., editor: Symposium on the healthy personality, New York, 1950, Josiah Macy, Jr., Foundation.

Erikson, E.H.: Identity and the life cycle. Psychological issues, vol. 1, No. 1, monograph I, New York, 1959, International Universities Press.

Erikson, E.H.: Childhood and society, ed. 2, New York, 1963, W.W. Norton & Co., Inc.

Ewing, C.P.: Crisis intervention as psychotherapy, New York, 1978, Oxford University Press.

Faberow, N., and Shneidman, E., editors: The cry for help, New York, 1961, McGraw-Hill Book Co.

Ford, D., and Urban, H.: Systems of psychotherapy, New York, 1963, John Wiley & Sons, Inc.

Frederick, C.J.: Organizing and funding suicide prevention and crisis services, Hosp. Community Psychiatry **23**(11):346, 1972.

Freud, S.: Collected papers, vol. 1, London, 1924, The Hogarth Press Ltd. (Translated by Joan Riviere, Alex Strachey, and James Strachey.)

Freudenberger, H.J.: Staff burn-out, J. Soc. Issues **30**(1):159, 1974.

Freudenberger, H.J.: Psychotherapy: theory, research and practice **12**(1):73, 1975.

Glass, A.T.: Observations upon the epidemiology of mental illness in troops during warfare. In Symposium on Preventive and Social Psychiatry sponsored by Walter Reed Army Institute of Research, Walter Reed Army Medical Center, and National Research Council, April 15-17, Washington, D.C., 1957, U.S. Government Printing Office.

Goffman, E.: Asylums, New York, 1961, Doubleday & Co., Inc.

Golan, N.: When is a client in crisis? Soc. Casework **50**:389, July 1969.

Goldman, G.D., and Milman, D.S., editors: Modern woman: her psychology and sexuality, Springfield, Ill., 1969, Charles C Thomas, Publisher.

Gouirand, Y., and Soubrier, J.P.: Possibilities of psychotherapeutic intervention in suicide attempters and those who are suicidal, Perspect. Psychiatriques **3**(47):153, 1974.

Granetz, R., editor: Middle age, old age, New York, 1980, Harcourt Brace Jovanovich, Inc.

Greene, B.L.: Sequential marriage: repetition or change. In Rosenbaum, S., and Alger, I., editors: The marriage relationship, New York, 1968, Basic Books, Inc., Publishers.

Guilford, J.P.: The nature of human intelligence, New York, 1967, McGraw-Hill Book Co.

Haas, K.: The middle-class professional and the lower-class patient, Ment. Hyg. **47**:408, 1963.

Hahn, M.E.: Psychoevaluation: adaptation, distribution, adjustment, New York, 1963, McGraw-Hill Book Co.

Hankoff, L.D., and others: Crisis intervention in the emergency room, Am. J. Psychiatry **131**:47, 1974.

Hartog, J.: The mental health problems of poverty's youth, Ment. Hyg. **51**:85, Jan. 1967.

Heine, R.W., and Trossman, J.: Initial expectations of the doctor-patient interaction as a factor in continuance in psychotherapy, Psychiatry **23**:275, Aug. 1960.

Hellerstein, H., and Goldstone, E.: Rehabilitation of patients with heart disease, Postgrad. Med. **15**:265, 1954.

Hendrickson, B.: Teacher burn-out: how to recognize it; what to do about it, Learning 37, Jan. 1979.

Hinckley, R.G., and Hermann, L.: Group treatment in psychotherapy, Minneapolis, 1951, University of Minnesota Press.

Hinkle, L.E., Jr.: Social factors and coronary heart disease, Soc. Sci. Med. **2**:107, 1968.

Hinsie, L.E., and Campbell, R.J.: Psychiatric dictionary, ed. 4, New York, 1970, Oxford University Press, Inc.

Hollender, M.H.: The psychology of medical practice, Philadelphia, 1958, W.B. Saunders Co.

Hollingshead, A.B., and Redlich, F.C.: Social class and mental illness, New York, 1958, John Wiley & Sons, Inc.

Holmstrom, L.L., and Burgess, A.W.: Assessing trauma in the rape victim, Am. J. Nurs. **75**(8):1288, 1975.

Horney, K.: Feminine psychology, New York, 1967, W.W. Norton & Co., Inc.

Inkeles, A.: Social structure and the socialization of competence, Harv. Ed. Rev. 36, 1966.

Jacobson, G.: Crisis theory and treatment strategy: some sociocultural and psychodynamic considerations, J. Nerv. Ment. Dis. **141**:209, 1965.

Jacobson, G.: Crisis theory, New Directions for Mental Health Services **6**:1, 1980.

Jacobson, G., Strickler, M., and Morley, W.E.: Generic and individual approaches to crisis intervention, Am. J. Public Health **58**:339, 1968.

Jacobson, G.F.: Emergency services in community mental health; problems and promise, Am. J. Public Health **64**(2):124, 1974.

Janis, I.L.: Psychological stress, psychoanalytical and behavioral studies of surgical patients, New York, 1958, John Wiley & Sons, Inc.

Jenkins, H.: Self concept and mastectomy, J.O.G.N. Nursing, p. 38, Jan./Feb. 1980.

Johnson, D.M.: The psychology of thought and judgment, New York, 1955, Harper & Row, Publishers.

Johnson, E.S., and Williamson, J.B.: Growing old: the social problems of aging, New York, 1980, Holt, Rinehart & Winston, Inc.

Kaplan, D.M., and Mason, E.A.: Maternal reactions to premature birth viewed as an acute emotional disorder, Am. J. Orthopsychiatry **30:**539, 1960.

Kaplan, D.M., and Mason, E.A.: Maternal reactions to premature birth viewed as an acute emotional disorder. In Parad, H.J., editor: Crisis intervention, New York, 1965, Family Service Association of America.

King, S.H.: Perceptions of illness and medical practice, New York, 1962, Russel Sage Foundation.

Knitzer, J., Allen, M.L., McGowan, B.: Children without homes, Washington, D.C., 1979, Children's Defense Fund.

Krouse, H., and Krouse, J.: Psychological factors in postmastectomy adjustment, Psychological Reports **48:**275, 1981.

Kubie, L.S., cited by Kaufman, J.G., and Becker, M.D.: Rehabilitation of the patient with myocardial infarction, Geriatrics **10:**355, 1955.

Kübler-Ross, E.: On death and dying, New York, 1969, Macmillan, Inc.

Kübler-Ross, E.: Questions and answers on death and dying, New York, 1974, Collier Books.

Larson, C., Gilbertson, D., and Powell, J.: Therapist burn-out: perspectives on a critical issue, Soc. Casework **59**(9):563, 1978.

Laurie, P.: Drugs: medical, psychological, and social facts, ed. 2, Middlesex, England, 1971, Pelican, C. Nicholls & Co., Ltd.

Lazarus, R.S.: Psychological stress and the coping process, New York, 1966, McGraw-Hill Book Co.

Lazarus, R.S., and others: The psychology of coping: issues in research and assessment. In Coehlo, G.V., and others, editors: Coping and adaptation, New York, 1974, Basic Books, Inc., Publishers.

Lecker, S., and others: Brief intervention: a pilot walk-in clinic in suburban churches, Can. Psychiatr. Assoc. J. **16**(2):141, 1971.

Lee, P.R., and Bryner, S.: Introduction to a symposium on rehabilitation in cardiovascular disease, Am. J. Cardiol. **7:**315, 1961.

Lindemann, E.: Symptomatology and management of acute grief, Am. J. Psychiatry **101:**141, Sept. 1944.

Lindemann, E.: The meaning of crisis in individual and family, Teachers Coll. Rec. **57:**310, 1956.

Linn, L.: Psychiatric program in a general hospital. In Bellak, L., editor: Handbook of community psychiatry and community mental health, New York, 1964, Grune & Stratton, Inc.

Linton, R.: Culture and mental disorders, Springfield, Ill., 1956, Charles C Thomas, Publisher.

Lowenstein, R.M.: Psychology of the ego. In Alexander, R., Eisenstein, S., and Grotjahn, M., editors: Psychoanalytic pioneers, New York, 1966, Basic Books, Inc., Publishers.

Luchins, A.S.: Group therapy: a guide, New York, 1964, Random House, Inc.

Maguire, P., Chir, B., and others: A conspiracy of pretense, Nursing Mirror, p. 17, Jan. 10, 1980.

March, J.G., and Simon, H.A.: Organizations, New York, 1963, John Wiley & Sons, Inc.

Maslach, C., and Jackson, S.E.: Burned-out cops and their families, Psychol. Today **12**(12):59, 1979.

Maslach, C., and Pines, A.: The burn-out syndrome in the day care setting, Child Care Q. **6:**100, 1977.

Mason, E.A.: Method of predicting crisis outcome for mothers of premature babies, Public Health Rep. **78:**1031, 1963.

Masserman, J.H.: Principles of dynamic psychology, Philadelphia, 1946, W.B. Saunders Co.

McDonald, J.M.: Rape, offenders and their victims, Springfield, Ill., 1971, Charles C Thomas, Publisher.

McGee, R.K.: Crisis intervention in the community, Baltimore, 1974, University Park Press.

McGee, R.K., and others: The delivery of suicide and crisis intervention services. In Resnik, H.: Suicide prevention in the 70's, Rockville, Md., 1973, National Institute of Mental Health.

McIver, J.: Psychiatric aspects of cardiovascular diseases in industry. In Warshaw, L.J., editor: The heart in industry, New York, 1960, Harper & Row, Publishers.

McMahon, J.T.: The working class psychiatric patient: a clinical view. In Riessman, F., and others, editors: Mental health of the poor, New York, 1964, The Free Press.

Mechanic, D.: Social structure and personal adaptation: some neglected dimensions. In Coehlo, G.V., and others, editors: Coping and adaptation, New York, 1974, Basic Books, Inc., Publishers.

Merrifield, P.R., and others: The role of intellectual factors in problem-solving, Psychol. Monogr. **76**(10): 1962.

Merton, R.K.: Social theory and social structure, enlarged edition, New York, 1968, The Free Press.

Moore, H.E.: Tornadoes over Texas: a study of Waco and San Angelo in disaster, Austin, 1958, University of Texas Press.

Morales, H.M.: Bronx Mental Health Center, N.Y. State Division Bronx Bull. **13**(8):6, 1971.

Morley, W.E., and Brown, V.B.: The crisis-intervention group: a natural mating or a marriage of convenience? Psychother. Theory Res. Prac. **6**:30, Winter 1968.

Morley, W.E., Messick, J.M., and Aguilera, D.C.: Crisis: paradigms of intervention, J. Psychiatr. Nurs. **5**:537, 1967.

Murphy, L.B.: Coping, vulnerability, and resiliency in childhood. In Coehlo, G.V., and others: Coping and adaptation, New York, 1974, Basic Books, Inc.

Murphy, L.B., and Moriarty, A.: Vulnerability, coping, and growth from infancy to adolescence, New Haven, Conn., 1976, Yale University Press.

Myers, J.K., Bean, L.L., and Pepper, M.P.: A decade later: a follow-up of social class and mental illness, New York, 1968, John Wiley & Sons, Inc.

Myers, J.K., and Roberts, B.H.: Family and class dynamics in mental illness, New York, 1959, John Wiley & Sons, Inc.

Nagi, S.: Child maltreatment in the United States: a challenge to social institutions, New York, 1977, Columbia University Press.

O'Brien, J.: Mirror, mirror, why me? Nursing Mirror, p. 36, April 24, 1980.

Opler, M.K.: Culture, psychiatry and human values, Springfield, Ill., 1956, Charles C Thomas, Publisher.

Ovesy, L., and Jameson, J.: Adaptational techniques of psychodynamic therapy. In Rado, S., and Daniels, G., editors: Changing concepts of psychoanalytic medicine, New York, 1956, Grune & Stratton, Inc.

Palmore, E.B.: Social factors in mental illness of the aged. In Busse, E.W., and Pfeiffer, E., editors: Mental illness in later life, Washington, D.C., 1973, American Psychiatric Association.

Parsons, F.: The social system, New York, 1951, The Free Press.

Piaget, J.: The child's conception of the world, Totowa, N.J., 1963, Littlefield, Adams & Co.

Pines, A., and Maslach, C.: Characteristics of staff burn-out in mental health settings, Hosp. Community Psychiatry **29**:233, 1978.

Pumpian-Mindlin, E.: Contributions to the theory and practice of psychoanalysis and psychotherapy. In Alexander, F., Eisenstein, S., and Grotjahn, M., editors: Psychoanalytic pioneers, New York, 1966, Basic Books, Inc., Publishers.

Rapoport, L.: The state of crisis: some theoretical considerations, Soc. Service Rev. **36**:211, June 1962.

Rapoport, R.: Normal crises, family structures, and mental health, Fam. Process **2**:68, 1963.

Rappaport, D.: A historical survey of psychoanalytic ego psychology. In Klein, G.S., editor: Psychological issues, New York, 1959, International Universities Press.

Redlich, F.C.: The concept of normality, Am. J. Psychother. **6**:551, 1952.

Rehabilitation of patients with cardiovascular diseases, technical report series, Geneva, 1966, World Health Organization.

Reiff, R.: Mental health manpower and community change, Am. Psychologist **21**:540, 1966.

Reiser, M.F.: Emotional aspects of cardiac disease, Am. J. Psychiatr **107**:781, 1951.

Reisman, D.: Individualism reconsidered, New York, 1954, The Free Press.

Reissman, C.K.: The supply-demand dilemma in community mental health centers, Am. J. Orthopsychiatry **40**:858, Oct. 1970.

Resnik, H.L.P., and Hathorne, B.C.: Summary of recommendations of the task force on suicide prevention. In Resnik, H.: Suicide prevention in the 70's, Rockville, Md., 1973, National Institute of Mental Health.

Riessman, F., and Miller, S.M.: Social change versus the psychiatric world view, Am. J. Orthopsychiatry **34**:29, Jan. 1964.

Riessman, F., and Scribner, S.: The underutilization of mental health services by workers and low income groups: causes and cures, Am. J. Psychiatry **121:**798, Feb. 1965.

Roberts, S.: Behavioral concepts and nursing throughout the life span, Prentice-Hall, Inc., Englewood Cliffs, N.J., 1978.

Ross, M.: Extramural treatment techniques. In Bellak, L., editor: Handbook of community psychiatry and community mental health, New York, 1964, Grune & Stratton, Inc.

Rubenstein, D.: Rehospitalization versus family crisis intervention, Am. J. Psychiatry **129**(6):715, 1972.

Rubenstein, D.: Family crisis intervention as an alternative to rehospitalization, Curr. Psychiatric Ther. **14:**191, 1974.

Rusk, T.: Future changes in mental health care, Hosp. Community Psychiatry **22:**7, Jan. 1972.

Salzman, L.: Developments in psychoanalysis, New York, 1962, Grune & Stratton, Inc.

Selkin, J.: Rape, Psychol. Today, p. 71, Jan. 1975.

Seward, G.: Psychotherapy and culture conflict, New York, 1956, The Ronald Press Co.

Shubin, S.: Burn-out: the professional hazard you face in nursing, Nursing '78 **8**(7):22, July 1978.

Sifneos, P.E.: A concept of emotional crisis, Ment. Hyg. **44:**169, 1960.

Singh, A.N., and Brown, J.H.: Suicide prevention: review and evaluation, Can. Psychiatr. Assoc. J. **18**(2):117, 1973.

Slater, P.: Cultural attitudes toward the aged, Geriatrics **18:**308, 1963.

Slavson, S.R.: A textbook in analytic group psychotherapy, New York, 1964, International Universities Press.

Smitson, W.: Focus on service, Ment. Hyg. **56**(4):22, 1972.

Stone, L.: Psychoanalysis and brief psychotherapy, Psychoanal. Q. **20:**217, 1951.

Storaska, F.: How to say no to a rapist and survive, New York, 1976, Warner Books, Inc.

Strickler, M., and Allgeyer, J.: The crisis group: a new application of crisis theory, Soc. Work **12:**28, July 1967.

Sullivan, H.S.: Conceptions of modern psychiatry, New York, 1953, W.W. Norton & Co., Inc.

Tarachow, S.: An introduction to psychotherapy, New York, 1963, International Universities Press.

Tershakovek, A.: An observation concerning changing attitudes toward mental illness. Am. J. Psychiatry **121:**353, Oct. 1964.

Tierney, K.J., and Baisden, B.: Crisis intervention programs for disaster victims: a source book and manual for smaller communities, Washington, D.C., DHEW Pub. No. (ADM)79-65, 1979, U.S. Government Printing Office.

Torop, P., and Torop, K.: Hotlines and youth culture values, Am. J. Psychiatry **129:**106, Dec. 1972.

Tyhurst, J.A.: Role of transition states—including disasters—in mental illness. In Symposium on Preventive and Social Psychiatry sponsored by Walter Reed Institute of Research, Walter Reed Medical Center, and National Research Council, April 15-17, Washington, D.C., 1957, U.S. Government Printing Office.

United States House of Representatives: A bill to provide for the assistance in the construction and initial operation of community mental health centers and for other purposes, No. 3688, Eighty-eighth Congress, first session, 1963.

Vernick, J.: The use of the life space interview on a medical ward, Soc. Casework **44:**465, 1963.

Wales, E.: Crisis intervention in clinical training, Professional Psychology **3**(4):357, 1972.

Wilson, S.E., and others: Evaluating mental health associates, Hosp. Community Psychiatry **22:**371, Dec. 1971.

Yamamoto, J., and Goin, M.L.: On the treatment of the poor, Am. J. Psychiatry **122:**267, Sept. 1965.

Zachry, C.B.: Emotion and conduct in adolescence, New York, 1940, Appleton-Century-Crofts.

Zinberg, N.E., and Robertson, J.A.: Drugs and the public, New York, 1972, Simon & Schuster, Inc.

Index